Śāṅkara Vedānta for Environmental Harmony

(A Novel Interpretation of the Age-old Advaita Vedānta Darśana)

by
DR. VANDANA SHARMA 'Diya'

MLBD® PUBLICATIONS

Motilal Banarsidass Publications

MOTILAL BANARSIDASS
PUBLICATIONS
4741/23, Ansari Road, Daryaganj, New Delhi - 110002 (India)
Email: mlbd@mlbd.com | sales@mlbd.com
exports@mlbd.com | publications@mlbd.com
Website: www.mlbd.com

Śāṅkara Vedānta for Environmental Harmony
by
Dr. Vandana Sharma 'diya'

First Edition Published in 2021

Published in India by Motilal Banarsidass Publications

ISBN : 978-93-917-596-9-8 (HB)

Printed and bound in India

Dedication

The present book *Śāṅkara Vedānta for Environmental Harmony*' is dedicated to **Jagadguru Ādi Śaṅkarācārya** who is the source of all knowledge and is the Highest Reality '*Brahman*'. It is merely by submitting in His holy feet that one can realise the non-dual esence of all existances.

Om Jñānadāyakāya Namaḥ

(I bow in reverence before Śaṅkara who is the bestower of the Ultimate Wisdom of Non-duality.)

Guruvaṇdana

श्रुति स्मृति पुराणानाम् आलयम् करुणालयम्।
नमामि भगवद्पादम् शङ्करम् लोकशङ्करम्॥

śrutismṛtipurāṅānāṃālayamkruṅālayam I
namāmibhagvadpādaṃśaṅkaramlokaśaṅkaram II

(I bow in reverence before Jagadguru Ādi Śaṅkarācārya who is an incarnation of Lord Śiva and is the fountainhead of the unmatched wisdom of the Vedas, Upaniṣads and Purāṇas. He is an embodiment of utmost compassion and is the One who causes the welfare of all beings.)

Foreword

The present scholarly book '***Śāṅkara Vedānta for Environmental Harmony***' authored by Dr. Vandana Sharma 'Diya' is a novel attempt to highlight the practical dimensions of Ādī Śaṅkarācārya's Vedāntic insight in the context of environmental harmony.

Advaita Vedānta is both a view of reality and a way of life. It has a strong theoretical foundation drawn from the Prasthānatrayī in terms of experiential certainty (anubhava), scriptural support (śruti) and logicality (yukti). Based on these it propounds a viable practical mode of life. The Prasthānatrayī teach the same spiritual truth metaphysically and morally.

There have been several Vedāntic Ācaryas expounding the Vedāntic lore from different perspectives. Among them, Ādī Śaṅkarācārya remains outstanding. The distinguishing feature of Ādī Śaṅkarācārya's philosophy is the advocacy of the doctrine that the Ultimate Reality is unitary, all-pervasive, pure-consciousness *'Brahman'*. All multiple objects are phenomenal manifestations of the same reality. They are real from an empirical point of view but cease to be so ultimately at the transcendental level. The world we live in is real and we have to reckon with it, but not so ultimately. The world is empirically diverse real but intrinsically it is the same unitary Brahman which is ultimately real. There is, therefore, fundamental unity among all existences. All of them share the same essence. They come from the same source, are sustained by It and get absorbed in It. All are equally valuable and there is no existential hierarchy. Of course, there are differences in terms of names and forms. This constitutes diversity. So, there is unity at the transcendental level and multiplicity at the empirical level.

Ādī Śaṅkarācārya has been a profound thinker. His approach has been holistic. His writings have stemmed from different perspectives. They present a symbiosis of theory and praxis. He was deeply concerned with the betterment of all existences, neglecting none. For Him, inanimate existences are as valuable as animate ones as all are the same Brahman. So, we should have equanimity leading to equal respect for all existences. All are equally valuable and have a specific place and function in the scheme of the cosmos. Every existence has its own nature and distinct role in the cosmic process. So, it is our duty to preserve and protect the existence and essence of every entity. Then only there can be peace and harmony in the world.

The Upaniṣadic averments, such as '*sarvam khalvidam brahma*', *īśāvāsyamidaṁ sarvam*' and many more, highlight that the entire Nature is benevolent and bountiful. All objects of Nature exist for others in the mode of sacrifice. Ādī Śaṅkarācārya placed great emphasis on caring and protecting Nature. In His compositions, He exhorted us to worship Nature as 'The Divine'. Self-sacrifice is the hallmark of divinity. Anything, which is divine, is to be worshiped and since everything is Divine, it is to be revered.

From the above-stated position, Ādī Śaṅkarācārya constructs a logically sound system of thought in metaphysical and moral spheres. From the transcendental point of view, metaphysics is important and must be taken into account. However, from the empirical standpoint morality is significant. Both need to be attended to. So long as we live in this world, moral code of conduct has to be abided by. This is practical Vedānta that Swami Vivekanand highlighted.

Scholars have mostly attended to the metaphysical aspect of Ādī Śaṅkarācārya's thought but the ethical one has not been given due consideration. Further, they hold a truncated vision in terms of confining to external environment only. The internal environment is more fundamental and the external one is only its outer manifestation. This apart they only raise environmental concerns but do not care to cultivate environmental consciousness.

Dr. Vandana Sharma 'Diya' in this scholarly work has dwelt on this matter, which is much needed from the worldly perspective. In doing so she has done full justice to Advaita Vedānta. She has brought to fore Ādī Śaṅkarācārya's valuable contribution for environmental protection, which is essential and inevitable for realizing peace and perfection. This book is a rich contribution to not only Śaṅkarite literature but also world thought and culture for all times to come. Dr. Sharma's approach is fresh and novel. It is not only scholarly with profuse references but also insightful. Her research on the current area is of immense value to the country. The way she has gone beyond the realms of metaphysics and has highlighted the practical aspects of Ādī Śaṅkarācārya's thought is indeed commendable.

I wish her all the success in her academic and spiritual advancement

Prof. S.R. Bhatt

Chairman - *Indian Phiosophical Congress, Asian-African Philosophical Congress*

Former Chairman - *Indian Council of Philosophical Research, MHRD, Govt. of India*

Former Head - *Dept. of Philosophy, University of Delhi*

Blessings

H.H. Patyas Swami Chidanand Saraswati Ji
President Parmarth Niketan

The present book ***'Śaṅkara Vedānta for Environmental Harmony'*** authored by ***Dr. Vandana Sharma (Diya)*** is a scholarly and unusual attempt to show up the practical dimensions of Ādi Śaṅkarācārya's philosophy of non-dualism in relation to environmental harmony. This work not just highlights the author's unmatched devotion towards Śivāvtāra Jagadguru Ādi Śaṅkarācārya but alo throws light on her deep and insightful bond with 'Mother Nature' and her precise understanding of the Advaita Vedānta Darśana.

Bhagvāna Jagadguru Ādi Śaṅkarācārya has been one of the most intense, deep and reflective thinker, philosopher and ascetic of all times. Śivāvtāra Śrī Śaṅkara was Jñānayogī, Bhaktiyogī and at the same time a Karmayogī. The uniqueness of His philosophy remains its all-embracing spirit. It advocates that behind the variedness of names and forms remains *'The Non-dual Brahman'* which is the essence of all movable and immovable beings. Those scholars who have bluntly misunderstood the philosophy and message of Ādi Śaṅkarācārya have gone a bit to far in comprehending that the world is completely unreal. The world is only ultimately not as real as the Brahman is but that must not make us interpret that it is non-existent or not real. Having understood this, all objects of the world are worthy of reverence and respect. Thus, there exists vital unity among all existences. Jagadguru Ādi Śaṅkarācārya's Advaita Vedānta goes on to disregard any hierarchy at the ultimate level and motivates the seeker to develop a non-dual vision through which he can see the 'Ultimate Truth' behind the varied forms. Therefore, if seen in the right light Śaṅkara Vedānta is both 'Metaphysicially sound and Moral'.

Dr. Vandana Sharma through this extraordinay, well-researched and well-referenced work goes on to bring to light the ethics of Ādi Śaṅkarācārya and how they can be practically applied in dealing with environmental catastrophe.

The book definitely is essential in today's time when the entire globe is facing the fury of Nature. Surely, if man starts walking on the path and teachings left behind by Ādi Śaṅkarācārya, there will be all embracing peace and calm prevailing throughout the world. This book is also an important and innovative contribution to Śaṅkara Advaita Vedānta literature, Indian philosophy and culture and to world literature.

Dr. Vandana Sharma's research and work holds immense value for India and to the academic world. I shower upon her my blessings for her holistic expansion.

(Swami Chidanand Saraswati)

Blessings

Divine Shakti
FOUNDATION

Sadhavi Bhagwati Saraswati

The beautiful, commendable book 'Śaṅkara Vedānta for Environmental Harmony' by ***Dr. Vandana Sharma (Diya)*** weaves scholarly study together with practical applications of Ādi Śaṅkarācārya's non-dualistic philosophy, and applies this to environmental harmony. By concentrating on the practical aspects of Bhagvāna Ādi Śaṅkarācārya's Advaita-Vedānta *Dr. Vandana Sharma (Diya)* inspires the reader to see traditional philosophies in a new light. Our philosophies and values are timeless; however their application and expression will very as societal norms change and evolve. Re-application of age-old philosophies to modern dilemmas and challenges is the need of the hour.

Words cannot do justice to the glorious impact of the teachings of Jagadguru Ādi Śaṅkarācārya upon the people, the culutre and the nation of India. His logical and compelling teachings show us the way to understanding and experienceing true unity. His concept of *'Brahman'* elevates every entity of the cosmos (humans, animals, insects, trees, objects) to being 'Supreme Reality'. Thus the dog, the river, the tree, the human, the water bodies, all are embodiments and expressions of the the Supreme and therefore are worthy of worship. Tragically, Ādi Śaṅkarācārya's deep, profound thought has been only narrowly interpreted, typically. When the depth of these meanings are truly understood, we grow deeply in our understanding of our own Self and of all those beings with whom we share this divine universe, as well as ethical lessons about how to move through the world with wisdom and dharma.

I am so impressed to see the great work that ***Dr. Vandana Sharma (Diya)*** has accomplished in extracting ethical and moral codes of peaceful co-existence from the metaphysics of Jagadguru Ādi Śaṅkarācārya. These highlight very clearly what our dharma and duty are with regard to protection and preservation of the natural enviornment. Her work is a beautiful synthesis of the life of Ādi Śaṅkarācārya, His philosophy of non-dualism, His works and His establishments. The work is detailed, well-researched and well-referenced.

This book will be of immense value at a time when humanity seems tragically willing to become a witness to what has been called, "Mother Nature's Irrepressible Fury" in the form of pandemics, natural disasters including floods, earthquakes, tsunamis, draughts and diseases. These are taking place alongside the preventable tragedies of hunger, thirst, poverty and oppression. If all of our global family vows to practically apply the teachings of Ādi Śaṅkarācārya in our lives, we will be able to successfully overcome the distress, disaster and dis-ease plaguing our societies and our world.

Dr. Vandana Sharma's (Diya's) book holds great value for both laymen and scholar, across India and across the world.

I wish her great success in her academic and spiritual journey.

With love and peace,

In His seva,

Sadhvi Bhagawati Saraswati, PhD
Secretary-General, Global Interfaith WASH Alliance
President, Divine Shakti Foundation
Parmarth Niketan, Rishikesh

Acknowledgement

This book could successfully be completed because of the spiritual, mental and emotional support and grace of various beings. Herewith, I take the opportunity to extend my gratitude to all of them.

First and foremost, I bow in humility and express my gratitude to **Sākṣāta Śiva Jagadguru Ādī Śaṅkarācārya**. Without His benevolence and blessings, I could not have concluded this work. He alone is the source of all knowledge. His presence in various names and forms assisted and motivated me to complete this book without any doubts and confusions. I also outstretch my indebtedness to **Gaumātā** (the source of wisdom, health and wealth) the entire **Sanātanadharma Saṁskṛti, the Daśnāmīsaṁnyāsisaṁgha, Nāgāsādhusaṁgha** and to the **Advaita Guru-Paraṁparā** that starts with **Lord Śiva**; **The Supreme Non-dual Brahman**.

I express utmost indebtedness to **H.H. Jagadguru Shankaracharya Swami Nishchalananda Saraswatiji Maharaja (Puri Math), H.H.Pujya Swami Chidananda Saraswatiji Maharaja, Pujya Swami Govindgiriji Maharaja (Treasurer-Shree Ram Ayodhya Mandir), Pujya Parivrajaka Swami Gyanananda Saraswatiji Maharaja (Founder and Chairman-Jagadguru Shankaracharya Vedic Shodha Sansthanam, Varanasi), Pujya Swami Vigyananandaji (Jt.General Secretary-Vishwa Hindu Parishad) and Pujya Sadhavi Bhagwati Saraswatiji (Divine Shakti Foundation).** Without the support, blessings and grace of these realized saints, I would not have been in a position to conclude this work.

I express my sincere gratefulness to Parmarth Niketan (Rishikesh), Divine Shakti Foundation (Rishikesh) and all the four Maṭhas of the Advaita Vedānta Order (Puri, Shringeri, Dwarka, Jyotir) as these institutions have polished me into a human being and scholar of value by assisting me in attaining the vision to look beyond the material world.

I thank **Pujya Dr. Karan Singh Ji** for his utmost grace and compassion. His persona and charisma can not be described in the finest of words.

I also thank **Shri Shyam Jaju Ji** for always standing by me through thick and thin. His support has been unconditional and encouraging.

I proffer my profound gratitude to **Param Pujya Prof. S.R. Bhatt** who I admire, value and revere deeply. He has been a constant source of motivation, encouragement and positivity in my life. His proficiency, wisdom, compassion and insight were extremely crucial in concluding this book. He has been a teacher who has not only taught me various complex concepts with ease but has also ingrained in me his own qualities of truthfulness, hard work and patience. He has further played the role of a guide, mentor and philosopher in my life and I am extremely fortunate to have his blessings by my side.

I thank **Prof.L.P.Singh** for extending unconditional love and support. His unmatched wisdom and encouragement have always motivated me to put my best foot forward.

I extend my humble and profound appreciation to **Dr. J. Thirumal** *(Associate Professor & Head, Department of Philosophy, Annamalai University)* who has not just been an inspiration for me but has also extended enormous support. His Knowledge, strength of character, clear and concise thought and his interest in Ādī Śaṅkarācārya's philosophy were motivators while I gave shape to this work. He is a figure who I hold dear for he is a living example of compassion and humanity.

I also thank **Prof. Satheesha K.S.** *(Dept. of Advaita Vedanta, Central Sanskrit University, Tirupati)* for teaching me various complex concepts and supporting me in concluding this work successfully.

I further thank my Grandparents (Late) **Col. T.N. Spolia** and (Late) **Kamla Spolia** for installing in me virtues of the highest order. I am indebted to my mother **Smt. Sudha Sharma** who is the source of my very being and who has been my anchor and friend as I worked on this book. I also thank my aunt **Kumārī Radha Spolia** for all the kindness and support that she has outstretched. I offer my appreciation to **Dr. Kaushalendra Singh (Banaras Hindu University)**, who has provided valuable insights while I worked on this book. His suggestions and philosophical discernments enabled me to give shape to this work in the most appropriate fashion.

I extend my heartfelt gratitude to my canine children **Bhairava Sharma (Goofy-1)**, **Rudra Sharma (Mushy)** and **Krishna Sharma (Goofy-2)** for teaching me various practical lessons of Ekātmavāda. They practically taught me that despite varied names and forms, the Brahman is ever-present, ever-shining and ever-knowing.

I profer my sincere appreciation to **Motilal Banarsidass Publications,** Daryaganj, New Delhi and their entired team for assisting me in concluding and publising this piece of work.

Last but not the least, I thank **all living sentient beings** of the cosmos who have directly or indirectly added to my wisdom, experience and to this work.

Oṁ Sarvadigvijayaprabhave Namaḥ

(*I bow before Śaṅkara who with the light of His non-dual wisdom has successfully influenced and conquered all the ten directions*).

Dr. Vandana Sharma *'Diya'*

Contents

Abbreviations

e.g. - Exempli gratia, for example

ed. - Edition, editor, edited by

etc. - Et cetera, and so forth

i.e. - That is to say

Ibid - Short for ibidem, meaning the same place

Op. cit., - 'Opere Citato' In the work cited

p. – Page

pp. – Pages

Tr. - Translated by

Vol. – Volume

V. – Verse

S. - Sūtra

1. Introduction

The present book is an analytical exposition of Ādi Śaṅkarācārya's life, philosophy, practical enterprises and works. The book attempts to deduce environmental ethics from the subtle metaphysics of Advaita Vedānta as propounded by Ādi Śaṅkarācārya. It also looks at His works intricately in order to highlight an environmental and eco-esthetical view that raises environment to the level of the '*All-pervasive Truth, Highest Good, Supreme Beauty and Ultimate Reality*'. One can particularly see this view in Śaṅkara's Prakaraṇagranthas. The book further goes on to take into consideration His life and practical initiatives in order to identify lessons of universal compassion in view of environmental harmony.

The most startling situation today is the degradation of environment. There is a perpetual deterioration of environment internally, externally and cosmically. Environmental pollution is rooted in *'Avidyā'*. It is ignorance that becomes the root cause of greed, stress, disease, ruining of internal peace, balance, accord and a gamut of other vices. These perverted internal states lead to external unrest in the name of pollution and cause disharmony in the five great elements (Pañcamahābhūtas), deforestation, animal brutality, acid rain, melting glaciers and a hoard of other environmental issues. The corruption of internal and external environment leads to cosmic disturbance, disorder and disruption.

It becomes important to reinterpret the term '*Environment*' and look at it from a holistic point of view. Environment is not merely external rather it is all-enveloping. It is internal, external and cosmic. It is not only limited to trees, animals, air and water but embraces every spec of the universe including humans. The book uses the popular contemporary word '*Environment*' with the meaning as expounded by the Vedic texts. As a result, the same must not be comprehended in the Western context of living and non-living entities that exist outside a human being and with which he has an outwardly relationship. On the other hand, the word '*Environment*' is to be understood as whole, complete, all-inclusive, all comprehensive and Absolute Reality. Therefore, *'Environment'* connotes to the Highest Principle in the material world called '*Īśvara (God)*' and the Highest of Reality at the transcendental sphere known as '*Brahman*'.

The word '*Environment*' includes internal, external and cosmic states of all the creatures of the world. It refers to birth, life and death of all lives in accordance with the cosmic order (*Ṛta*). It also refers to the cosmic principles of creation, preservation and destruction. '*Environment*' should further be understood as that which is the essence of the cosmos, which defines the 'Svabhāva' and 'Dharma' of each being in the universe and establishes their intrinsic worth and value at an individual, social and cosmic level. Additionally, '*Environment*' is to be comprehended as the divine body of the '*Supreme Being*' while humans, animals, birds, insects, trees, water bodies, earth, planets and all other entities are to be cognized as wholesome parts of the same. Just as in a body each organ is wholesome, has its own function, is interdependent and co-exists in harmony with other parts likewise all entities of the world are wholesome parts of the '*Supreme Spirit*' which have a specific function to play in the universe, they are interdependent and co-exist in harmony within the scheme of cosmos. It is also to be realized that just as Ātman pervades the whole of body and illumines each organ likewise there is only one Universal Spirit that pervades all entities of the world and lights-up their very being. Therefore, '*Environment*' is to be understood as division-less, continuous and uninterrupted '*Universal Spirit*'. Internal, external and cosmic environments are merely segregated for the sake of explanation and intellectual understanding. However, there exists no real compartmentalization of the same.

The book makes an earnest effort to see external environmental miseries of the cosmos like deforestation, animal cruelty, pollution, climate change and more in the light of Ādi Śaṅkarācārya's sublime philosophy. It further highlights that the same is merely a manifestation of the perversion of man's internal environmental conditions which become the very cause of cosmic disharmony. With this backdrop,

- The book approaches '*Environment*' in view of Ādi Śaṅkarācārya's holistic philosophy of non-dualism (Advaita Vedānta) and examines the term '*Environment*' with a wholesome perspective.
- The book brings to fore Ādi Śaṅkara's scheme of Sādhanā comprising of Sādhanacatuṣṭaya, fifteen-fold Yoga and the process of Śravaṇa, Manana, Nidhidyāsana and Niṣṭhā in order to realize a state of absolute non-duality in which all material entities melt away and shine as the '*Self*'.
- The book goes on to feature the practical endeavors of Jagadguru Ādi Śaṅkarācārya in establishing the four Maṭhas, the Daśanāmīsaṃpradāya, the Nagāsādhusaṇgha, the Pañcadevopāsanā and the Chāradhāmayātrā in view of environment. Further, it will emphasize His '*Works*' in the light of environmental ethics and aesthetics.
- The book makes desirable efforts to highlight that reducing Ādi Śaṅkara's philosophy to sheer metaphysics is downgrading the very understanding, glory and novelty of His unique thought which is wholesome, all-enriching, all-inclusive and all-embracing.

- The book ventures to derive environmental ethics from Ādi Śaṅkarācārya's metaphysics that will assist the society in realizing self-sameness with all existences.
- The book undertakes to establish that the Highest Reality '*Brahman*' can be realized only when one develops a vision to see the '*Self*' in all existences and all existences in the '*Self*'. Only when one fosters ethics as the very foundation on the path to realization and holds reverence towards all lives can he attain the state of Realization/ Liberation/ Wisdom/ Mukti/ Nirvāṇa.
- The book attempts to establish that the world is not an '*Illusion or Void*' as has been commonly misinterpreted. All entities of the world are not annulled or hollowed rather they hold seminal value in the Vyāvahārika Jagat.
- The book endeavors to uphold that the realization of non-duality at the highest level in no way contradicts the very experience of duality in the material world.

The book '*Śāṅkara Vedānta for Environmental Harmony*', focuses on the elucidations in accordance with Śāṅkara's philosophy of non-dualism. It makes an effort to practically apply Advaita Vedāntic teachings and wisdom for wholesome wellness and coherence.

As long as humans continue to see duality as ultimately real, the issues related to environmental degeneration will persist. Even if the entire world comes together in order to address the problems related to environmental deterioration by merely indulging in external acts of planting trees, restricting the use of plastic and voicing opinions against animal cruelty, there will be a negligible difference and the problems related to the same will linger on. The only way to deal with environmental glitches or for that matter any other snag including social issues like violence, thefts, murders and more is by being established in non-dualism. It is merely by non-dualistic approach that exploitation of environment, killing of sentient beings and degeneration of resources can come to a complete halt because when everything is realized as the '*Self*, who will exploit whom? and, who will kill whom? Therefore, the present book will address the problems related to environment by emphasizing that all issues are generated due to seeing dualism and considering apparent names and forms to be 'Ultimately Real'. Dualism leads to likes and aversions which generate feelings of greed, possession, hate and jealousy. The mother of all apparent dualities is none other than '*Avidyā*'. Thus, merely by fighting ignorance can one fight the demon of duality and consequently get rid of environmental and social upheavals.

The present book takes into consideration a comprehensive collection of primary as well as secondary sources. It judiciously makes use of an array of primary sources from the Advaita Vedānta literature of Ādi Śaṅkarācārya. It also goes on to cite references from a wide range of books, journals, articles and materials available in print as well as on the internet related to Advaita Vedānta as expounded by Śaṅkara. However, it is desirable to mention here that finding references for the present work has been an extremely arduous task due to a lack of research in the specific area. However, the same makes use of the following sources,

1) **Primary Sources:** These offer a direct account of an original philosophy, thought and discovery. These texts are considered to be an authority and become the foundation of any original research.

a) **Prasthānatrayī:** These are the three literally sources, namely; Upaniṣads, Bhagvadgītā, Brahmasūtras. The Vedānta school of philosophy recognizes the Prasthānatrayī as texts of authority. The study of Vedānta is not considered complete unless these three texts are taken into consideration. The present work takes into account the Bhāṣyas of Ādi Śaṅkarācārya on Prasthānatrayī as primary sources. Let's have a look at the same in brief,

i) **The Bhagvadgītābhāṣya:** Bhagvadgītā is a text that is based upon the understanding of the Vedas and is revered as the Pañcaṃveda (fifth Veda)'. It is further referred to as the Smṛtiprasthāna (derivative text). Ādi Śaṅkara's commentary on the Bhagvadgītā remains one of the most prominent and celebrated works of all times. Despite hundreds of commentaries available on the Bhagvadgītā, the Śāṅkarabhāṣya till date holds seminal value and authority. It must be noted that though no known work has been done on the present topic that this book deals with yet if one comprehends the Bhagvadgītā in view of the same; it is not difficult to find references and draw implications in view of 'Environmental harmony'.

ii) **The Upaniṣadbhāṣya:** Upaniṣads are the text of revelation and are said to be the Śrutiprasthāna (primary texts). Though, there are a number of Upaniṣads yet only 108 Upaniṣads remain well-known. Out of 108 Upaniṣads Ādi Śaṅkarācārya wrote Bhāṣyas on the principal Upaniṣads (Pramukhopaniṣads) namely; Aitareyopaniṣad, Īśopaniṣad, Kenopaniṣad, Bṛhadāraṇyakopaniṣad, Taittirīyaopaniṣad, Kāthopniṣad, Praśnopaniṣad, Śvetāśvataropaniṣad, Chāndogyopaniṣad, Māṇḍūkyopaniṣad and the Muṇḍakopaniṣad.

The Upaniṣads are the philosophical parts of the Vedas. Ādi Śaṅkarācārya's Bhāṣyas on the Upaniṣads establish the non-duality of Jīva and Brahman. Śāṅkara Upaniṣadbhāṣyas have been applauded since time immemorial and hold an eminent position in the history of literature. They become the bedrock of ethics, morality, and universal benevolence. These can be the guiding light in case of cosmic environmental harmony. One can clearly see the seeds of compassion in the Upaniṣads. For instance, Chāndogyopaniṣad comprises of one of the initial avowals of Ahiṃsā (non-violence) as an ethical edict.[1] It also includes the examination of other ethical foundations of Damaḥ, Satya, Dāna, Ārjava, Dayā and more.[2]

Ādi Śaṅkarācārya's Bhāṣyas further propound on the above-said ideas by seeing them from a wholesome point of view and considers imbibing these qualities as a basic foundation for realizing the Highest Reality '*Brahman*'. Therefore, Upaniṣadbhāṣyas provide enough material that stands in favor of environmental harmony, cosmic reverence and compassion towards all forms of lives which will be brought to light in subsequent chapters of this book.

iii) **The Brahmasūtrabhāṣya:** The Brahmasūtras are said to be Nyāyaprasthāna (expositional text). Ādi Śaṅkarācārya wrote a profound and novel commentary on Sage Bādarāyaṇa's Brahmasūtras. In merely 555 aphorisms the magnificent text goes on to systemize the philosophy of the Upaniṣads. There are no direct references to *Environment* that can be found in the Brahmasūtrabhāṣya if one comprehends the term '*Environment*' from a contemporary point of view. However, it is important to understand that the present book uses the popular word '*Environment*' to merely denote that which is all-pervasive. Further, nowhere in the Brahmasūtrabhāṣya the word '*Jiva*' is used exclusively for human beings. In case, one concludes that the word '*Jiva*' is only meant for human beings then he is going against the very idea of '*Advaita*'. If a person argues that trees, animals or rivers are not specifically mentioned in the text then again it is to be considered that nowhere are women and children mentioned in the text, so is the Brahmasūtrabhāṣya

---

1 Paul Deussen, '*The Six Upanishads of the* Vedas, Vol.1 ', Motilal Banarsidas, Delhi, 2010, pp.114-115.

2 Kane Pandurang Vaman, '*History of Dharmashastra (Samanya Dharma), Vol.2* ', Bhandarkar Oriental Research Institute, Pune, 1962, p.5

meant only for humans and within humans are they only applicable to men? Such arguments are pointless and illogical. The wisdom of Brahmasūtrabhāṣya is applicable to all beings of the world irrespective of their caste, creed, sex, religion, form and shape because wisdom is beyond divisions. Thus, from a wholesome point of view lessons of all pervasive compassion can be deduced from this text.

b) **The Prakaraṇagranthas:** Ādi Śaṅkarācārya left behind a series of lucid and modest collection of work that spoke about the principles of non-dualism (Advaita Vedānta) in the simplest of manner. This collection of work is called '*Prakaraṇagranthas*'. They are elementary in nature and become the foundation of Advaita Vedāntic teachings. They elucidate upon the philosophy, ideas, and thoughts of Sarvabrahmavāda (All is the Brahman/ All is Divine). They use a wide range of examples, analogies and illustrations to make the seeker well versed with deep and intellectual concepts related to Ekātmavāda. The book makes the most of a wide variety of Prakaraṇagranthas written by Ādi Śaṅkarācārya.

It must be noted that many scholars hold distinct views concerning the authenticity of these works. However, the aim of this book is not to dwell on the controversy of authenticity. Based upon material available from the four Maṭhas it has been deduced that the Prakaraṇagranthas used in this book are the original works of Jagadguru Ādi Śaṅkarācārya.

Śrī Śaṅkara was not only a philosopher, logician, metaphysicist and a yogī of high stature but was also a compassionate writer and poet. His writings throw light on His deep understanding of life as a whole while His poems highlight the intricate bond that He shared with nature and all its creatures. It is impossible for someone to write such deep, subtle and sensitive poems unless he has deeply understood, observed, interacted, and contemplated upon the various entities of the cosmos with a wholesome vision.

The current work uses some of Ādi Śaṅkarācārya's most rejoiced hymns like Ānandalaharī, Bhajagovindam, Maṇīśāpañcakam, Kaṇakadhārāstotram, Nirvāṇaṣatkam, Viṣṇuśaṭpadī, Dakṣiṇāmurṭiaṣṭakam, Gaṇgāṣṭakam, Yamunāṣṭam, Dhanyāṣṭakam, Ātmapañcakam, Sādhanapañcakam, Maṇikarṇikāṣṭakam, Hari-Harā Stotram, Śrī Mūkaṃikāpañcaratnastotram, Yogatārāvalī and more. All the above said are written in an easy and comprehendible language. One can enjoy the fragrance of non-duality in these beautiful works and can further witness a sense of compassion, aesthetics and devotion of the highest order. Some of these works in a unique way make use of sentient entities such as rivers, birds, flowers and animals to describe the paramount beauty of '*Īśvara*' and refer to them as the '*Supreme Brahman*'. Therefore, one can witness how Ādi Śaṅkarācārya's inner state of purity led Him to see purity and beauty at an external level. The book will go on to throw light on these works in the subsequent chapters.

2. **Secondary Sources:** These sources include analysis, explanation, or assessment of the primary sources. They endeavor to elucidate upon the same. The book makes use of some of the most celebrated secondary sources written by eminent philosophers and scholars who possess an intricate knowledge of the subject and have a wholesome vision.

   Various secondary sources and the wisdom of several scholars and philosophers have assisted in developing and concluding this book. However, it is to be pointed out that no known research or book related to Ādi Śaṅkarācārya's philosophy and Environment has been carried out or published in India or abroad. Therefore, this book emerges as a unique, innovative and critical work of all times.

The aim of this book is not merely to see environment in view of Ādi Śaṅkarācārya's philosophy rather it also endeavors to kick start a new era where ancient thoughts, philosophies, teachings and visions will be reinterpreted in order to deal with the current environmental, social, political, religious, scientific and cosmic chaos. While we innovatively try to reinterpret the age-old philosophies, we must take utmost care of being in harmony with their metaphysics and basic principles. Ascertaining that the basic principles of Advaita Vedānta are not violated, the present work was undertaken to deal with current environmental disharmony that is sweeping the world. This book endeavors to give a new insight and aims at becoming the bedrock of many other researches and works that would study similar environmental issues in view of Ādi Śaṅkarācārya's sublime philosophy.

Oṁ Jagadgurave Namaḥ

(I bow in reverence before Śaṅkara who is the Universal Guru)

2.
Vedic References of Environmental Harmony

Today, the entire planet is at a critical juncture. As a man's internal states are corrupted with greed, competitiveness, ego, and an unwavering drive to govern the globe, his external states degenerate, manifesting as pollution, wars, riots, cruelty on other sentient beings, rapes, murders, and a slew of other problems. All of the world's exterior problems, i.e. environmental, social, political, religious and more have their roots in the inner pollution of man's being. So long as the internal condition of the human race remains in a state of flux, the external states will continue to rot.

As previously stated, the distinctions between the interior, exterior, and cosmic environments are purely for the sake of convenience and comprehension. These are non-dual, interconnected, and in sync with one another.

Our inner states manifest as the world we create for ourselves and this manifested world affects our Antaḥkaraṇa. A disturbed internal environment combined with a degraded external environment results in cosmic environmental discord. It is unfortunate that humans have not only become unmindful towards their internal states but have convinced themselves into believing that all peripheral states and all beings that exist in the so-called '*External Realms*' have sheer material value and are to be manipulated for the benefit of mankind. It is this self-centered approach that has led to massive environmental discord at an internal, external and cosmic level.

The Vedas are flowing with verses that point towards not merely the realization of inner purity but also aim at the accomplishment of external harmony, reverence and peace. The eventual aim of the Vedas is spiritual progress that culminates in liberation or the realization of '*Self*'. This aim is unattainable so long as man suffers from internal and external environmental pollution and degradation.

The present chapter will look into the Vedic averments that talk about holistic harmony of one's being. It will throw light upon how Vedas have held the external states and the varied manifested beings as the '*Very Self*'. It is this all-enveloping approach of the Vedas that promotes inner well-being, outer reverence and cosmic wholesome vision of non-dualism. The holistic approach of compassion and oneness present in the Vedic text becomes the bedrock of comprehensive environmental purity and reverence.

It must be understood that though this chapter highlights the Vedic voices in terms of one's external states yet it is internal environment as Mana, Buddhi, Ahaṁkāra and Citta that needs to be purified through various techniques that the Vedas and the Advaita Vedānta Darśana recommends. Unless one has attained inner perfection, outer acts of compassion will be considered as merely initial. Therefore, in order to understand the essence of the Vedic verses emphasized in this chapter, it is recommended that one develops purity of internal environment. Only a pure state of one's inner being will ensure that he/she understands the significance of these verses in the right light and in view of holistic cosmic environmental wellness.

2.1. The Vedas: An Overview

The Vedas is the most ancient and the largest sacred text of the world. The divine text is composed in Saṃskrit and is revered as an authority by the people belonging to the '*Sanātana Dharma*', also known as the '*Hindus*'. Nonetheless, the text is intended to benefit everyone and is not limited to any caste, creed, gender, religion, species, or nationality. Sanātana Dharma is devoid of any divisions or ideologies. It doesn't refer to any sect, creed or religion as in the case of Christianity, Islam and Judaism. It focuses more on a natural code of conduct and an all prevailing cosmic law that includes every spec of the universe from a tiny ant to the humongous galaxies.

The word '*Veda*' means '*Wisdom/ Knowledge*'. It is derived from the Saṃskrit word '*Vid*' which means '*To Know*'. It aims at the wisdom of the '*Self*' called '*Parāvidyā*'. However, it also deals with material knowledge of the world called '*Aparāvidyā*'. The Vedas are regarded as authorless, divine revelation and are known as '*Apauruṣeya (not written by any human)*'. It is a single body of text that has been divided into four parts, namely; Ṛgveda, Yajurveda, Sāmaveda and Atharvaveda. Each of the Veda is further divided into four sections called,

- **Saṁhitā** (The text of methodologically arranged Maṅtras, hymns, prayers.)
- **Āraṇyaka** (The text that explains the philosophy behind rituals.)
- **Brāhmaṇas** (The text associated with Saṁhitā that explains the symbolism of ceremonies.)
- **Upaniṣad** (The philosophical texts of non-dual wisdom that are the culminating part of the Vedas and are also referred to as Vedānta.)

The six schools of Indian philosophy, namely; Nyāya-Vaiśeṣika, Sāṃkhya-Yoga and Mīmāṃsā-Vedānta are rooted in the Vedas and accept the undisputed authority of the same. The Vedas are said to be '*Śruti*' which means '*they were heard*' by the seven realized sages (Saptaṛṣi)[1] in the deepest states of contemplation.

The Vedas voice that there is comprehensive harmonization among all aspects of existence. The Vedic principle of '*Ṛta*' embodies the sublime, regulated and harmonious operation of the cosmos as also the inner ethical, moral, symphonic and orderly demeanor of the human race. The divine text talks about an intrinsic relationship of Self-sameness between an individual and the entire cosmos. Therefore, just as the human body is the dwelling of an individual being, the cosmos is the divine abode of the Supreme Being.

With the above said in mind, anyone who purposes to settle conflicts of any sort (environmental, political, social and more) in order to realize coherence, concord and synchronization has to initiate with the immediate rather than the mediate, proximate rather than the remote and with the visible rather than the invisible. Further, it must also be lucidly understood that one is never in conflict with others instead the conflict is always with one's own inner states. The seed of discord, greed, hate and jealousy sprouts within us and manifests into external issues, struggles and pollutions. Subsequently, one continues to oscillate between opposites such as truth and falsity, light and darkness, mortality and immortality, ethics and wickedness. Therefore, if we want global environmental peace, we must first be at peace with ourselves.

2.2. 'Environment' in the Abrahamic Religions

The Encyclopedia of Britannica states,

"Environment is the complex of physical, chemical, and biotic factors that

1 Swami Madhavananda, '*Brihdarnayaka Upanishad with* Commentary of Shankaracharya', Advaita Ashrma, Himalayas, 1950, pp.326-327. (V.2.2.4) (Names of the Saptarishi- *Vashishtha, Kashyapa, Atri, Jamadagni, Gautama, Vishvamitra and Bharadvaja).*

act upon an organism or an ecological community and ultimately determine its form and survival."[2]

The Cambridge dictionary defines the same as,

"The air, water, land in or on which humans, animals and plants live."[3]

Wikipedia defines '*Environment*' as,

"Environment includes the living and non-living things that an organism interacts with or has an effect on. Living elements that an organism interacts with are known as biotic elements; animals, plants, etc. Abiotic elements are non-living things that include air, water, sunlight, etc. Studying environment means studying the relationships among these various things."[4]

From the above-said definitions of environment, it is generally understood that,

- Environment is something external and complex in or on which living organisms survive. It is the interaction of oneself with other organisms in a certain way.
- Environmental elements are divided into living (animals, birds, plants, etc.) and non-living (air, water, sunlight, etc.)
- An understanding of the relationship that exists between these living and non-living organisms is said to be the study of environment.

Therefore, it is evident that '*Environment*' is everything around us and how we interact with all of it. A clear distinction is drawn between an individual and everything that surrounds him. While interacting with everything that surrounded a man, he became the centre of the creation

---

2 Encyclopedia Britannica, 2020, '*Environment Biology*', Online, https://www.britannica.com/science/environment (Accessed;1 April 2021).

3 Dictionary.cambridge.org,2021, '*Environment*', Online, https://dictionary.cambridge.org/dictionary/english environment, (Accessed: 1 April 2021).

4 Wikipedia.com,2021, '*Environment*', Online, https://simple.wikipedia.org/wiki/Environment, (Accessed 1 April 2021).

and the whole of Nature was meant for the satisfaction of his needs and desires. This thought gained prominence due to the attitude held by Abrahamic faith systems and verses that appear in the Bible and the Quran respectively,

'And God said, "Let us make man in our image after our likeness and let him have dominion over the fishes of the sea, the birds in the air, over the cattle, livestock and all wild animals and over every creature that crept upon the earth."'[5]

"Oh believers! Lawful to you is the slaughtered meat of flocks, camels, cattle, sheeps and all gazing animals. If you find the fetus in the slaughtered mother's belly, you may eat it.[6] The meat of all animals that comes from hunting done by trained animals and birds are lawful as your food. All fish of the sea are made lawful for you to eat. He has created horses, mules, and donkeys, for you to ride and use for show and entertainment."'[7]

There are hundreds of verses in the Bible and the Quran which throw light on the idea that man is the epicenter of the creation and all plenteousness of Nature was meant for him to support his existence, consumption, gratification and amusement. Slowly, Nature's bounties were getting lost and soon environmental crisis stood up as a demon that threatened the very survival of the human race. It was this crisis that gave rise to '*Environmental Ethics*'. Therefore, it is to be understood lucidly that in the Abrahamic faith systems and in the western world '*Environmental Ethics*' were developed in order to deal with the emerging environmental catastrophe. These were needed to protect '*Human's Survival*' that was at the mercy of Nature. Environmental ethics had nothing to do with spirituality or reverence for Nature. Its emergence was solely meant to control and preserve resource depletion, concluding biodiversity,

---

5 Biblehub.com, 2004, Genesis. 1:26KJV, '*The Holy* Bible', Online, https://biblehub.com/kjv genesis/1-26.htm, (Accessed:1 April 2021)

6 Quranx.com. 2012, A-maida, 5.1-5.2 '*The Holy Quran*', Online https://quranx.com/5.1 , https://quranx.com/5.2 (Accessed:1 April 2021)

7 *Ibid.*, 5.4, https://quranx.com/5.4.\

deforestation, cessation of aesthetics, boosting of economy and for the attainment of various material benefits. Trees, animals, birds and all creatures being equivalent to a human remains meaningless for the only worth that Nature holds in Abrahamic faith systems is to support the center of Lord's creation '*Humans*'.

The division made in the name of living and non-living organisms by science also had a materialistic approach. All those entities that could be seen taking birth, growing, aging and dying were called '*Living*' while water bodies, mountains, sun, and the air were referred to as '*Non-Living*'. Therefore, living and non-living entities were segregated based upon what appeared living or non-living to the external senses.

The dipping environmental harmony was pushing the intellectuals of the society to reconsider religion and reinterpret it in a new light. It was only during the 1970s that philosophers like Arne Naess,[8] J. Baird Collicot[9] and Richard Sylvan[10] began thinking about the issue of environment which was soon becoming the most crucial concern before humanity. It was in the late 1970s and early 1980s that a debate started between people about whether environment had inherent value which was independent of human values or whether its significance was limited to being instrumental. Therefore, on one hand, there was the emergence of deep-ecology approaches and on the other hand, pragmatic anthropocentric approaches were originating. Unfortunately, all of this had an insignificant effect on the deteriorating condition of '*Mother Nature*' and on all beings of the planet.

---

8 En. wikipedia.org. 2004, '*Arne NÊss*', Online, https://en.wikipedia.org, (Accessed 1 April 2021)

9 En. wikipedia.org, 2005, '*J. Baird Callicott*', Online,https://en.wikipedia.org, (Accessed 1 April 2021).

10 En.wikipedia.org, 2004, '*Richard Sylvan*', Online,https://en.wikipedia.org, (Accessed 1 April 2021).

With scientific and technological advancements, the entire health of the planet and its species including human beings were at the receiving end. This appalling scenario continues even today. Man has gone all out to destroy Nature in the name of scientific discoveries and technological advancements. He has heartlessly indulged in destroying forests, damaging biodiversity, polluting the five great elements and killing animals for the sake of vogue and amusement.

The entire world is facing the fury of Nature in the form of natural disasters, resource exhaustion, disappearance of species, climate change, global warming and ozone layer depletion. This situation is not only proving to be detrimental for other sentient beings but has also damaged humans to a great extent. Today, man commonly suffers from diseases like asthma, bronchial issues, cancer, depression, and the recent pandemic adversity (Covid-19). It is to be observed here that the undesirable world of suffering is created by none other than the human race. It is human alone who has broken the laws of the cosmos and has pushed the entire globe into a depressing state of mental, physical, social, environmental and cosmic melancholy. All his efforts to preserve Nature in the name of planting trees, restraining the use of plastic and opting for eco-friendly products have had a trivial effect on the health of the planet.

The above said throws light on the fact that no matter how much one tries to change things at an external level or in parts he will surely fall flat. The need of the hour is total change, wholesome approach, holistic view, and organismic well-being.

2.3. 'Environment' as Understood in the Vedic Traditions

Contrary to the Western and Abrahamic thought where environment is considered as isolated from humans, the Vedic vision of looking at environment is wholesome. It is devoid of any bifurcations, parts or compartments. The same remains unbroken and all-inclusive. In this regard the Yajurveda declares,

aum nārāyaṇāya vidmahe vāsudevāya dhīmahi।
tanno viṣṇu pracodāyat॥[11]
(May in order to realize the Absolute 'Nārāyaṇa', we contemplate upon 'Vāsūdeva, the 'One' who indwells all.)

The Bhagvadgītā states,

samo'ham sarvabhūteṣu na me dveṣyosti na priyaḥ।
ye bhajanti tu mām bhaktyā mayi te teṣucāpyaham॥[12]
(I equivalently indwell within all the creatures. I have no likes or aversions towards any life form.)

Further, the *Īśopaniṣad* asserts,

īśā vāsyamidaṁ sarvam yatkiñca jagatyāṁ jagat।
tena tyaktena bhuñjīthā mā gṛdhaḥ kasyasviddhanam॥[13]
(The entirety of cosmos is pervaded by the Īśvara (Lord) who is the 'Self' of all movable and immovable entities. Therefore, only by renunciation can one enjoy the bounties of Mother Earth and not by possession of the same.)

From the above one can unambiguously understand that the entire cosmos is a manifestation of the non-dual '*Ultimate*'. In this light, the trees, animals, birds, mountains, rivers, humans, and every spec of the universe is not just equal in essence but is the very Divine. It is also to be considered that the Divine not just envelops the entire cosmos in accordance with the Vedic literature, but also indwells all entities of the universe and Himself appears as

---

11 Pt. Sri Ramananuja Acharya, '*Sukta Sangraha*', Shrimatham, 2017, p.9 (V.1, Vishnu Gyatri Mantra)

12 Shankaracharya, '*Shrimadbhagvadgitabhashya*', Manav Prabodhan Pranyasa, Bikaner, Rajasthan, 2016, pp.146-147 (V.9.29).

13 Swami Gambhirananda (Tr), '*Eight Upanishads: Isa, Kena, Katha, Taittirya, Vol.1 with commentary of Shankaracharya*', Advaita Ashrama, Himalayas, 1957, pp.4-6. (V.1, Ishopnishad)

the dog, the sparrow, the Ganges and the entire world of material and the immaterial. The following verses throw light on the same,

ekam sat viprā bahudhā vadanti'[14]
(The Ultimate truth is 'One' known by the wise as many).

Just as the white light passes through the prism and splits into seven colors likewise the Divine who is non-dual appears as the assorted names and forms in which the world exists due to the effect of Māyā[15]. In this regard, the Cāndogyopniṣad avers that,

'eko'hambahuśyāmaḥ'[16]
(I am one and I become many)

Therefore, in view of the Vedic texts Environment is to be comprehended with the connotation of '*Brahman*'[17] which is all-pervasive, omnipresent, omnipotent and omniscient. From this point of view, all entities of the world are the Divine who exist in the Divine, are pervaded by the Divine, are indwelled by the Divine; they are born from the Divine, live in the Divine and merge back into the Divine.

India is a country that worships and reveres Nature as the Highest Reality. The term '*Nature*' must not be limited to trees, animals, birds, rivers and mountains, rather '*It*' is internal, external, individual, cosmic, and takes into account every spec of the cosmos. It is the very '*Self*. Thus, a human being is not perceived as the centre of the cosmos rather the entire cosmos is seen as interwoven and interdependent.

---

14 Griffith Ralph T.H, '*The Rigveda*', Védico Antiguo Einglés, Spain, 1896, p.275 (V.1.164.46).

15 See chapter-4 (4.5, Maya- the power through which the infinite appears as finite), P. 128

16 Swami Nikhilananda, '*The Upnishad-Taittirya and Chandogya with Commentary of Shankar Acharyaa, Vol.4, (Chandogya Upanishad)'*, Harper & Brothers Publisher, New York, 1959, pp.294-295 (V.6.2.3).

17 See chapter-4 (4.2, Brahman-the ultimate principle), P. 111

Each life is whole and is a wholesome part of the '*One Whole Reality*' and therefore, the cosmos has multiple wholesome centers. Indian culture has since time immemorial worshiped trees, animals, rivers and mountains as the very manifestation of the Self. India has not just been environmentally protective but has been environmentally conscious and has realized '*One Divinity*' pervading multiplicity. It has been held that the external, internal and cosmic environments are non-dual. Therefore, internal peace extends, manifests and is established at an external and cosmic level. It is the inner contamination, unrest and mental greed that manifests as pollution, degradation and discord outwardly.

Nature in the Vedic tradition has been revered as the '*Mother of all*'. Thus, there exists unity among all entities that are born and nourished in Her compassionate lap. Environment as '*Mother*' fosters every being only till the time we revere and respect Her. However, if we try to overpower Her, exploit Her or malign Her, She reacts. She responds in the form of mental stress internally, as diseases physically, as natural calamities environmentally and as comprehensive disharmony at a cosmic level. Planting of trees, being kind to animals, restricting the use of plastic can help us in our mission to support the cosmos but it is surely not the cure for internal, external and cosmic environmental disharmony that we continue to face. In this regard Svāmī Vivekānada aptly states,

"The miseries of the world cannot be cured by physical help alone. Unless a man's nature changes, physical needs will continue to arise and miseries will continue to be felt. No amount of physical help will cure these miseries. Ignorance is the mother of all evils and of the misery that we see. Let man have light, let them be pure, spiritually strong and educated; then alone misery will cease. We may convert every house of the country into a charitable asylum and fill the land with hospitals but the misery will continue to exist until man's character changes"[18]

---

18 Swami Vivekananda, '*Complete Works of Swami Vivekananda*', Partha Sinha Digital Publication, 2019, p. 36.

From the above, it can be concluded that external acts combined with internal change can alone lead to holistic environmental harmony.

The Vedic view of Environment is based upon divinity, spirituality, equality, reverence, co-existence, co-operation, accord, concord, coherence, compassion and universal oneness of all lives. This view aborts any sort of preferences, divisions, dualities and compartmentalization. Each life and each form has its own role to play in the larger scheme. Realization of non-duality with all lives leads to harmony in the truest sense, as says the Yajurveda,

yastu sarvāṇi bhūtāni ātmanyevānupaśyati ।
sarvabhūteṣu cātmānaṁ tato na vijugupsate ॥
yasmin sarvāṇi bhūtāni ātmaivābhūd vijānataḥ ।
tatra ko mohaḥ kaḥ śoka ekatvamanupaśyataḥ ॥[19]

(He who sees the Self in all and all in the Self has no sense of revulsion by the reason of the vision of non-duality. When all beings have been realized as the 'Self' there remains no delusion and no sadness).

2.4. Vedic References in View of Environment

oṃ dyauḥ śāntirantarikṣaṃ śāntiḥ
pṛthivī śāntirāpaḥ śāntiroṣadhayaḥ śāntiḥ ।
vanaspatayaḥ śāntirviśvedevāḥ śāntirbrahma śāntiḥ
sarvaṃ śāntiḥ śāntireva śāntiḥ sā mā śāntiredhi ॥
oṃ śāntiḥ śāntiḥ śāntiḥ ॥[20]

(May the cosmic atmosphere be peaceful, may peace prevail in the earth, water, and medicinal herbs. May peaceful be the plant kingdom, the presiding deities of the great elements and the Supreme Consciousness 'Brahman'. May all be peaceful, may peace be rooted in peace, may you be that peace. Peace (within), Peace (without), Peace (in the cosmos))

The above said is one of the many hymns of the Vedas that talk about universal amity and coherence. The Vedas are bejeweled with innumerable references that speak of

19 Swami Gambhirananda, p.12-13, (V.6, Ishavasyaopnishad, Yajurveda)

20 *Yajurveda*, Shanti Mantrani, Taittirya Aranyak, V. 4.42.37.

environmental harmony. The Vedic tradition and sages have seen environment as all-encompassing and have shared an intimate bond with it. Thus, one can see that when they speak of the sun, moon, stars, animals, trees, birds and other forces of nature, they refer to them as the '*Highest Reality*'. One can also see them intimately referring to these as mother, father, protector, friend, son and more. It is to be taken note of that the Vedas and our revered sages have repeatedly spoken of a Unitary Principle that permeates and enlivens the entire cosmos and all entities. This Principle is known by varied names and it manifests itself in diverse forms. Environment is seen as that Ultimate Principle. All beings of the universe are indwelled, saturated and are that very '*Principle*' which they mistakenly consider as distinct. This non-dual Vedic approach to environment becomes the guiding light that holds '*Mother Nature*' at the highest plinth. Therefore, the Vedas give us the necessary vision to see the entire cosmos in the 'Self' and the 'Self' in the whole of cosmos. They advised us to work for the benefit of all beings and not merely be restricted to the advancement of the human race. They enlighten us to not foster hate for any creature and give us the valuable lessons of compassion, love, universal amity and cosmic coherence. Let us now see various references from the Vedas that speak of environmental harmony.

2.4.1 Vedic References for the Origin of the Divine Cosmos

The origin of the cosmos and all its sentient beings find mention in the Vedic literature. It is affirmed in the Vedas that the '*One Eternal*' manifests as the entire material world of beings. The thought can be seen in various Vedic verses i.e.,

oṃ ārdraṃ jvalati jyotirahamasmi jyotijrvalati
brahmāhamasmi। yo'hamasmi brahmāhamasmi। ahamasmi
brahmāhamasmi। ahamevāhaṃ mā juhomi svāhā॥[21]

[21] Swami Vimalananda, 'Mahanarayanopnishad', Shri Ramakrishna Matha, Madras, 1968, pp.86-87, (V.67)

(Just like a drenched seed sprouts, that Absolute Light manifests itself as the diverse universe. I am that Supreme Light 'Brahman' which shines as the very essence of all existences. I experience myself as finite due to the effect of ignorance. However, in essence, I am the 'Supreme Spirit' and with the dint of wisdom, I realize My true nature).

puruṣa evedaṃ sarvaṃ yadbhūtaṃ yacca bhavyam।
utāmṛtatvasyeśāno yadannenātirohati॥[22]

(All this is nothing but the Supreme Being, the 'One' that is, the 'One' that was, and the 'One' that will be. Though He appears as the material universe of names and forms yet He is the immortal 'One' behind the mortals.)

It is to be clearly understood that the Vedas consider the entire cosmos as an undivided living entity. It is propagated that the water, earth, air, space, fire, sun, moon, planets, animals, birds, insects, humans, mountains, rivers, trees and every spec of the universe is pulsating with life and consciousness,

tasmādaśvā ajāyanta ye ke cobhayādataḥ।
gāvoḥ ha jajñire tasmāt tasmājjātā ajāvayaḥ॥
candramā manaso jātaścakṣoḥ sūryo ajāyata।
mukhādindraścāgniśca prāṇādvāyurajāyata॥
nābhyā āsīdantarikṣaṃ śīrṣno dyauḥ samavartata।
padbhyāṃ bhūmirdiśaḥ śrotrāttathā lokāṃ akalpayan॥
vedāhametaṃ purucaḥ mahāṃtamamṛtaṃdhruvam।
ādityavarṇaṃ tamasaḥ parastāt saṃsthitaṃprabhum॥
sarvāṇi rūpāṇi vicitya dhīraḥ।
nāmāni kṛtvā'bhivadanyadāste॥[23]

(From 'That' came the horses and all animals having two rows of teeth. From 'That' came the cow, the goat and the sheep. From 'His' mind came the moon, from 'His' eyes the sun was born. From 'His' mouth was born Indra and Agni and 'His' very breadth became the air. The astral world was born out of 'His' naval and the world beyond was made from 'His' head. 'His' feet became the earth and 'His' ears became the space. 'He' exists as the color of the sun, the

---

22 Swami Lokeshwarananda, '*Shvetasvatara Upanishad (Translation and notes based on Shankara*'s commentary)', Ramakrishna Mission Institute, Kolkata, 1994, pp.107-108 (V.14, Adhyaya-3).

23 *Rigveda,* Purushasukta, V.10.90.10; 10.90.13-10.90.16

dispeller of darkness. 'He' is omniscient and creates from 'Himself' the world of multiple forms and names.)

From the above, it can be established that all existences of the cosmos are Divine in their essence because that which is born out of the Divine is itself '*The Divine*'. Along these lines, the God or Reality that we search for is our '*Very Self*'. This Self alone appears as the world of variation. However, under the control of ignorance, we elect to see duality and reject the non-dual '*Truth*' from which all creatures of the universe are born, in which they live and in which they are ordained to merge.

Prosperity, joy, and overall advancement flourish in a society where Nature is held in reverence and all lives are respected. Cosmic reverence leads us to being established in Dharma. It allows us to appreciate every life form. We start seeing divine value and purpose attached to each creation. In this respect the Atharvaveda states,

sarvo vai tatra jīvati gauraśavaḥpuruṣaḥ paśuḥ ।
yatredaṃ brahm kriyate paridhijīrvanāyakam ।।[24]
(Where there is complete purity, humans, animals, birds and all other existences live in glee and congruence).

2.4.2 Vedic References for the Pañcamahābhūtas

The Pañcamahābhūtas or the five great elements bring to life the entire world. Every entity of the cosmos from an ant to the heavenly galaxies are a subtle amalgamation of these elements. As long as accord exists within and among these elements, the entire cosmos is established in harmony. However, the moment their coherence is bothered it leads to diseases at an individual level and natural catastrophes, pandemic maladies, floods, draughts, earthquakes and other undesirable events at a universal level. Let's see how the Vedas view the five great elements.

---

24 *Atharvaveda*, V. 8.2.25.

(i) Bhūmi: The Vedas behold '*The Earth*' as the '*The Mother*' who nurtures and fosters all living creatures without any discrimination. She is venerated and is approached with reverence. Ample amount of hymns of Her magnificence decorate the entire body of the Vedas. She is described in the Vedas as a compassionate, benevolent, nurturing, and bountiful Mother. She is the one who blesses everyone with peace and prosperity. It is further stated that the preserver Viṣṇu exists within Her seven layers.[25] This indicates that She is Supremely Divine. Her grandeur can be understood by the following Vedic verses,

gandhadvārāṁ durādharaṣāṁ nityapṣtāṁ karīṣiṇīm।
īśvarīṁ sarvabhūtānāṁ tāmihopahvye śriyam॥[26]

(I evoke here the Goddess of prosperity 'Mother Earth'. The 'Divine One' who nourishes all creatures.)

bhūmi-rdhenurdhariṇī lokadhāriṇī॥[27]
mṛttikè pratiṣthti sarvam tanme nirṇuda mṛttike।
tvayā hatená pāpena gacchāmi páramāṁ gatim॥[28]

(The 'Earth' just like the Mother Cow, confers upon all the creatures the gifts of delight. She nurtures and provides for all. May Goddess Earth, the nourisher of all beings eradicate all evils and lead us to the highest state of being.)

The Mother Earth is not only the source of all lives but is also the physical body of all sentient beings. She is present in all beings for as long as they are in their physical bodies, and they exist in Her once they give up their material form. As a result, when She is bruised, injured, or exploited, the entire cosmic harmony is jeopardized. Her well-being is directly proportionate to the well-being of all lives. The amount of suffering and pain that the human race has inflicted upon Her is unfathomable. However, this compassionate Mother has silently suffered every evil and

---

25 Divedi Kapildev, '*Vedon Mein Vijnan*', Vishvabharti Anusandhana Parishad, 2014, Bhadohi.p.283 *(ato devā avantu no yato viṣṇuvircakarame। pṛthivya sapt dhāmbhiḥ॥)*

26 Pt. Sri Ramanuja Acharya, p.11, V.9

27 *Rigveda*, Durva Mrittika Suktam, V.5 (10th Mandal); (Also see Mahanarayanopnishad)

28 *Mahanarayanopnishad* (V.10.1.9)

continues to forgive and bless all living beings. Unfortunately, today humans have crossed all margins of insensitivity and She has reacted by giving forewarnings in the name of earthquakes, volcanoes, floods, famines, draughts and more. These warnings are to remind the human race that the vision of unity in diversity can alone save the entire cosmos. However, if they disregard this oneness, continuc to exploit Her, abuse other sentient beings (animals, trees, birds, plants) and persistently injure the harmony of the planet, they are on the path of self-destruction. It is time that humans approach the entire globe and all existences with a sense of veneration, regard, benevolence, self-sameness and compassion. As humans continue to mar the earth and ruin Her glories, the Vedas continue to caution us,

'Do not harm the earth for if 'She' gets angry we will face the wrath of Her fury helplessly.'[29]

It must be noted that the Earth has silently witnessed all our actions and all the forms in which we have appeared through several births. In every form, birth and through the spaces of time, She has unconditionally nourished us and has led to our material and spiritual evolution. She has also been a silent witness to our ancestors, instances in time and all events of the world. She has provided every living creature with food and has held for us the waters, the plants, mountains, deserts, animals, humans and everything simultaneously. No being on the earth can ever pay off Her debt and therefore bowing before Her unexplainable compassion is all that we can do. The Bhūmisūktam or the Pṛthvīsūktam of the Atharvaveda affirms the above said emotion towards the '*Mother Earth*'.[30]

The Divine Earth is called '*Viṣvaṁbharā*'[31] for she nurtures all the creatures as her children. She is referred to as '*Vasudhā*' for She is the provider of material and spiritual

29 Dwivedi Kapildev, pp.265-266.

30 *Atharvaveda*, Bhumisukta, V.12.1.7

31 *Ibid.*, 12.1.6

wealth. She is '*Hiraṇyavakṣa*'[32], the one who holds in Her breast '*gold*' and fosters every creature with valuable nutrition and worldly fortune. She is called '*Viṣvadānī*'[33], the one who gives magnanimously at all times, in all seasons, through all situations and without discriminating amongst any creature. She is '*Dhruva*'[34], the one who is firm and gives an unshakable base to all existences, thus making the world operate meticulously.

The Mother Earth is the undisputed provider of vegetation, herbs, medicines, minerals, and various other organic and inorganic materials. It, therefore, becomes our duty to hold Her at the highest pedestal rather than exploiting Her bounties. The Hills, mountains, water bodies, deserts, trees, forests, humans, animals, birds, insects, rocks and more are Her various ornaments. '*Mother Earth*' is not merely a material entity instead She is the source of all existences. In this view, the Yajurveda states that,

yate bhūme vikhnāmi ṣipraṁ tadpi rohatu।
mā te marma vimṛgvari yā te hṛdayampirpam॥[35]
(Whatever part of the Mother Earth you dig into, it must at once be replenished. Never injure the heart or the sensitive parts of Her.)

Thus, for the sake of maintaining the equilibrium, we must refill the vacuum of the earth with manure, ashes from Yajña and provide Her with complete nourishment as we do to a breastfeeding mother. If this care is not given and if She is ruthlessly exploited, it will lead to provoked disaster. Also one must not hurt the internal layers of the earth which are extremely delicate and sensitive.

The Vedas establish a unique bond between Mother Earth and all living creatures. This bond is based upon essential

---

32 *Atharvaveda,* V.13.1.6.

33 *Ibid.,* V.7

34 *Ibid.,* V. 12.1.11.

35 *Yajurveda,* 12.1.65.

unity and apparent diversity. As a result, when we recognize this fundamental non-duality, we naturally venerate the seeming differences. The Vedas emphasize this connection by saying,

mātā bhūmiḥ putroahaṁ pṛthivyāḥ[36]
(The Earth is my mother and I am her child)

pṛthvimātā dyauṣpitā[37]
(The Earth is my Mother and the Sky is my Father)

(ii) Āpaḥ: The Vedas clearly speak of Water as '*Life*', '*Nectar*' and as the finest of '*Physicians*'. It is also venerated as the elixir of life. Water, according to the Vedas, is '*Divine*' and has an inbuilt therapeutic potential that can cure all maladies. It is the best of all medicines[38] and can even cure genetic and cardiovascular disorders.[39] It is well known that no medicine can work without water. Water is said to be the greatest of all doctors[40] and acts as a therapeutic medicine for all living creatures.[41] In this regard states the Yajurveda that,

śaṁnó devīrbhiṣṭaya āpó bhavantu pītaye।
śaṁ yorbhī stravantu naḥ ।। īśāṇā-vāryāṇāṁ kṣayántīś-carṣaṇīnām।
āpo yāccāmi bheṣajam।।[42]

(May the 'Divine Waters' protect us and flow down on us for quenching our thirst and lead us to peace and perfection. O Water! You are Supreme and Divine. We seek your healing powers.)

sumitrāṇa āpah ouṣadhayaḥ santu durmitrāḥ-tasmai।
bhūyāsuḥ asmān dveṣṭi yam ca vayam dviṣmaḥ ।।[43]

---

36 *Atharvaveda*, V.12.1.12.

37 *Yajurveda*, V. 2.10-2.11.

38 *Rigveda*, V.1.23.20.

39 *Atharvaveda*, V. 3.7.5; 6.24.1-6.24.2.

40 *Ibid.*, V.1.5.4.

41 *Ibid.*, V.1.5.4.

42 *Yajurveda*, Taittiriya Aranyaka, V.4.42.19.

(O Divine Waters! You are benevolent, we seek nourishment from you.
Bless us with a part of the Supreme bliss that you possess.
We approach you with reverence so you may lead us to the highest abode,
purify us and let us be reborn with splendor.)

***apsu me somò abravīdantarvīśvānī bheṣajā*[44]**

(A skilled physician states that in the 'Water' lies the capacity to heal all ailments.)

The Vedic civilization regarded '*Water*' as Godly. In the material world, it is of paramount importance. It is no wonder that all important pilgrimages and temples were set up near water bodies. Water is considered to be the most essential for all existences (men, animals, birds, plants and all life forms). None can carry on without it. It is the source of peace and calm.[45] Water is regarded as nectar, which is chaste, flawless, and celestial. The Ṛgveda refers to the water as,

***'The Mighty One'*[46]**

Unfortunately, the modern man has forgotten that he exists in non-dualism with Water and this duality has led him to exploit water bodies in the most pitiless manner. Degradation of aquatic ecosystems, surface water pollution, marine pollution, and ground water pollution caused by excessive use of chemicals and pathogens, contamination of water bodies, plastic debris, sewage pesticides, industrial leaks, and hydraulic fracturing are just a few of the many issues associated with water pollution. These problems have harmed not just the ecosystem, but have also ruined the health and beauty of water bodies, the well-being of air, land, sea species, and the overall health of the planet. Furthermore, water contamination has a severe impact on plants, trees, and crops, which are rapidly losing their distinct

---

43 *Yajurveda*, Taittiriya Aranyaka, 4.42.26

44 *Atharvaveda*, Navgrehsuktam, V.1.6.2.

45 *Shatapathabrahman*, V.1.2.2.11

46 *Rigveda*, Hiranyagarbhasuktam, V.121.7-121.8.

traits. Pollution prevents sunshine and oxygen from reaching sentient beings dwelling in aquatic bodies, causing them to perish. It is time for the human race to recognize that harming these sentient and conscious water bodies is unquestionably paving the way to the end. It is to be remembered that in the wellness of life-enriching waters bodies lies the wellness of the entire cosmos. In this regard announces the Chāṅdogyaopniṣad,

āpo vāvānnādbhūyastasmādyadā suvṛṣṭirna bhavati
vyādhīyante prāṇā annaṃ kanīyo bhaviṣyatītyatha yadā
suvṛṣṭirbhavatyānandinaḥ prāṇā bhavantyannaṃ bahu
bhaviṣyatītyāpa evemā mūrtā yeyaṃ pṛthivī yadantarikṣaṃ
yaddyauryatparvatā yaddevamanuṣyāyatpaśavaóca vayāṃsi
ca tṛṇavanaspatayaḥ śvāpadānyākīṭapataṅgapipīlakamāpa
evemā mūrtā apa upāssveti॥[47]

(The 'Divine Waters' are undoubtedly superior to food. That is the reason why in the absence of rain, all living creatures worry about the scarcity of food. However, when there is rainfall in abundance, all living beings rejoice and are gleeful. All these creatures are nothing but 'Water' in various forms. The earth, atmosphere, space, mountains, Gods, animals, birds, reptiles, creepers, trees, worms, insects and ants all are nothing but Water. Thus, one must revere 'The Water' which is the essence of all lives.)

(iii) Vāyu: Air is the life and cosmic breath. It is because of Air that life dances. There is not a single being that can exist without air. In Air exists all beings of the world and in all beings of the world exists the Air. '*Vāyu*' is considered Divine in the Vedas and there are various hymns that glorify the Divine Vāyu as the Highest Reality. While revering the Godly Air, the Vedas say,

---

47 Swami Nikhilananda, p.338. (V. 7.10.1 Chandogyaopnishad)

namaste vāyo! tvameva pratyakṣaṁ brahmāsi ।।
tvameva pratyakṣaṁ brahm vadiśyāmi ।
ṛtam vadisyāmi । ***Satyam vādiṣām*** । ***tanmāmavatu*** ।[48]

(Salutations to Vayu! You are the living, manifested Brahman. You are the Divine. You are the subtle seer. You are the knower of the cosmic order, the knower of truth and the subtle essence of all).

It must be noted that the meaning of the word '*Vāyu*' has been made clear in the Śatapatha Brāhmaṇa where it is stated,

The entire universe is woven in a string and that string is 'Vāyu'.[49]

Therefore, the word '*Vāyu*' has a broader meaning and is only casually translated as '*Air*' which has a much limited connotation. '*Vāyu*' refers to a cosmic principle that pervades every entity and indwells within all. It is itself living and thus it becomes the essence of all lives. Air becomes the instrument through which herbal medicinal properties reach us during Yajña. Thus, says the Ṛgveda,

tanno vāto mayo bhuvātu bhesjaṁ tanmātā ।[50]

(May the air waft to us the pleasant medicine from the particular fire which is healing).

Further, even the Yajurveda refers to the air as a universal healer that bestows immortality and perishes away all evils,

āvātavāhi bheṣajaṁ vivātavāhi yadrapaḥ ।
tvaṁ hi viśvabheṣajodevānāṁ dūtaīyase ।।[51]

(O Divine Wind! Bestow us with healing powers for you are the universal healer and the carrier of the message of Gods. You alone are the medicine of all ailments.)

Sadly, the new age man under the veil of duality, greed and ignorance has caused unfathomable damage to the air

---

48 (i) Yajurveda, Taittiryopnishad, Shikshavalli, Dvadashonuvaka, V.1
(ii) Goel Aruna, '*Environment and Ancient Sanskrit Literature*', Deep & Deep Publications, Delhi, 2003, p.139.

49 Raja Ram Mohan Roy, '*Vedic Physics, Scientific Origin of Hinduism*', Golden Egg Publishing, Toronto, 1999, p.84. (V.1.192, Jaiminiya Brahman; V.1.24, Yajurveda; V.8.7, 3.10, Shatapatha Brahman).

50 *Rigveda,* a no bhadrah suktam, V.1.89.4 (Vishvadeva).

51 *Yajurveda,* Taittiriya Aranyaka, Shanti Mnatrani, V.4.42.5.

and has inflicted unimaginable harm to all beings of the earth. He has destined the entire globe to serious ailments like respiratory problems, heart issues, chronic obstructive pulmonary diseases, cardiovascular disorders and lung cancer. All these maladies spring from contaminated air. Polluted air not only proves to be a hazard for humans but also harms animals, birds and puts unbearable stress upon trees and plants. Many humans, animals and birds are destined to premature death every year because of air pollution. Unfortunately, India has the highest death rate.[52] Smoke from industries, fossil fuel power stations, motor vehicles, marine vessels, aircrafts, greenhouse gasses, fumes from paints, hair sprays and nuclear weapons become a few of the many causes of air pollution.

(iv) Ākāśa: Space and sound are interrelated and that becomes the basis of noise pollution. Taittiryopaniṣad which is associated with the Yajurveda discusses two types of Ākāśa i.e., the one within the body and the one outside.[53] The inner spaces or Antahkaraṇa of a human being exist in perversion. From within, a human is infected with greed, power and ego which has its roots in Avidyā and these inner states end up polluting the external spaces. In this regard, the Yajurveda advises the human race that,

ghāṁ mā lekhīrantarikṣaṁ mā hiṁsīḥ।[54]
(Do not destroy the space)

Therefore, one needs to be peaceful, calm, positive and tranquil within to make sure that the same is manifested in the entire cosmos. Accordingly, Indian philosophy propagates that all problems that become the cause of grief, unrest and

52 Wikipedia Contributors, 2021, '*Air Pollution*', Online, https://en.wikipedia.org (Accessed April 1, 2021).

53 Swami Gambhirananda, p.248, V.1.6.1, Taittiriyaopanshad (*sa ya eṣo'ntahrdaya ākāśḥ*)

54 *Yajurveda,* V. 5.43.

chaos have their solution within. External manifestations are merely the effects and the cause lies within the inner spaces of our hearts.

The Vedas are flowing with Ricās where one seeks the purity of inner states. It will be worth the while to mention the Śivasaṅkalpasūkta of the Yajurveda where one prays for the sake of attaining purity, calmness, nobility and divinity of the inner states.[55] Though contemporary environmental science doesn't recognize inner states to be the reason for environmental disharmony yet Vedas do profess that it is the internal pollution that leads to outer pollution.[56]

(v) Agni: '*Fire*' is one of the five elements in the Vedas. It is Divine and purifying. It is this fire in the Yajña that leads to purity. At a philosophical level, the fire of wisdom and Ṭapah consumes all that is negative and evil. It is the destroyer of greed, passion and ignorance. It burns away selfish interests and leads one to a state where cosmic welfare becomes his vision and mission. In this relation says the Navagṛhasūktam of the Yajurveda,

udbudhyasvāgne prati jāgṛha tvamiṣṭāpart saṁsṛjethāmayaṁ ca ।
punḥ kṛṇvaṁstvāpitaraṁyuvā namanvātāṁ
sīttvayitantumetam ॥[57]

(The light of wisdom Agni! Let us be vigilant while we work for ourselves and the well-being of all creatures of the cosmos. May we all remain together, even with the departed souls of our forefathers with whom you connect us like a thread.)

yo rudro agnau[58]
(Salutations to Rudra who is the very Agni)

---

55 Kapoor Rajive, '*Shivsankalpasutra*', Ideal Print Links Pvt Ltd, Mumbai, 2016, (V. 34;1-6, *Vajasaneyisamhita, Yajurveda*)

56 Sanghvi Nandita, '*Vedon Me Paryavarana*', Sonali Publications, Jaipur, 2004, pp.313- 356.

57 *Yajurveda, Vajasaneyi Smhita, Navgrahasuktam,* V.5; 15.55.5.

58 *Ibid., Rudram,* V.4.5.29.

In addition to the above, the Tṛsuparṇamantrāṇi of the Atharvaveda states,

hā (gā) ṁsasasuciṣada vasurantarikṣasadadhotā
***vedaśādatithirduronāsata* ।**
nṛṣada varasadṛtāsada vyomasadābajā
***goja rītja adṛjā ṛtam bṛhat* ॥[59]**

(That which appears as the brilliant sun in the clear skies and as the moving air in the mid-regions is none other than the 'Divine Fire'. This Fire indwells within all and is the wellness of the guest (the beings who appear in this world momentarily). This Fire shines in all beings as the very 'Self'. This Fire is consecrated in the Yajña, and it pervades the sky as air, it is born in the ocean as the sublime submarine heat, and it shines as the rays of sun. It is the essence of light and appears as the newborn sun on the mountains. 'Fire' is indeed the Supreme Reality which is the essence of all creations.)

From the above, it can be comprehended that fire is not just Divine but is also meant for the welfare of all. Unfortunately, this fire is being manipulated by humans in the most inauspicious manner. In order to capture land for the sake of high-end infrastructure, this fire is being used to burn up forests and various animals that live in them. This fire is used to instigate riots and destroy the property of the nation and this fire is used to burn a young girl for the sake of dowry. All these crimes are due to the polluted states of our Antaḥkaraṇa and as long we do not purify our inner states; we will go on destroying the world. This state will ultimately lead to our very own destruction.

2.4.3 Vedic References for Divine Animals, Birds and other Sentient Beings

Today animals, birds, reptiles and all other sentient beings exist in fright. Under the guise of ignorance, man has exploited them to the point of absurdity. He ruthlessly kills these divine sentient beings for the sake of their skin, organs,

---

59 *Yajurveda,* Taittirya Aranyaka, Trissuparnamantrani, V.38-40.13.

to hang them up as a piece of décor or merely to relish them as a meal. The pitiful condition of these celestial beings is a question mark on human morals, ethics, education and life. They are beaten up, kicked, enslaved and abandoned. Contrary to this view the Vedic society perceived them in a different light altogether. Animals, birds and insects are considered to be the Divine manifestation and are also referred to as God's Vibhūtis.[60] They have deep significance and have been an integral part of the Vedic, Upaniṣadic, Purāṇic texts, Indian culture, religion, philosophy, astrology, history, Yoga, art, and life. The Nārāyaṇasūkta of the Yajurveda states,

yacća kiñcit jágat sarvaṁ dṛśyate śrūyate'pivā I
antar-bahiścá tatsarvaṁ vyāpya nārāyaṇaḥ sthitaḥ II[61]

(Whatever in the universe is known through perception is pervaded and indwelled by Nārayaṇa.)

In this regard states the Vibūtiyoga of the Śrīmad Bhagwadgīta that,

uccaiḥśvasam aśvānāṁ vidudhi māṁ amṛtodbhvam I
airāvataṁ gajendrāṇām narāṇām ca narādhipam II
āyudhānām ahaṁ vajraṁ dhenūnām asmi kāmadhuk I
prajanaś cāsmi kandarpaḥ sarpāṇām asmi vāsukiḥ II
anantaś cāsmi nāgānām varuṇo yādasām aham II
pitṛṇāṁ āryamā casmi yamaḥ saṁyamatām aham II
prahlādaś cāsmi daityānām kālaḥ kalayatām aham II
mṛgāṇām ca mṛgendróham vainateyaśca pakṣiṇām II
pavanaḥ pavatām asmi rāmaḥ śastrabhṛtām aham II
jhaṣāṇāṁ makaraś cāsmi srotasām asmi jāhnavī II[62]

(Amongst the horses I am 'Ucchaṣvā' that emerged during the churning of the ocean. Amongst the elephants, know Me as 'Airāvta', and I am the 'King' amongst the humans. Amongst weapons, I am 'Vajra'. Amongst the cows, I am 'Kāmadhenu'. For the sake of maintenance of the world, I am 'Kāmadeva'

60 Shankaracharya, '*Shrimadbhagvadgitabhashya*', (Ch.10: Vibhūtiyogaḥ).

61 *Yajurveda*, Narayanasuktam, V.10.13.5.

62 Shankaracarya, '*Shrimadbhagvadgitabhashya*', pp.157-158 (V.10.27-10.31).

and amongst snakes, I am the 'King Vāsuki'. Amongst the Nāgas, I am 'Ananta' and amongst water beings, I exist as 'Varuṇadeva'. Amongst the dead ancestors, I am 'Aryamā' and in terms of discipline, I am 'Yamarāja'. Amongst demons, I am 'Prahlāda' and in terms of account, I am 'Kāla'. Amongst the animals, I am 'Mṛga', 'Simha' and amongst birds, I am 'Gruḍa'. As a purifier of all lives, I am 'Vāyu' and as the protector that holds the weapon, I am 'Rāma'. Amongst the beings of sea, I am 'Magara' and amongst sacred rivers, I am 'The Gaṇgā')

ahaṁ sarvasya prabhavo mattaḥ sarvaṁ pravartate |
iti matvā bhajante māṁ budhā bhāvasamanvitāḥ ||[63]

(From Me sprouts the entire cosmos. I am the source of everything. I am the foundation of all spiritual and physical realms. The wise ones who are fully aware of this, worship and devote themselves to Me.)

aham ātmā guḍākeśa sarvabhūtāśayasthitaḥ |
aham ādiśca madhyaṁ ca bhūtānām anta eva ca ||[64]

(I exist as the Ātman in the hearts of all living creatures and I am the beginning, middle and end of all these beings).

The Vedas profoundly talk about these Divine sentient beings, their personalities, character, food and well-being. The Ṛgveda classifies them into six categories[65] as those who fly in the air (flying birds, virus, flies, etc.), live on the land (dear, cow, fox, humans, etc.), exist in waters (fishes, octopus and other marine animals), live both in water and on land (tortoise, frogs, ducks), stay in forests (tigers, fox, wolf) and the ones that live along with humans (dogs, cats, cows, bulls). Each animal, bird, reptile and insect is associated with a deity and embodies the 'It's' energies. As a result, worshiping that animal entails worshipping that Deity. Bulls, dogs, snakes, the nīlkaṇṭhī bird, lizards, ants and scorpions are associated with *'Lord Śiva'* and His varied forms. The cow is worshiped as '*Śrī*' and is said to be the home of all Deities. Elephants

---

63 Shankaracharya, '*Shrimadbhagvadgitabhashya*, p.151 (V.10.8)

64 *Ibid.*, p.155 (V.10.20)

65 *Rigveda*, V.10.90.8; (Also see; Atharvaveda, V.19.6.14; Yajurveda, V.3.1.6.)

are worshiped as '*Gaṇeśa*'. Lions are associated with '*Ādi Śakti Durgā*'. Crocodiles are connected to '*Goddess Gaṇgā and Yamunā*'. The eagle-Garuḍa and serpent-Ananta in ancient texts are associated with '*Viṣṇu*'. Further, in order to re-establish Dharma, '*Mahāviṣṇu*' appears as a Matsya (fish), Kūrma (tortoise), Varāha (pig), and Nṛsiṃha (half man and half lion). Swan is associated with the goddess of wisdom '*Saraswatī*'. Crows are associated with '*Śani*'. Owls are connected with Goddess '*Lakśmī*'. Peacock is associated with '*Kārtikeya*'. Even the smallest of insects are associated with a certain deity. '*Bhrāmarī*', a wasp who ended the demon Aruṇāsūra is associated with '*Goddess Pārvatī*'. Animals have been revered in the Vedic literature as '*Ṣodaśkalāḥ* (the ones who are bejeweled with sixteen celestial arts).[66] They are also revered as '*Maḥ* (the ones who are great and worthy of worship for their unconditional love and grace).[67]

Gaumātā is a subject of devotion, emotion and reverence in India. She occupies an extraordinary position in the Vedic literature. Hurting, killing or disrespecting the cow is forbidden in the Indian culture. The Vedas glorify the importance of the cow at a physical, emotional, psychological, religious, economic, environmental, social, cosmic, and spiritual level. '*The Mother Cow*' is home to all the deities and divine energies. She is said to be Goddess Lakṣmī.[68] She must never be killed, hurt or injured (Aghnayeyam).[69] The Vedic texts refer to the cow as a noble being that is decorated with glory, brilliance, divinity, purity, beauty, non-violence, calmness, tranquility, wisdom, compassion, love and the ability to nurture all beings.[70] She is an emotional and harmless animal who remembers every pain and affection

---

66 *Samveda,* Tandaya Brahman, 6.12.2, (*sodaśkalāḥ paśavaḥ*)

67 *Shatpatbrahman,* V.11.8.1.3 (*paśvo vai maḥ*)

68 *Atharvaveda,* V. 2.26.3.

69 *Ibid.,* V.7.73.8

70 *Ibid.,* V.1.4.2.53-58

that is extended to her. She is the giver of wealth.[71] Every society that invests in her health, wellness and well-being flourishes by leaps and bounds.

In India, bulls are equally revered and are said to have divine powers.[72] It is a symbol of the unity of physical strength and gentleness. The bull is an animal that is decorated with the virtues of patience, calmness and dedication. The Vedas have not only praised the bull's physical vigor but have also announced it as the '*Lord of animals*'.[73] It is seen and worshiped as the beloved one of 'Lord Śiva' '*Naṇdī*'.

The '*Ṣvāna*' or the dog is declared as Godly in the Vedic texts. The Rudraṁsūkta of the Kṛṣna Yajurveda states that,

vo namo namo mṛgayubhyáś śvanibhyáś ca।
vo namo namaḥ śvabhyaś śvapátibhyaś ca vo namaḥ॥[74]

(I bow to Rudra, the One who controls dogs, the One who is Himself the dog and the One who protects the dogs.)

The Atharvaveda yokes and represents Rudra (A fearsome form of Lord Śiva) with dogs.[75] The Ṛgveda further refers to the dogs as the messenger of God who resides amongst human beings in order to lead them to the auspicious path,

urūṇa sāvá sutṛpā udambalau yamasyá dūtau cárato janāguṁ anú। tāv asmabhyáṁ dṛśaye sryáya punár dātām asúmadyeha bhadram॥[76]

(Salutations to the two Divine broad-nosed messengers (Śyamā and Śabla) who take away our souls. For the sake of leading humans to auspiciousness, you graced mankind by staying amongst them (as dogs))

---

71 *Shatpatha Brahman* V. 1.8.1.36

72 *Atharvaveda*, V. 9.4.5; 9.4.11; 9.4.15.

73 *Samveda*, Tandya Mahabrahman, V. 19.12.6.

74 *Yajurveda*, Taittiryasamhita Rudramsukta, V.4.5.4.

75 *Atharvaveda*, V. 11.12.30.

76 *Rigveda*, Yamasuktam, V., 10.4.12.

The Goddess Dog 'Saramā' appears in the Ṛgveda.[77] She is the beloved daughter of Prajāpti Dakṣa and Virani (Asikni). She is the one with fortunate feet. *Saramā* was married to Maharṣi Kaśyapa. She is also the celestial companion of Devrāja Indra.[78] In Maṅdala five of the Ṛgveda dogs are described as those who know the '*herbs*' and the ones who are *'all wise'* suggesting that they have high intuitive powers and high realms of existence.[79] They are also referred to as '*Vastoṣpati* (the lord and protectors of the house)'.[80] It is believed that all negativities and evils remain at bay in a household that fosters and reveres dogs.

In the '*Aṣṭādhyāyī*' of Maharṣi Pāṇini there are over two hundred names given for dogs that describe them externally, and internally. Some of these names are '*Maṇḍala* (he who moves in circles), *Rātrijāgara* (the one who remains awake at night), *Vakrapuccha* (the one who has a tilted tail), *Sūcaka* (the one who informs of any unforeseen danger), *Śīghracetanaḥ* (the one who awakens before the dawn of any trouble), *Grāmasiṁha* (the lion of the village), *Sārmeyaḥ* (the one whose feet bring luck and prosperity).

Dogs also form an important part of the great epic Rāmāyaṇa[81] and to the surprise of many, the Māhābhārata starts and ends because of the *'Divine Dog'*.[82] Before the battle of Māhābhārata, Arjuna prays to '*Kokāmukha*' a form of

---

77 *Rigveda*, .62.3; 1.72.8; 3.31.6; 4.16.8; 5.45.7; 5.45.8

78 *Ibid.*, V.1.62.3; 1.72.8

79 *Ibid.*, V.45.8

80 *Ibid.*, V.7.55.1-5

81 *Ramayana*, Ch.60-61.

82 *Mahabharata* starts with *Janmejaya* and his brothers who were all set to perform a sacrificial ceremony. Suddenly, a pup appeared and the brothers mercilessly beat him up. The injured puppy, went crying to its mother and narrated the incident. The mother went up to the brothers and asked "Why was my child beaten-up when he had committed no crime?" She thus cursed them. *Mahabharata* ends with *Yudhishthir* refusing to enter heaven without his dog and realizing that the dog was none other than Lord in disguise.

Goddess Durgā who has the face of a dog. Further, Lord Dattātreya who represents the non-duality of *Brahamā-Viṣṇu-Maheśa* accepted dogs as His Guru and Ādi Śaṅkarācārya realized the dogs as the source of all wisdom '*Vedas*'.

The elephant has been described as the most intelligent and physically strong sentient creature with immense power to remember. It is calm, loving, friendly, non-violent, caring and protecting. The first six verses of the Atharvaveda talk about the glory and divinity of the elephant.[83] Similarly, the Vedas in-depth talk of siṁha (lion), aṣva (horse), uṣtha (camel), mayūra (peacock), ulūka (owl), garuḍa (eagle), muṣaka (rat), sarpa (snake), fish (matsya) and many more.

The Śatapathabrahman goes on to announce humans as also animals.[84] It has been further declared that animals and birds have natural knowledge of herbs and can treat themselves.[85] Animals have the innate wisdom of seasons and make changes in their life and food following the weather. While birds are often seen migrating, insects and reptiles hibernate as per the weather and season. They also possess inner wisdom and can sense natural disasters, undesirable events and death.[86] Animals and birds are said to be natural navigators and can find their way through air, water and land. The Yajurveda also states,

"If one wants to understand the ocean, one must understand the water animals. If you want to know the surface of a water body study Śiśumāra (porpoise), to understand the mid of the ocean, study the Maccha (fish), and to understand the depths of it, study the Magara (crocodile)".[87]

The Vedas go on to announce that all animals (including humans) and birds have the qualities of the sun and the

---

83 *Atharvaveda,* V.3.22.1-6 (*hastivarcasvaṁprathatāma*).

84 *Shatapathabrahmana,* V. 3.8.4.1.

85 *Atharvaveda,* V. 8.7.23-25

86 *Yajurveda,* V.24.20 (*vasantāyekapiñjalāna*).

87 *Ibid.,* V. 24.21 (*samudrāyeś iśumārāna*)

moon in them.[88] All animals and birds live in communities or groups and grieve the death or injury of their member.[89] The Vedas also declare that one must not hurt, harm, injure or kill any animal. The text authoritatively states,

abhyaṁ naḥ paṣubhyaḥ|[90]
(Animals must live without any fear)

The Atharvaveda speaks of establishing Gauśālā and Paṣuśālā for the protection of old, injured, disabled and sick animals.[91] It further states that for animals to live happily, forests and trees must be preserved. The society must provide them with adequate food, medicine, grass, leaves and pure, fresh water[92] which are essential for their wellness and well-being.

2.4.4. Vedic References for the Celestial Forests, Trees, Plants and Herbs

Forest, trees, plants and herbs are said to be Godly in the Vedic culture. There are a plethora of Vedic verses that revere them as divine, conscious, and the provider of Amṛta (oxygen), Ouśadhi (medicinal herbs), Anna (food), Phala (fruits), Puṣpa (flowers), Cāyā (shade), Saundarya (beauty), Jīvan (life). These forests, trees and plants are also home to millions of animals, birds and smaller beings who completely depend upon them for survival. A tree is bejeweled with divinity and therefore every part of the tree (Pañcāṅga) is a blessing for all beings of the cosmos. It's Jada (roots), Prakāṇda (trunk), Śākhā (branches), Patra (branches), Phala (fruits) and Puṣpa (flowers) are a boon to the universe. The Ṛgveda is embellished with an entire Sūktam in the glory of Ouśadhi that the divine trees and plants bestow us

---

88 *Yajurveda,* V.24-35.

89 *Rigveda,* V. 8.46.31 (*carthegaṇe, śivatneṣu*)

90 *Yajurveda,* V. 36.22.

91 *Atharvaved,* V.3.14.1-6

92 *Ibid.,* (V.7.13.11; 7.75.1-2)

with. It makes some of the most important revelations concerning trees, herbs, and plants,

'The Divine trees and curative herbs appeared three Yugas before the emergence of Deities and billions of years before the origin of any other being. The 'Divine' manifested as trees, herbs and plants at various places on the earth (on the mountains, deserts, under the water, in plains and more). These Godly appearances were meant to destroy pain, suffering, ailments and heal wounds of all living creatures. They further remove infections and weakness. They have a positive and wholesome effect and lead to complete wellness. These Divine celestial beings nurture, protect and bless all lives with material and spiritual advancement like a mother and thus they are also referred to as 'Mātraḥ'. The holy trees and plants lead us to Mokṣa by destroying diseases, misery and take us beyond the realm of birth and death. Trees and herbs have supreme powers and those creatures who submit to them are bestowed with lifelong wellness. Without any discrimination between man and animal, these saintly trees and herbs have equally blessed all lives.[93]

Just as poison can annul the effect of poison and iron can cut through iron, likewise, trees that are living, conscious and pulsating with consciousness have the ability to provide life and breath to the cosmos. It is to be comprehended that life springs from life and not from that which is inert and lifeless. Therefore, uprooting a tree is uprooting the whole of cosmos and cutting down a tree is cutting down one's own survival. Undoubtedly, trees protect us, nourish us and promote our well-being. They are the destroyer of poison (pollution) and are called *'Viṣdūṣṇī'*.[94] However, they can also lead to complete destruction if they are ruthlessly exploited. The Kauṣītakibrahmaṇa forewarns the human race,

93 *Rigveda, Oushadhisukta,* 10.97.1 to 10.97.23

94 *Atharvaveda,* V8.7.4.

All trees and plants are the fire element. They are the source of fire and destruction. In the event, that humans continue to exploit them, they will merge themselves with the earth and this will lead to the end of the world. Thus, trees as nurturers are Śiva and as destroyers are Rudra in disguise.[95]

The Śatpathbrahmaṇa states that the Highest Truth '*Śiva*' manifests as the trees. Yajurveda's Rudrādhyāya states that trees, vegetables, forests, herbs, creepers and bushes are indeed Śiva.[96] The reasons why these have been referred to as 'Śiva' are,

- The name '*Śiva*' means '*the auspicious one*'. Thus, Śiva becomes the cause of auspiciousness. As Brahma, He creates the world out of Himself and becomes everything visible and invisible, moving and stationary, within and without. As Viṣṇu, He sustains the entire cosmos and in the form of Rudra, He destroys everything. Just like Śiva, trees, vegetables and the plant kingdom become our bodies as they nourish us with food, they become our breadth and they become the source of cosmic life and birth. They also preserve all creatures and sustain them and finally if they are exploited, they self-dissolve themselves and lead to the destruction of the universe.
- Śiva alone can absorb all the poison of the world and bestow the cosmos with longevity, health and auspiciousness likewise trees alone can absorb the poison of carbon dioxide (Co_2) and bestow the cosmos with oxygen which becomes the reason for longevity, health and auspiciousness.
- Śiva is the Highest Reality and nothing in the cosmos including trees, plants, herbs and forests can be anything else other than Śiva.

---

95 *Shatpathbrahman;* V.6.1.3.12 *(auṣdhyo vai paśupatiḥ); (also see; Kaushitakibrahman,* V.6.5 *(yadugro deva auṣdhyovanaspatayastena))*

96 *Yajurveda, Rudradhyaya,* Ch.16.

As far as taxonomy or naming of trees and plants is concerned, the Vedic culture has been extremely conscious and scientific in naming then. The trees are named keeping in mind their Guṇa and Dharma besides which a philosophical, religious and spiritual consideration has also been made while naming them.

The western world uses the Linnaeus technique to name the trees and plants. Carl Linnaeus was a Swedish botanist (1707-1778).[97] However, the great philologist Sir William Jones (1746-1794)[98] in his introduction of the book '*Botanical Observations on Select Indian Plants*' states in regards with Indian plant names and the Saṃskṛt language that,

"I am very solicitous to give Indian plants their true Indian appellations; because I am fully persuaded that Linnaeus himself would have adopted them, had he known the learned and ancient language of this country (Bhāratvarṣa)"[99]

Keeping the above said in mind the fig tree is known as '*The Bodhi Tree*'. It is the tree that leads to realization and it is under this tree that Lord Buddha was enlightened. The Saraca Asoca tree is known as '*The Aśoka Tree*'. This tree eradicates all sorrows and it was this Aśoka tree that ended all the sorrows of Sītā Maiyā. The poisonous plant of thorn apple, commonly known as Dhattura due to its medicinal qualities hidden in its toxicity is known as '*Śivaśekhara*'. Not only trees and plants are auspiciously named but are also planted in a certain quality of earth, in a certain direction and in a certain auspicious Nakṣatra.[100] Further, the name of the land in which we live '*Jambūdvīpa*' comes from the

97 Wikipedia Contributors, 2001, '*Carl Linnaeus*', Online, https://en.wikipedia.org/ (Accessed: April 1, 2021).

98 Wikipedia Contributors, 2001, '*William Jones (philologist)*', Online, https://en.wikipedia.org (Accessed April 1, 2021)

99 Jones William, *'Botanical Observations on Select Indian Plants'*, Vernor and Hood Museum Publication London, 1879, Introduction.

100 *Varahamihira, Brihatsamhita,* V. 55.61.

tree '*Jaṁbū*' and means the land of Jambu trees (Jāmun or Indian berry). The word '*Dvīpa*' refers to an island, continent or planet. There are seven continents described in the Matsyapurāṇa, Viṣṇupurāṇa, Varāhapurāṇa, Nīlamatapurāṇa and other Purāṇic and Vedic texts.[101] Further, in regards with trees, herbs and plants the Vedas state,

mā auṣadhīrhiṁsiḥ।[102]

(Extend no violence towards medicinal herbs and trees.)

mā kā kaṁbīram ud vṛho vanaspatim aṣastīvir hi nīnśḥ।[103]

(Do not cut or uproot trees for they are the destroyers of pollution)

āp auṣdhīruta novantu, dyorvanā giryo vṛkṣkeśa।[104]

(Forests, trees, herbs and mountains are said to be the protectors of all.)

The Atharvaveda further states that,

Trees and plants are both; male and female.[105]

Therefore, there exists sex discrimination in the plant world also. Further, the Charakasaṃhitā says,

bṛhatphalaḥ ṣvetapupaṣpaḥ snigdhapatraḥ pumāna bhavate।
śyāmā cāruṇapuṣpā strī phalavṛntaistathaṇ bhiḥ।[106]

(Those trees that are large, with bigger fruits, have white or corresponding colored flowers, dense, shiny and slippery leaves are male. However, those trees that are shorter in height have smaller fruits, have red or corresponding colored flowers are female).

---

101 *Vishnupurana*, Ch.2; *Varahapurana*, Ch.74; *Matsyapurana*, 121-122. (*Jambudvipa is one of the seven continents mentioned in the Vedic texts which is devided into: Bharatavarsha, Harivarsha, Kimpurusvarsha, Ramyakvarsha, Ramanvarsha, Kuruvarsha, Bhadrasvarsha, Ketumalvarsha, Ilavarsha. These seven continents are divided by seven seas and the eleven mountains mark their boundary which are: Mandar, Gandhamadana, Vipula, Suparshva, Nichadha, Hemakunda, Himadri, Shringavana, Shvetanchala, Nilagiri and Sumeru*).

102 *Yajurveda* V. 6.22.

103 *Rigveda*, V. 14.8.

104 *Ibid.*, p.72 (V.5.41.11)

105 *Atharvaved*, V. 6,16.2 (*vilaho nāma te pitāmadāvatā*)

106 *Charaksamhita*, *Kalpa*, V. 5.5.

The Vedas also go on to state that the plant kingdom is not only conscious but they are as sensitive as humans and animals. They are born and they die, they feel pain and pleasure, joy and sorrow, they sleep and are prone to sickness, they get hurt and bleed when they are broken, uprooted or cut down.[107] In fact, the Atharvaveda states,

asthuvṛkṣā ūdharvasvapnaḥ![108]
(They sleep while they stand)

The Vedas also propound that a dead ancestor, animal or a near and dear one may be reborn as a tree, plant, herb, shrub or creeper.[109] Thus, do no harm to them. Never hurt their trunk or roots. Only for the sake of wellness or to save a life, make use of their fruits, leaves and twigs. Even in such a case one must bow down to the plant, seek its consent, seek forgiveness and pluck only the amount needed for the sake of food or medicine. After one plucks the leaves, fruits or breaks the twigs, it is important to water the plant mixed with sugar and turmeric in its roots. One must also take care of not touching, breaking or plucking any plant, tree, vegetable or herb after sunset.[110] The *Mahābhārata* in this regard states,

"Trees, plants and herbs drink water through their roots and make their food through sunlight. They digest the food due to the presence of Vāyu and Agni that is within them. When they are injured, they experience unimaginable pain. They are affected by pleasant and foul smells. They do fall sick and feel weakness and wellness. A creeper exactly knows how and where to climb, this proves that they have a divine vision (in Indian philosophy vision and sight are separate. A creature may not have sight

---

[107] Dwivedi Kapildev, pp.79-80.

[108] *Atharvaved*, V.6.44.1.

[109] Dwivedi Kapildev, p.80.

[110] *Ibid.*, p.85.

***which is connected to material eyes but it has a vision which is connected to the inner states of being). Despite being physically strong, trees are extremely sensitive to weather, kind-harsh words, pure-impure thoughts, good-bad touch*'.[111]

Forests are considered extremely essential in the Vedic literature. Forests are home to millions of plants, trees, herbs, animals, birds and other smaller celestial beings. They protect all the lives that live in them and further nurture them. They are a source of food, water, and shade for these creatures. These sentient beings live in the forest with peace, calm and without fear.[112] Along with other creations of the cosmos, forests add to the splendor and beauty of the earth. The Vedas in fact view the whole cosmos as a forest where all beings must live in accordance with their Dharma. In order to make sure that the beauty of the world is maintained, the forests have to be preserved and revered.

For thousands of years' plants and trees have decorated the Indian culture, art, architecture, philosophy, religion, traditions, occasions and have been the foundation of life. They are worshiped and are held in high esteem. Sadly, the modern man has turned a deaf ear to the wise Vedic voices and has been exploiting these conscious beings mercilessly. He has cut down forests and destroyed the homes of zillions of animals. Deforestation has led to ruining of Biodiversity, dipping levels of oxygen, extinction of various plant and animal species, injuring of the ozone layer, global warming, natural disasters and climate change. Mass destruction of forests has not only affected the glaciers but has adversely injured the overall health of the planet and its sentient beings including the human species.

---

111 *Mahabharata, Shantiparva* (*Adhyaya* 1.8.4), V.184.10-18.

112 *Rigveda*, V.10.146; 1-6.

2.4.5. Vedic References for the Celestial Water Bodies, Clouds and Rains

As mentioned before '*Water*' in general and all water bodies in specific are revered in the Vedic literature. Each water body in India has been specifically named, is attached to a deity, has a certain Guṇa and accordingly has a prescribed function and duty. Water bodies such as oceans, seas, rivers and streams help in nourishment, preservation of life, spiritual and material upliftment and bestow all beings with liberation. The Vedas particularly talk about the importance of those water bodies that originate from the Himālayas and how their divine qualities make them beneficial for all lives.[113]

Water bodies have been seen as pulsating traditions, breathing cultures, all-encompassing philosophies, living religions and are the lifeline of the entire cosmos. The importance attached to water bodies cannot be summed up in the best of words. An example of one such living tradition is '*The Gaṇgā*'. She is revered and worshiped not just as the Highest Reality at a transcendental plane but is supremely revered at a material level as '*The Mother*'. She becomes the link between the physical world and the trans-physical spheres and it is merely through '*Her*' that one can attain liberation. At a religious level, no ritual can be complete without the Ganges. At a philosophical level, She is the Supreme Brahman and the cause of all lives. At an ecological level, She is not only home to thousands of sentient beings but also supports their existence. At a medicinal level, Her water is rich in minerals and helps in curing various ailments and in terms of belief, it is strongly held in the Sanātana Dharma that only once you merge with Her, your journey in the world is said to be complete. Lord Kṛṣna in the Śrīmad Bhagwadgītā states,

---

[113] Dwivedi Kapildev, p.267.

srotasām asmi jāhnavī ।[114]
(Amongst the rivers, I am the Gaṇgā)

Likewise, the Yamunā, Saraswatī, Narmadā, *Kāverī*, Kṛṣnā, *Godāvrī* are rivers that are held in great reverence in the Vedic traditions. The Nādistutisūkta of the Ṛgveda is a dedication to the '*Divine Rivers*'.[115] In addition, the Vedas also speak of large water bodies called '*Samudra*'. The word '*Samudra*' is of Saṃskṛta origin. It is made of roots '*Saṁ* (gathering)' and '*Udra* (water)'. Therefore, the word refers to the confluence of smaller water bodies. The Vedas never speak of flowing of the ocean or the Samudra rather it is a place where all smaller water bodies end their journey and expand their identity.[116] Thus, the Ṛgveda states,

agriṃ viśvā abhi prakṣaḥ sacante samudraṁ na sarvataḥ ।
sapta yahvīḥ । nā jāmibhirvi cikite vayo no vidā deveṣu ।।[117]
(The seven Divine Rivers seek the Samudra. They eagerly flow into the 'It' but are unable to fill it.)

It has also been stated in the Ṛgveda[118] and the Atharvaveda that the ocean within it holds the wealth of magnificent precious stones.[119] The Samudra is further to be a source of rain and electricity.[120] The Advaita Vedānta Darśna often cites the example of the ocean as '*Brahman*' and waves as the various entities of the world to describe the non-duality of the Transcendent Reality and the world of material. Thus, oceans are worshiped as the very Divine along with all other water bodies.

---

114 Shankaracharya, '*Shrimadhagvadagitabhashya*', p.158 (V.10.31)

115 Wikipedia Contributors, 2006,'*Nadistutisukta*', Online, https://en.wikipedia.org (Accessed April 1, 2021).

116 *Rigveda* V. 6.36.3; 8.44.25.

117 Griffith Ralph T.H, pp.113-114; 870-872, (*Rigveda,*V.1.71.7 ; 7.33.8,)

118 Rigveda, V. 1.97.44, *Rigveda*

119 *Atharvaveda,* V. 1.13.3.

120 Dwivedi Kapildev, p.269.

The Vedas not only talk of the scientific manner in which the clouds are formed by the evaporation of sea water in six and a half months but also suggest Yajña as a remedy to hasten the entire process which helps the vapors to move up at a faster pace and thus the rains take place. In this regards says the Yajurveda,

samudra dūrmirmadhumāna udārata amṛtasyan।[121]
(In the naval of the ocean lies the rain)

Clouds have been seen as Godly and Divine. Only if they bless the world, it rains. The rains are essential for the health and well-being of the earth and all its creatures. In the absence of rains, draught, lack of food, water, electricity, the occurrence of diseases, heat wave and a whole lot of other issues take shape. It is unfortunate that due to the pollution of water bodies, air and earth we are now facing a decline in rains. We are also destined to acid rains due to man's uncontrollable greed which is severely affecting the entire planet.

2.4.6. Vedic References for Time, Heavenly Planets, and Constellations

The Vedas have revered 'Time' as '*Kāla/ Mahākāla*' and have considered it Divine. Kāla or Mahākāla' is also referred to as '*Lord Śiva*' or the Great Time. It is further refered to as '*Death*' and is associated with the deity of '*Yamrāja*'.[122]

A common '*Hindu*' is often heard saying that '*nothing happens before time*', '*time decides everything*', '*time is a great healer*' and '*none can stay alive once his final time has arrived*'. This throws light on the fact that despite modernization the concept of the divinity of time is deeply ingrained in an Indian mind. In the Bhagvadgītā, Lord Kṛṣna describes Himself as,

---

121 *Yajurveda*, V.17.89

122 WikipediaContributors,2005, '*Kaal*', Online,https://en.wikipedia.org (Accessed April 1, 2021).

***kālośmi lokaṣyakṛt prvṛddho lokān smāhartum iha pravṛtaḥ*।[123]**
(I am the Supreme destroyer called 'Kāla')

The Atharvaveda talks about the heavenly planets.[124] '*Sūrya*' or the Sun is not seen as a mere planet in the Vedic culture rather and it is revered as the soul of the cosmos. The Vedas referer to the Sun as being multiple. The Sun is also the source of energy, rain, light, and color. In this regard, the Vedas highlight,

***sūrya ātmā jagatsta syupaśch*।[125] *yasmin sūrya arpitaḥ sapta sākam*।[126]**
daṣam diṣo nānā sūryaāḥ*।[127] *ava divastārayanti sapta sūryasya
raṣmayaḥ*।[128] *ye trişptāḥ priyanti viṣvārūpāṇi bibhrataḥ*।[129] *ṣāḥśuṣṇaṁ
***pari pradakṣiṇata*।[130] *suṣumṇaḥ sūryaraśimaścandramā gaṅdharvaḥ*[131]**
***ādityaḥ na kadācanāstameti*।[132] *dhāryanta ādityāso jagata stha*।**
***ahorātre pari sūryaṁ vasāne*। *prāsya viṣvā tirto vīryāṇi*।[133]**
***aho rātrairvimitaṁ triṁ śaddgaṁ*।[134]**

(The Sun is the cosmic soul. Just like our solar system, there are seven other divine solar systems. There are ten directions and multiple suns in the cosmos. The Sun has seven rays that cause rainfall. The rays of the sun gives color to every object of the world. The earth revolves around the sun and rotates on its axis. The moon shines because of the reflected light of the same. The Sun neither sets nor does it ever rises.)

From the above, it can be comprehended that the Sun is the essence of life. It energizes our being and creates a

---

123 Shankaracharya,'*Shrimadbhagvadgitabhashya*', p.175. (V.11.32)
124 *Rigveda*, V.1.115.1; *Yajurveda*, V.7.42; *Atharvaveda*, V.13.2.25
125 *Ibid.*,
126 *Atharvaveda*, V. 13.3.10,
127 *Rigveda*, V. 9.114.3.
128 *Atharvaveda*, V. 7.107.1.
129 *Ibid*, V. 1.1.1.
130 *Rigveda*, V. 10.22.14,
131 *Yajurveda* V. 18.40.
132 *Rigveda, Aittaryabrahmana*, V. 3.44.
133 *Atharvaveda*, V. 13.2.32.
134 *Ibid.*, (V. 13.3.8)

platform for us to live and experience the various facets of the material world. The Vedic culture philosophically sees the Sun as the '*One*' who showers upon all beings the light of wisdom, brilliance and splendor. It is the eradicator of the darkness of ignorance, evil and fear. Therefore, one bows in humility before the Sun and seeks knowledge. In this regard the Yajurveda states,

mayī medhāṁ mayī prajāma mayī sūryobhrājo dadhātu।[135]
(Sūrya! Bestow us with wisdom and prudence)

There also exists an Upaniṣad in the glory of '*Sūrya*' known as the '*Sūryaopaniṣad*'. It is associated with the Atharvaveda and refers to '*Sūrya*' as the Ultimate Reality '*Brahman*',

ye evam vedasa vai brahmanaḥ।[136]
(The Sun that is the Brahman becomes the essence of the Vedas)

sūryādvai khalvimāni bhūtāni jāyante।[137]
(All the creatures are born out of Sūrya)

Other than the Sun, eight more Godly planets have been spoken about in the Vedas, they are: Caṅdra (Moon), Buddha (Mercury), Śukra (Venus), Maṅgala (Mars), Bṛhaspati (Jupiter), Śani (Saturn), Rāhu (north lunar node), and Ketu (South lunar node). They all are the governor of the universe and the ones who execute ethical, moral and cosmic codes. They have been seen by the Vedic texts as living, conscious, all-knowing and all-seeing planets. Each planet has a specific Guṇa (quality) and accordingly affects the cosmos and all beings. They not only have astronomical and scientific significance but also play a pivot role in terms of astrology, religion, spirituality, philosophy, karma, ethics, morals, virtues and environment. Further,

---

135 *Yajurveda, Medhasuktam* V. 4.10.46.

136 Joshi, Bimali, Trivedi, '*112* Upanishad', Parimal Publication, Delhi, 2013, p.298, (*Atharvarveda, Suryaopnishad,* V. 63.1,)

137 *Ibid.*, p.299. (V.63.2).

each planet is associated with a tree, plant, herb, animal, stone and more. For example, the planet Śani is said to be the Lord of justice. He accordingly makes a person enjoy or suffer in order to take him at a higher physical, mental, emotional, spiritual, cosmic and ethical sphere. It is a symbol of righteousness, Tapas, Tyāga, kindness towards all, dedication, honesty and discipline. The Pīpal tree represents the energies of planet Śani and in terms of animals, the buffalos, dogs and crows are His representations. It has been further advocated that telling lies, causing harm to any living creature (man, animal, bird, tree, plants, etc.), cheating, backbiting or ruining someone's reputation can induce the '*Vakradṛṣṭi*' of the deity and thus the being will suffer from ill health, misery, misfortune, loneliness, depression, mental fatigue and financial losses. The ones who are well-wishers of all lives are blessed by Śani and if He has to take someone towards spiritual asceticism He will give pain, pleasure and loneliness for the sake of spiritual advancement. Likewise, the planet Bṛhaspati (Jupiter) is associated with, banana trees, elephants and horses.

In addition to the above, the Navagraha (nine planets), the twenty-eight Nakṣatras (constellations), Māsa (month), Tithi (dates), Dina (day) have been considered divine and have been associated with the Highest Energy. For example, Revatī Nakṣatra (zeta piscium constellation)[138] is associated with the fish and with water as its element. Likewise, the month of Śrāvaṇa, which is the fourth month of the Indian National Civil Calendar (Śālivāhana Śāka calendar)[139] marks

138 Wikipedia Contributors, 2007, '*Revati Nakshatra*', Online, https://en.wikipedia.org (Accessed April 1, 2021).

139 *Shalivahana Shaka Calendar* is used along with the Gregorian calendar as per the The Gazette of India. The *Shalivahana Shaka* or the *Shaka Samvata* Hindu calendar is also prevalent in Java, Bali and Indonesian. Bali, goes on to celebrate 'Nyepi or the Day of Silence' as its official new year. The 'Nepal Sambat' used by Nepal has its origin in the Saka calendar. The calendar has also been used in the contemporary Philippines before colonization according to the Laguna Copperplate Inscription.

the starting of the rainy season. It is supposed to be the holiest month dedicated to the worship of Lord Śiva.[140] During this month farming, journey of any kind, plucking of plants, etc. are prohibited because this is the month of breeding for all beings. As an act of compassion and reverence to Lord Śiva, devotees eat only once a day and sacrifice their two meals for the sake of other animals and birds who are in the process of mating and require food and energy for the sake of well-being and reproduction. Similarly, in terms of dates, people observe fast on the '*Caturthī*' or the fourth day that falls after the new moon. The date is associated with *Lord Gaṅeṣa* and is a symbolism of the *'Fourth State of Being (turīya avasthā)'*. The fourth state of being is a state of complete non-duality and this day aims at the achievement of a state where one realizes complete non-dualism with the rest of the creation. The fast observed on this day is a symbolism of material sacrifice for the wellness of the entire cosmos and the realization of the highest state of being.

Along the above-mentioned lines it is clear that the stated entities are considered living, conscious and at a high pedestal by the Vedic seers. It is unfortunate, that science considers them as mere material and in the desire to overpower outer space, it has led to space pollution which is a result of dysfunctional spacecraft, abandoned launch vehicles, mission-related and fragmentation-associated debris.[141] This pollution not just fetters outer space but harms the entire universe and affects each of its beings. Further, it is disheartening to see that time has merely been reduced as a scale of calculation while fasting in modern times has become a fad for the sake of detoxing our bodies.

---

140 Wikipedia Contributors, 2004,' *Shraavana'*, Online, https://en.wikipedia.org (Accessed: April 1, 2021).

141 Wikipedia Contributors, 2004, '*Space Debris'*, Online, https://en.wikipedia.org (Accessed April 1, 2021).

2.4.7. Vedic Yajña, Mantras, and Bali for Cosmic Harmony

1. The Vedic Yajña: The Vedas speak highly of Yajña or havan. It has been prescribed by the Vedas as an act that is beneficial for the entire cosmos. It is through Yajña that one can attain balance with Nature. Yajña promotes environmental wellness, atmospheric purity, inner and outer well-being. It removes pollution on an overall level and promotes quality of life. Yajña is a scientific process that strikes a balance between O_2 (oxygen) and CO_2 (carbon dioxide) in the atmosphere. It is an amalgamation of science, spirituality, culture, compassion and faith. It is through inner awareness and Yajña that the purity of earth, water and air can be attained. There is a natural cycle in the cosmos through which each substance is established and based on which seasons, day-night, solar system, etc operate. This natural cycle is technically known as '*Yajña*'. The Ṛgveda and the Yajurveda describe the same as,

yatpuruṣeṇa haviṣā devā yajñamatanvata |
vasantosyāsīdājyaṁ grīṣma idhamḥ śaruddhviḥ |[142]
(In the cyclic rainy Yajña, spring is the Ghī, summer is firewood and the autumn season is the offering).

The above-said process operates throughout the cosmos. The minutest of atoms and the massive galaxies operate as per this process. It is this process alone that is responsible for the continuous change and operation of everything visible and invisible. Thus, the Vedas declare that,

ayaṁ yajño bhuvnasya nābhiḥ[143]
(Yajña is the very core of the cosmic cycle)

As mentioned before, Vedic Yajña is meant to promote cosmic wellness, well-being, health, happiness and harmony. In this regard, Prof. S.R. Bhatt in his book '*Indian Spirituality: Theory and Praxis*'[144] states,

---

142 *Rigveda*, 10.90.6; *Yajurveda*, 31.14

143 *Ibid.*, V.1.64.35

144 Bhatt S. R., '*Indian Spirituality: Theory and Praxis*', Indian Council of Philosophical Research, Delhi, 2018, p.24.

"Yajña is the principle of co-existence, harmony, co-operation and partaking. It is the 'Anāsakta Karma' as enunciated in the Bhagvadgītā. It is the best of Karma to be performed[145] as it is the pivotal principle of the cosmos.[146] It has been defined as a collective endeavor, preserving and enhancing of natural resources, and it is to be performed with the aim of equitable and distributive sharing of fruits.[147] Thus, after the performance of Yajña, it is said that 'Idam na mama (it is not for me alone)'.[148] Therefore, it is a process through which there is a transition from 'Mama (mine)' to 'Sarva (all)'"

Further, the Yajurveda states that,

'Yajña is the source of joy. It eradicates all pessimisms and all pollutions from the Pañcamahābhūta and leads to physical, mental, emotional, spiritual and cosmic wellbeing.'[149]

Yajurveda's chapter-18, Mantra-1 to 29 also talks about the removal of all kinds of pollutions; attainment of tranquility, prosperity, cosmic health; fruitful farming, plenty of grains; glories of trees, plants, vegetables and benefits of seasons. All of these can be attained with Yajña.

The Yajña has to be performed in a sacred fire pit called '*Havankuṇda*' as per the mathematical and geometrical directions laid down in the Śulvasūtras.[150] The size of the Kuṇda is ascertained by the intent and kind of performance of the Yajña. It is to be noted that Yajña elevates the levels of oxygen and reduces pollution. It leads to the overall health of all beings. Dr.Swami Satya Prakash Saraswati in his book

---

145 *Śatapathbrahmaṇa*, V. 1.7.1.5, *(yajñovai śreṣthatamam karma)*

146 *Atharvaveda*, V.9.11.94, *(yajñoviśvasyabhv̆anasyanābhi)*

147 *Ibid.* (*sāmudāyikamyogakṣmamuddiśyasamudyāyāṅgataya Kriyamāāṇam Karma yajñaḥ*).

148 *Idamna mama*' (The fruit of yajna is prasada and is not meant for oneself but is to be enjoyed and distributed amongst all.)

149 *Yajurveda*, V. 9.21

150 *Shulbhsutras* is the text of Geometry that has Sutras related to the Havankuṇda construction.

'*Aum Agnihotra - An Ancient Process of Fumigation (A Study From the Chemical Standpoint)*' states,

"in the materials of Agnihotra some elements produce the formaldehyde gas (CH_2O) which spreads in the atmosphere without undergoing any change. Even carbon dioxide (CO_2) transforms to a large extent into formaldehyde gas (CH_2O) which is a strong germicide. This gas is activated only when it comes in contact with water vapors. This is the reason why the Havankuṇda is sprinkled with water from all four sides."[151]

The Central Pollution Control Board, Delhi has done various experiments with Yajña and all the experiments had an outstanding result. One of the experiments is given below,

'An experiment was conducted in the open at the Karawal Nagar, East Delhi. Here, 108 Havanuṇdas were made and Yajña was performed. The sampling was done based upon the comparison of the microbe colony counts before, during and after the Yajña. The results showed a drastic reduction of 55% in bacteria, 15% in fungi, and 79% in the pathogens on the next day after the Yajña was over'.[152]

Yajña has a bunch of benefits. It maintains the inner, outer and cosmic environment. It helps in decreasing air, water, and land pollution. It also leads to mental and spiritual wellness and eradicates negativities of all kinds. Scientifically, it has been proven that Yajña produces certain gasses like ethyl oxide (C_2H_4O), propylene (C_3H_6), Acetylene (C_2H_2) and more that combat pollution.[153] Let's have a look at the material (*sāmagrī*) used in Yajña,

---

[151] Swami Prakash Satya, '*Aum Agnihotra - An Ancient Process of Fumigation (A Study From the Chemical Standpoint)*', Jan Gyan Prakashan, India, 1974, pp.71-73.

[152] Sharma Pushpendra, Tripathi C.N, Ajnavi S and Dubey S.K, '*Agnihotra- A Non-Conventional Solution to Air Pollution*', International Journal of Innovative Research in Science & Engineering, UP, 2014, p.2.

[153] Dwivedi Kapildev, p.278.

(i) Wood: for the sake of '*Agniprajvalana*' the Vedas prescribe collecting wood only from those trees that burn away swiftly, have negligible smoke and emit the least CO_2. Such wood converts into holy ash and leaves behind no charcoal (C). Since these wood emit the least CO_2 they cause no harm. Further, only the branch of a tree which has fallen on its own or that has no new or young leaves can be taken after praying and seeking consent from the tree for the sake of cosmic welfare. No trunk of the tree is allowed to be cut nor is any tree allowed to be uprooted. The Vedas sanction the branches of trees such as Āma (Mang)/Mangi) era Indica), Gular (Ficus Raccmosa), Pīpala (Ficus Religiosa/ Sacred Fig Tree), Śamī (Prosopis Cineraria), Palāśa (Butea Monosperina), Bargad (Banyam Tree), Bilva (Bael, Aegle Manmelos)

(ii) Agni: The Vedas consider fire to be the greatest of all purifiers which destroys negativities, diseases, infections, impurities, pollution and more. It is the symbol of light, wisdom and health.[154]

(iii) Ghī: is the main ingredient in Yajña. The Ghī that has been obtained from the Mother-cow is said to be the finest of all. Ghī purifies the environment and eliminates all toxins from it. Further, Ghī is said to be an antidote to poison and therefore, a person who is bitten by a poisonous snake is fed with Ghī. Ghī used in Yajña also disinfects the atmosphere and leads to overall health and prosperity.[155]

(iv) Havya: is the oblation burnt in the Havankuṇda. When the oblations are ingested by the Agni, they are dissolved and bifurcate into minute particles. These particles purify the environment efficiently and effectively. The more a material is diluted, the greater potency it has. The Homeopathic and the Bio-chemic medicine systems are

---

154 Griffith Ralph T.H, *Rigveda,* p.118-119, V.1.74.3, (*uta bruvantu jantava udaghnirvṛtrahājanid dhanaṃjayo raṇe-raṇ*||) (Also see, *Rigveda,* V. 7.13; 7.14)

155 *Atharvaveda* V. 6.32.1.

based upon this concept. The Vedas state that no element is ever destroyed rather it merely exists in a different form. Science also accepts the same thought. The material used in Havana changes its form, becomes lighter and spreads in the environment in order to purify it and benefit all beings as they breathe. Just as a small ice cube melts into half a glass of water, likewise a small amount of '*Havan offerings*' have the potency of benefiting thousands of beings. There are four different types of Havyas called '*Homa Havya*', i.e.,

- **Puṇyagaṃdha Havya**: It includes aromatic spices such as Elā (cardamom) Jaiphala (Nuhmeg) Kesar (saffron) Chandan Sandalwood) etc. This Havya helps to detoxify the surroundings while also adding to the natural therapeutic aroma.
- **Prapuṣyati Havya:** This Havya is nutritiously abundant in materials that add to the general wellness of the environment and benefits all living beings. It uses environmentally enriching products, i.e. milk, Ghī, roots, fruits, grains, herbs, etc.
- **Rogahara Havya:** The Havya is both medicinal and remedial. It uses medicinal herbs like Somalatā (Moon plant) Gugala (Commiphora wightii), Giloye (Tinospora Corditolia), Kapūra (camphor), etc. These offerings are effective against a wide range of bacterial and viral infections.
- **Madhurama Havya:** This Havya includes special sweet offerings i.e: Laddū, Khīra, Mīthī Khichaḍī. These Miśthānas are prepared as per the Vedic instructions. The same is known as Sthālīpāka in which cow milk becomes one of the essential ingredients. This Havya leads to curing specific diseases and further purifies the entire environment.

2. The Vedic Maṇtras: Maṇtras are a set of sacred and holy collection of words, sounds, phonemes, and syllables. These are sounds that are pronounced according to Vedic guidelines and produce a certain resonance and effect. Each

'*Maṇtra*' is a codification of a certain cosmic force. Thus, Maṇtras act as a bridge between the material world and the Supreme Consciousness.

The Vedic Maṇtras are recited in the present day for the sake of phonology rather than semantics. These divine Maṇtras are said to be the primordial rhythms of creation.[156] As they are recited, the cosmos is rejuvenated for they invigorate and nourish all forms of creation.

These Divine Maṇtras are recited by a qualified priest during a sacrificial ceremony for the sake of bringing about peace and harmony within and without, on an individual as well as on the cosmic level, in the Pañcamāhābhūtas and for the sake of Sarvbhūtahita. This is done because natural elements are home to varied energies. Therefore, these Deities/energies are evoked by the utterance of certain Maṇtras during a ritual or ceremony. Hence, each Deity is a symbol of a certain natural force (i.e.-Indradeva-lightning, wind and thunder. Varuṇadeva-sky and water, Agnideva-fire, Kṣetrasyapati-deity of fields) and is evoked as per the Vedic instruction for cosmic harmony. It is further declared that,

apo ousadhiruta no, vantu dyaurvana girayo vṛkśkeśaḥ[157]
(May the medicinal plants, the waters, the sky, the forests, the mountains, and the trees protect us.)

There are uncountable Manṭras in the Vedas that highlight environmental wellness, care and concern, i.e. Apahsūkta, Bhūmisūkta, Satyam Ṛtaṁ Bṛhat Maṇtra, Agni Sūkta and more. Therefore, Vedic voices have a deep-rooted significance which is meant for cosmic harmony, environmental wellness and a general spirit of unification.

3. The Vedic Bali : The Vedic wisdom is of paramount importance. If one judiciously reads the Vedas, he will

---

156 Holdrege Barbara, '*Veda and Torah: Transcending the Textuality of Scripture*', Sunny Press, New York, 1996, pp.347.

157 *Rigveda*,V. 5.41.11

conclude that the crux of the Vedic teachings and rituals is indeed cosmic concord. This coherence is based upon the realization that we all are interdependent, and as a result, one must foster ethical codes of conduct towards oneself and towards the whole of creation. The Vedas advocate only that which is meant for the welfare of all. For this reason, the reciting of Maṇtras, the performance of Agnihotra, certain prescribed gestures and codes were recommended for the highest good of one and all. Nevertheless, a few people misinterpret the Vedic rituals and deem them to be such in which an animal like goat, owl or horse is sacrificed in order to appease a Deity and earn rewards. This is a very sad interpretation of Vedic injunctions. Instead, sacrifice is to be understood as,

'Service and giving up of passions that creates bondages. Sacrificing one's comforts, luxuries, sleep, food, time, lust, and alms in order to feed, teach, serve and work towards the welfare of the needy. This is the right meaning and understanding of the term 'Sacrifice/Bali'. Sacrifice is when you give up a share of your meal for the sake of a hungry animal or human. Sacrifice is when out of your busy schedule you take out time to water a thirsty plant or teach a deprived child. Sacrifice is when you elect to heal an ailing human, animal, bird or invest in any act of welfare rather than exuberantly spend on luxuries. Sacrifice is when we elect cosmic welfare over the pacification of the greed of senses.

In the Śābarabhāṣya inflicting of injury has been pronounced 'forbidden'. Further, it is said that '*Śyena*' which may be interpreted as a ceremony where the intention is to cause harm to others is not propagated anywhere in the Vedas. In fact, the Vedas announce that,

"If a man desires Śyena (to inflict injury upon any another), one must do so entirely because he wishes to do so and not because of any text"[158]

---

[158] Jha Ganganatha,'*Śābarabhāṣya*', Oriental Institute (Sadhna Press), Badroda, 1933, p.7.

The Vedas, on the other hand, are replete with injunctions of universal coexistence, cosmic harmony, and environmental reverence. The following verse from the Yajurveda lucidly announces the message of universal concord,

mitrasyāhaṁ chkṣuṣā sarvāṇi bhūtāni samīkṣe।
mitrasya chkṣuṣā Samī Kṣāmahe॥[159]
(May all the creatures look at me affectionately. May I look at all the creatures affectionately. May we all look at each other affectionately.)

The Practice of '*Ahiṃsā*' is an important part of the Indian thought. It appears on numerous occasions in the Śatapathabrahman as '*Non-injury*' with the connotation of morality. The Vedas repeatedly instruct that Nature and animals must not be harmed. However, human's selfish and self-centered approach has driven him to misconstrue the Vedic voices following his whims and fancies. The Yajurveda declares animals to be '*Aghanya*' and announces that,

aghanyā yajamānasya paśūnpahi।[160]
(Animals are not to be killed or harmed)

"All humans and Deities are dependent upon animals for they are the essence of life.[161] ***Animals are the bedrock of a prosperous society.***[162] ***They must be protected and must live fearlessly.***[163] ***Almighty! Safeguard the two and the four-legged species. Bequeath upon them the abundance of food and water. May they and we have more vigor and stature. Save all of us from any harm.***[164]

---

159 *Yajurveda* V. 36.18 ; (Also see, Bhatt S. R, p.4)

160 *Atharvaveda,* V.7.73.8, '*aghnyeyama*'; (Also see, Dwivedi Kapildev, p.90.)

161 *Yajurveda, Shatpathbrahman,* V.6.2.1.14 (*ubhaye devamanuṣyāḥ paúuna upjñvanti*).

162 *Samaveda, Tandayabrahman;* V. 13.1.3 (*sarvam paśubhirvindate*).

163 *Yajurveda;* V. 36.22, (*abhayaṁ naḥ paśubhyaḥ*).

164 *Rigveda;* V.10.37.11 (*asmākaṁ devā ubhayāya janmane śarma yachata dvipadecatuṣpade adat pibadūrjayamānamāśitaṁt adasmeśaṁ yorarapodadhātanaæ*)

It is to be noted that the chief goal of Vedic rituals was never to savor distant fruits rather it was to break free from the captivities and bondages. We have a sense of attachment with food and often turn selfish when we have to share our food with others. We want to consume all the food and satisfy ourselves first. However, when we sacrifice our desire to eat in the name of rituals and fasting, it frees us from all slaveries. Likewise, the performance of Pañcamahāyajña[165] brings a sense of Divinity, sensitivity, self-sameness, reverence, and appreciation for the entire cosmos. It brings a sense of gratitude for the sacred texts, the Ṛṣis, for the living, the dead, for humans, animals, and for the inner and outer environment. While one performs actions, he must be aware that actions performed without proper understanding and executed with greed are futile and hollow. The performance of various rituals that are mentioned in the Vedas, elevate a person on a physical, mental, emotional, spiritual; individual and cosmic echelon. A being slowly but surely realizes that he is not a separate entity but co-exists in the Wholesome Reality. A being develops consciousness towards his daily tasks and gratefulness towards the entire cosmos. Therefore, rituals and Ahiṃsā have a greater significance than what people have understood.

Today, a handful of scholars who approach the Vedas with a sense of prejudice claim that the Divine Text is in favour of animal sacrifice *(paśu balī)*'. However, this is an extremely fallacious elucidation. Just as in the English language there are Homonyms[166], i.e. the word '*Round*' could mean circle, interview round, moving aimlessly or talking in a way that confuses someone. The word '*Crane*' means a bird, a device to pull up an object or a tiltin. The word '*Date*'

---

165 Panchmahayajna; 1.*Brahmain* - offering to the Ultimate Reality, Vedas, and Sages. 2. *Devrina* - offering to Deities and the great elements. 3. *Pitrain* - offering to deceased ancestors. 4. *Bhutrina* - offering to sentient beings, i.e. animals, birds, trees, insects. 5. *Manushyarina* - offering to human beings.

166 Homonyms-Words that have the same spelling, same pronunciations but have different meanings.

refers to a fruit, date of birth etc. Similarly, the word '*Balī*' has many meanings attached to it. Let's have a look at the same,

1) The word '*Balī*' stands as a technical terminology for '*Wrinkles*' in the Rasaśāstra text which is a chief branch of Ayurveda that deals with the chemical interaction of metals, minerals and herbs.[167]
2) The word '*Balī*' also appears as one of the 108 names of Lord Kṛṣna.[168]
3) The word '*Balī*' is respectively the name of the Demon King '*Mahābalī*' and suggests '*The One With Great Power and Strength*'.[169]
4) The expression '*Balī*' is also used for an austere or hermit.[170]
5) The term '*Balī*' connotes to self-sacrifice as '*Balīdāna*' (sacrificing one's comforts, alms, food or time for the sake of others).
6) The word '*Balī*' further refers to the name of the King of the Yādavas[171]
7) The word '*Balī*' appears as the name of the Monkey-king Ānav[172] in the great epic Māhābhārata.
8) The expression '*Balī*' is understood as the daily sacrifices that one offers to sentient beings i.e. sages, humans, dogs, cows, and crows.[173]

---

167 WisdomLib, 2015 '*Rasashastra*', Online, https://www.wisdomlib.org. (Accessed April 1, 2021)

168 Fifty eighth name of Lord Krishna *(Om Baline Namaha)*

169 Williams George, '*Handbook of Hindu Mythology*', Oxford University Press, London, 2008 pp.73–74.

170 Wisdom Lib, 2020,'*Bali*', Online,https://wwwwisdomlib.org. (Accessed April 1, 2021).

171 *Bhagavataskandha*, V. 10.

172 *Harivasa*, V.1.31; Ch.9: *Mahabharata, Adiparva*

173 King Shudraka, Ryder Arthur William (Tr), '*Mrichchakatikam –Samskrit Play (The Little Clay Cart)*', Harvard University, Massachusetts, 1905, pp.6-8, (V.1.9, *yāsāṃ baliḥ sapadimadgīhadehalīnāṃ haṃsaiś ca sārasa gaṇaiśca viluptapūrvaḥ)*

9) The term '*Balī*' suggests a compulsory tax or levy that is given to the King.[174]

10) '*Balī*' refers to a Deity who protects the Pātālaloka.[175]

11) '*Balī*' also means a ceremonial food offering to the Lord who protects all in accordance to the Śaivāgamas.[176]

12) Vāstuśāstra uses the expression '*Balī*' for a diagram with eighty-one squares and a cluster of Deities that are drawn on the ground and where the structural construction has to take place.[177]

13) In case of Jainism, '*Balī*' refers to the name of the sixth Prativāsudeva.[178]

Let us now also have a look at the various meanings of the word Paśu. Śaiva Siddhānta refers to an individual soul as '*Paśu*'. Thus, all beings embracing humans come under the category of '*Paśu*' while Patī is the '*Supreme Śiva*'.[179] The Śhilpaśāstra also considers all embodied souls including humans as Paśus.[180] Further, Ṛṣi Kaśyapa is said to be the ancestor of Paśus (humans, animals and plants) along with Gaṇdharva, Devas and Asuras[181] suggesting that despite varidness of forms we all have the same roots and heritage. The Vedic culture in general uses the term '*Paśu*' for all beings of the world. Therefore, it becomes clear that the word '*Paśu*' doesn't refer to merely an animal and has a variety of meanings. Similarly, the word '*Balī*' has multiple

---

174 *Bhagavatapurana*, V.I.13,40-41; *Brahmandapurana*, II.31, 48,.

175 *Parākhyatantra*, V. 5.44-45 (*10th cen Saiva-Siddhanta Tantra work*).

176 Wisdom Lib, 2015, '*Saivism*', Online, Wisdomlib.org. (Accessed;April 1,2021)

177 *Ibid.*,

178 In Jainism Prati Vasudevas are those who are considered anti-heroic or evil.

179 Banerjee Jitendra Nath, '*The Hindu Concept of God*', America Star Books, Maryland, 2011, pp.51-59

180 *Ibid.*, 'pp.51-59

181 *Vayupurana*, (V.69.290)

meanings and cannot be interpreted as '*Animal Sacrifice*'. This understanding seems to be pasted upon the Vedas and the Vedic rituals which are far from propagating any sort of ceremony that involves bloodshed or harm to any life. The reason why '*Balī*' has been misinterpreted could be due to various reasons, i.e.

- Lack of understanding of the original texts, their context, philosophy and the technique in which they must be understood (i.e. in accordance with place (deśa), time (kāla) and circumstances (paristhiti)).
- Lack of knowledge of Saṁskrit.
- Studying the Vedas with previous conditionings, biases and prejudices.
- Resolutely misinterpreting the Vedas for the sake of promoting violence, non-vegetarianism and divisions.
- Cunningly and purposefully pulling the Vedas down as a text of authority in order to uproot the Vedic culture, philosophy and history in due course.

It must be further noted that Vedas do not instruct or promote acts where any living being is killed or harmed for the sake of pleasing any Deity. On the contrary, animals have been raised to the level of the '*Supreme*' and are worshiped as the Highest Reality.

Every creature of the cosmos is associated with a Deity and is thus said to be Divine. e.g. Lord Śiva is associated with bulls and dogs as animals. Nīlkaṇthi is associated with Him as a bird. Snakes, scorpions and lizards are associated with Him as reptiles. Pīpal, Bilva, Dhattura, Bhāṇg, Āka, Pīli-kanera, Bera, and Rudrākṣ are associated with Śiva as trees and plants. Holy ash is associated with Him and is a divine reminder of our mortal natures. River Gaṇgā is associated with Śiva along with Kailaśa Mountain. The city of Vārānasi, Haridwār and Ṛṣikeśa. White color which gets manifested as all other colors is said to be His color. Destruction for the sake of reconstruction is His function and all five elements are associated with Bhūtanātha (Lord of the Bhūtas/ elements).[182] Hence, the Vedas is a body of text that teaches universal compassion and remains distant from any rituals, sacrifices and ceremonies that profess harm, disharmony, pain and suffering required to be inflicted on any being.

Conclusion

From the foregoing, it is clear that the Vedas adopt a holistic perspective and advocate for environmental protection and universal peace. It is adorned with rituals, verses and philosophies that intend to promote cosmic wellbeing. The heart of the Vedas is installed in compassion, love, concord and wisdom that leads to inner and outer joy. The Vedic scriptures recognize everything as being present in the Divine and the Divine being present in all entities of the world. There is absolutely nothing in the cosmos that is not '*The Divine*'. In fact, '*Nothingness*' is also pervaded and indwelled by the Divine. This makes the whole cosmos the very body of the Supreme. Along these lines, '*Environment*' is just another name for that '*Supreme*'. This Divine Environment in not something that is meant for the human race to exploit rather he is this very '*Environment*' that he elects to harm and so he damages his own survival. The Vedas since time immemorial have spoken about organic cosmology that sans any divisions. This non-dualism that underlines variedness is the most striking feature of the Vedic cosmology which makes it a universal philosophy that can be applied and practiced. It is no surprise that the Vedic vision of non-dualism has inspired many modern scientists, astronomers, philosophers, veterinarians, physicians, economists, management gurus, and others. Nothing is more appealing, rational, logical, compassionate, or universal than the concept of oneness without divisions.

---

182 Bhuta (*five elements*) + Natha (*Lord*) = Lord of the five elements

It is crucial to recognize that these timeless scriptures are incredibly scientific and have influenced many modern breakthroughs, hypotheses, researches and studies. Science and technology are not at odds with the Vedas. They are, in fact, in accord with material development as long as it serves to promote overall well-being. The schism between Vedic thought and science develops, however, when materialism becomes the motivator and the well-being of all other species is neglected in the quest to conquer environment under the guise of technology. Only when modern science wishes for human-centric development at the cost of ruthlessly destroying forests, water bodies and animals is when there is a prominent gap between Vedic thought and modern science. Selfish and greedy advancement is the first step in ascertaining the end of the world. Only when the whole cosmos is taken into account and when advancements are meant for the welfare of all lives will science be seen as all-encompassing and complete. At present science exists in a very limited space. It is for the humans, of the humans and by the humans. All its developments stand upon the graves of enumerable sentient beings and it exists in the spheres of greed, ego and the desire to extract the glories of '*Mother Nature*'. As long as science is not in harmony with Environment, it will be the cause of pain, misery and destruction of the world though outwardly it may appear to give us comforts.

Throwing light on how the Vedas view environment is essential before understanding Ādī Śaṅkarācārya's thought because Advaita Vedānta considers the Vedas (Śabda) as one of the chief Pramāṇa (Valid Source of Knowledge) along with Pratyakṣa (perception) Anumāna (infeulence) Upamāna (compaision) Arthapati (postulations) and Anupalabdli (non-apprehension). It must be noted that all six schools of Indian philosophy, namely; Nyāya-Vaiśeṣika, Sāṃkhya-Yoga and Mīmāṃsā-Vedānta have their roots in the Vedas and stand in favor of environmental harmony.

However, this book will throw light upon Ādi Śaṅkarācārya's Advaita Vedānta philosophy which can be a viable solution to the present-day environmental disharmony.

Oṁ Vedavedāntatattvajñāya Namaḥ
(I bow before Śāṇkara who is the knower of the root of the Vedas and the Upaniṣads)

3.
Ādi Śaṅkarācārya: A Life Sketch

The brilliance of Ādi Śaṅkarācārya can never be encapsulated. His life is a glaring example of compassion, devotion, duty and wisdom. In a span of merely thirty-two years, six months and ten days,[1] He propagated the doctrine of non-dualism through the lengths and breadths of Bhāratavarṣa. It was His endeavors that India even today remains a country that is established in essential unity despite evident diversity. He spoke of non-dualism in all the aspects in which we could think of '*life*'. To Him, all the fragments in which the world appeared were underlined by the non-dual principle '*Brahman*'. He saw humans, animals, birds, and trees as the '*Very Self*' and worked towards the welfare of all by strengthening India's culture and traditions.

Ādi Śaṅkarācārya's philosophy of non-dualism has not only established India's global spiritual identity but has also aided the world since time immemorial. His life and philosophy can be a game-changer in dealing with environmental disharmony, perishing ethics, and social chaos. Before expounding upon Ādi Śaṅkarācārya's philosophy, works and His enterprises in view of environmental harmony, it is desirable to be introduced to His life. The present chapter will make an effort to do the

1 Swami Gyananada Saraswati, '*Adi Shankara*, Neeta Publications, Delhi, 2006, Preface, p. 5.

same and highlight the important events of Ādi Śaṅkarācārya's life which will act as a foundation for the subsequent chapters.

3.1. The Precise Date of Śaṅkara

The date of Ādi Śaṅkarācārya's divine advent remains a mystery. However, prevalently it is accepted that He graced the planet during the 8th century. But before we accept this date as final, it becomes our responsibility to explore the anonymity of the thirteen hundred years that have been shelved in history (6th to 8th Cen.).[2] This can be done merely by taking a look at all the theories that revolve around the date of Ādi Śaṅkarācārya without any predispositions. However, while throwing light upon the date of Jagadguru Ādi Śaṅkarācārya, this book will take into account the records of the Maṭhas that were established by Him.

It must be brought to light that there also existed a person by the name Abhinav Śaṅkarācārya, who lived during the 8th Century. The scholars of the West often confuse Ādi Śaṅkarācārya with Abhinav Śaṅkarācārya. While the Maṭhas continue to acknowledge 509 BCE as Ādi Śaṅkarācārya's year of birth in order of the traditional accounts, the Western scholars continue to be baffled and consider the Great Saint to be born in the first half of the 8th Century. Let's have a look at the Maṭhas position in this regard before we turn the pages of Ādi Śaṅkarācārya's life,

1. The Dwārkā Śāradā Maṭha: This was the foremost Maṭha to be established by Ādi Śaṅkarācārya in the year 491 BCE on the Māgha Śukla Saptamī in the cyclic year of Sādhāraṇa.[3] The tradition of the Dwārkā Maṭha is based upon the Tāmraśāsana (copper charters) that was first issued by the 5th century king 'Sudhanvā'. The copper charters are now under the protection of the Govt. of India and lucidly

2 Swami Gyananada Saraswati, p.17.

3 *Ibid.*, p.17.p.47.

speak of Śaṅkara's advent.[4] The details of the same were published in the year 1872 by the Ācārya of Dwārkā Maṭha in a book called 'Vimarśa'.[5] The Maṭha announces the date of Ādi Śaṅkarācārya as 509 BCE.

2. The Govardhana Purī Maṭha: The Purī Maṭha was founded by Ādi Śaṅkarācārya in 485 BCE on the Vaiśākha Śukla Navmī in the cyclic year of Ānala.[6] The given date is in accord with the '*Guruparaṃparānāmamālā*' of the Govardhan and the Kāṇcī Maṭha which is preserved in the Adyar Library and Research central at Chennai.[7] Further, the list was based upon the Guruparaṃparānāmamālā which was issued by the then Pīthādhiśa Śrī Madhusūdan Tīrtha that includes the names of all the Śaṅkarācāryas starting with Padmapādācārya to Pīthādhiśa Śrī Madhusūdan Tīrtha.[8] From the available list, one can conclude that the birth year of Ādi Śaṅkarācārya is 509 BCE. Śrī Yogeśvarānanda, the former head of the Purī Maṭha also announces 509 BCE as the date of birth of Ādi Śaṅkarācārya.[9]

3. The Kāṇcī Kāmakoti Maṭha: This was established by Ādi Śaṅkarācārya in 482 BCE on the Vaiśākha Pūrṇimā in the cyclic year of Sidhārthī.[10] The Kāṇcī Maṭha records Ādi Śaṅkarācārya's date of birth as 509 BCE. Historic scholar Kota Venkatchalam[11] mentions that the Sātvāhana dynesty King

---

4 Subramanian V, '*Shankara's Date; A Discussion on Sudhanva 's Copper Plate*', 2015, p.25.

5 Swami Gyananada Saraswati, p.47.

6 *Ibid.*, p.17.p.48.

7 *Ibid.*, p.48.

8 *Ibid.*, p.49.

9 *Ibid.*, p.50.

10 *Ibid.*, pp.51-55.

11 *Kota Venkatchalam* is also known as 'Shankaracharya Shri Dvayanmada Shankarbharti Swami. He is a celebrated historian and scholar of Sanskrit who has been dedicated towards the upliftment of Indian Chronology by making references to primary sources. He has combined as well as worked on Indian Bhushastya, Ganitjyotish and more. He attained *Siddhi* on the 5060 Kartika Suddha Trayodasi (November 12, 1959 AD).

Hāla met Ādi Śaṅkarācārya in the year 494 BCE[12] and received His blessings. He further states,

"The chronology of Kāṇcī Maṭha is of utmost importance as it gives accurate dates for a number of historic Indian events. Therefore, all information is dated accurately, this is immensely important. There can be no doubt in the accuracy of the chronology of the Kāṇcī Maṭha"[13]

Therefore, from the accuracy of the records preserved at the Kāṇcī Maṭha one can deduce that the year of birth of Ādi Śaṅkarācārya is 509 BCE.

4. The Jośī Maṭha: The Maṭha is also popularly known as the 'Jyotir Maṭha'. It was initiated by Ādi Śaṅkarācārya on the Puṣya Śuddha Pañcamī of the 'Raktākṣa' cyclic year.[14] The Maṭha in its formal publication called 'The Maṭhānuśāsana (1946)' declares 509 BCE as Ādi Śaṅkarācārya's date of birth.[15]

5. The Kūdalī Maṭha: This is linked with the Śriṅgerī Maṭha and lies in the state of Karnataka. Officially, the Kūdalī Maṭha states that the birth year of Śaṅkara is 44 BCE. However, the 67th Śaṅkarācārya of the Maṭha firmly states that the year of Ādi Śaṅkarācārya is 509 BCE.[16]

6. The Virupākṣa Maṭha: The Maṭha rests in the state of Andhra Pradesh (Guntur). The head of the Maṭha Svāmī Kalyānānanda Bhārtī was previously known as Śrī Gantibāla Kāmeśwara Śarmā and is a scholar of great repute. He has authored many outstanding books on Indology and Sanātana Dharma. In his epical work '*Epochs of Bhāratavarṣa*' Svāmī Kalyānānanda Bhārtī announced the date of Ādi Śaṅkarācārya's as 509 BCE.[17]

---

12 Swami Gyananada Saraswati, pp.47-48.

13 *bid.*, p.49.

14 *Ibid.*, pp.49-50.

15 *Ibid.*, p.51.

16 *Ibid.*, p.52.

17 *Ibid.*, pp.53-55.

7. The Śriṅgerī Maṭha: This was set up by Ādi Śaṅkarācārya on the Puśya Pūrnimā of the '*Piṇgala*' cyclic year in 484 BCE. Till the year 1967 Śriṅgerī Maṭha recognized 44 BCE as Ādi Śaṅkarācārya's date of birth. However, in 1988, Śriṅgerī Maṭha celebrated the 1200th birth anniversary of Ādi Śaṅkarācārya and thus it is inferred that they accept 788 A.D as His date of birth.[18]

From the above, it can be lucidly concluded that all Maṭhas other than the Śriṅgerī Maṭha consider '509 BCE' as Ādi Śaṅkarācārya's date of birth.

3.2. The Divine Advent of Śaṅkara

Bhāratavarṣa was passing through unfathomable turmoil and dissonance. Vedic teachings were taken over by nihilism. Ethics, morals, and virtues had been abandoned. The society was torn into seventy-two sects like the- Śaivas, Kaulas, Kālamūkhas, Pāśupats, Vaiṣṇavas, Kapālikas, Śāktās, Sāṃkhya, Bauddhās, and Jainas. Delusion and superstition reigned throughout.[19] The society was split into conflicting groups and there was a situation of unrest and strife. People indulged in animal and human sacrifices. Black magic, wine, impure sex, meat and other mindless practices developed into an important part of the society in the name of '*Taṇtra*'. Virtue, humanity and Dharma were waning away. It was during this stage that Lord Śiva incarnated as Ādi Śaṅkarācārya for re-establishing Dharma, virtues and ethics which had lost their grandeur. Various texts i.e. Bhaviṣyapurāṇa, Mārkaṇḍeyasaṃhitā, Skaṇdapurāṇa, Kūrmapurāṇa, Liṃgapurāṇa, Śivarahasyam confirm that Lord Śiva incarnated as Ādi Śaṅkarācārya.[20] In the same regard Śrīmad Bhagavadgītā states,

---

18 Swami Gyananada Saraswati, p.56.

19 Sharma Vandana and Thirumal J, '*Praṣnottara Ratna Malika*', Originals Publications, Delhi, 2020, p.8.

20 (i) Swami Gyananada Saraswati , p.92.
(ii) Pande Govinda Chandra,' *Life and Thought of Shankaracharya*' Motilal Banarsidass, Delhi, 2011, p.82.

paritrāṇāya sādhūnāṁ vināśāya ca duṣkṛtām।
dharmasaṁsthāpanārthāya sambhavāmi yuge yuge॥[21]

(To bestow justice upon those who are pious, for the sake of demolishing those who indulge in evil acts, and to re-establish Dharma, I will appear millennium after millennium.)

Further, the Śaṇkaradigvijay aptly states in regards with Ādi Śaṅkarācārya's birth,

duṣṭācāravināśāya dharmasaṃsthāpnāya ca।
bhāṣyam kurvan brahmasūtratātparyārthavinirṇyam।
mohanprakṛtidvaitadhvāntamadhyāhnabhānubhiḥ।
caturbhiḥ sahitaḥ śiṣyaicautrairharivadbhujaiḥ॥[22]

(In order to abolish evil and for the sake of reinstating dharma (cosmic order), for the sake of commenting and giving a conclusive explanation of the Brahmasūtras and to put an end to all dualities that stem from ignorance, I will appear as 'Śaṅkara', the greatest of all abstainers along with my four disciples just as Viṣṇu appears with His four arms.)

Ādi Śaṅkarācārya descended in the Yuga of Kali, in the southern state of Kerala (Kalady)[23]on the Pañcamī Tithi during Śuklapakṣa of the Viśākhāmāha (2631 Yudhiṣṭhir Sāmvata). Today, this period falls roughly during April-May.

The extraordinary child was born to a learned Naṃbūdarī Brāhmaṇa couple; Śivaguru[24] and Āryamba[25]

---

[21] Shankaracharya, '*Shrimadhagvadagitabhashya*', Manav rabodhan Pranyasa, Bikaner, Rajasthan, 2016, V.4.8, p.76.

[22] Shastri N.S Ananthakrishna, (Ed), '*Shankaradigvijay*', Sringeri Matha, Shringeri 1956, V.41, p.6.

[23] Kalad, or Kalati means '*Footprints*'. It is a small town located in the midst of *Angamlay* and Perumbavoor in the Ernakulam district of Kerala. Kaladi stands on the eastern banks of the *Periyar* River (Churna River). It was previously known as *Sasalam.* This town was originally made by the tribal chief Rajashekana after being instructed by Lord Shiva in his dream.

[24] *Shivaguru* was the eldest son of the learned Brahmana scholar *Vidyadhiraja.*

[25] *Aryamba* was the daughter of a local legend and scholar Makha who belonged to a place called Melapalur that is situated 40 km from Ernakulam.

who belonged to the Atri-gotra of the Taittrīyaśākhā (Yajurveda).[26] They ardently revered and worshiped Lord Śiva. It is documented that His parents performed severe penance of forty-one days in the glory of Lord Śiva at the Vaḍakunāthana Temple in Trichur.[27] Responding to their prayers, Lord Śiva appeared instantaneously in the couple's dream and asked them if they wanted a child who lived long or a child who was extraordinary but was short-lived. The couple wished for the latter.[28]

Along with Ādi Śaṅkara, four of His Divine disciples were born in order to assist and further carry forward the mission of Lord Śiva who had descended to ward off all evils that were pushing the entire world into the darkness of dualism and wickedness. Lord Viṣṇu took birth as Sanandana, and later came to be known as Padmapādācārya.[29] The Deity Vāyu appeared in the form of yet another disciple, who is revered as Hastāmalakācārya.[30] Lord Śiva's beloved Nandī was born as Ānandagiri who was subsequently known as Toṭākāṣārya. He later composed Totakāṣṭkam in the glory of his Guru 'Śaṅkarācārya'.[31] Lord Brahma descended as Manḍana Miśra, who was later celebrated as Sureśvarācārya.[32]

3.3. The Joy of Nature at the Birth of Śaṅkara

It is averred that trees, animals, birds and the whole of Nature appeared jubilant at the birth of Ādi Śaṅkarācārya. The Madhavācārya Śāṅkaradigvijay affirms that,

---

26 Pande Govinda Chandra, p.82.

27 Vidyaranya Madhava, Svami Tpasyananda (Tr), '*Shankardigvijay*', Ramakrishna Math, Chennai, 2008, p.14.

28 Shastri N.S Ananthakrishna, (Ed),V.46-53, p.6-7.

29 Vidyaranya Madhava, Svami Tpasyananda (Tr), p.19.

30 *Ibid.*, p.20.

31 *Ibid.*, pp.21-23.

32 *Ibid.*, p.24.

***tasmin dine mṛgakarīndratarakṣusiṃha sarpākhumukhya-bahujantugaṇgā dviṣantaḥ। vairaṃ vihāya saha ceruratīva hṛṣṭāḥkaṇḍūapākṛṣta sādhutayā nighṛṣṭāḥ॥ vṛkṣā latāḥ kusumarāśiphalānyamuncan nadyaḥ prasannasalilā nikhilāstathaiva। jātā muhurjaladhaópi nijaṃ vikāraṃ bhūbhṛdgaṇādapi jalaṃ sahasotpapāta।*[33]**

(That day animals of contradictory nature like deer, lions, elephants, hyenas, snakes, and pigs came together with tranquility, serenity and mutual comradeship. Trees and creepers blossomed and showered flowers and fruits. Everything vibrated with pleasantness. The water bodies brimmed with purity and clarity. Clouds burst forth with exultation, and the streams cascaded joyfully from the mountains up above.)

The Śāṅkaradigvijay also records the joy of an Elephant named 'Diggaja' who was in conversation with his beloved wife and tells her,

***kemī kānta diva niśākarakarā dharmasya marmacchido mugdhey śaṁbhunavāvatārasugurorete guṇānāṁ gaṇāḥ karumādutpalsntatirvikasitā vismeradigyoṣitā-meṣāpāṅgaj harīti diggajavadhūprasnottare rejatuḥ।*[34]**

(Oh precious one! The calmness that we are relishing is not because of the moon but is because of the aura of virtue that the incarnation of Lord Śiva has brought along with Him.)

It is further recorded that all creatures irrespective of their shape and size were exultant at the auspicious and Celestial birth of Ādi Śaṅkarācārya. The following verse throws light upon the same,

***nākṣṇā mākṣikamīkṣitam kṣṇampi darākṣā muhuḥ śikṣtā kṣīrekṣū smupekṣitau bhuvi yayā sā śaṁaraśrīgroḥ। kāntānantadigantalṅakalājaḍghālatatatgruṇa kṣreṇī nir bharmādhurīmadadhurā dhanyeti manyāmahe॥*[35]**

(The bees were overtly joyous and refused to look at the grapes, sugar, candy juice and milk which they dote on for the aura of the 'Divine Child' was far sweeter than all of this).

---

[33] N.S. Shastri and Ananthakrishna (Ed), V.2.73-2.74 , p.17.

[34] *Ibid.*, V.4.67, p.35.

[35] *Ibid.*, (Ed) V.4.68, pp.35-36.

The above-mentioned gives us an occasion to ponder upon the fact that, the entire Nature and all living beings are conscious and flowing with emotions. The delight of Nature at the birth of Ādi Śaṅkarācārya highlights that all beings are sensitive to the changes that take place in the world. It also highlights that they not only comprehend various events that occur but they also become joyful and gloomy due to cosmic occurrences, changes and events.

3.4. The Early Years of Śaṅkara

Ādi Śaṅkarācārya demonstrated stupendous scholarship, immaculate intelligence and unmatched logic right from His childhood which is evident from the following verse,

***aṣṭavarṣe caturvedī dvādaśe sarvaśāstravit*।**
***śoḍaśe kṛtavānbhāṣyam dvātriṁśe munirabhyagāt*।।[36]**
(Mastered the Vedas by the age of eight, became well-versed in all the Śāstras by the age of twelve, commented upon the Brahmsūtras and Prasthāntreyī by the age of sixteen and attained Mahāsamādhī at the age of thirty-two).

In various texts He has been referred to as,

***'ekaśrutidhāra'*[37]**
(He, who remembers and retains all that He hears once)

It is further stated that Śaṇkarā began speaking and developed mastery on words and grammar in the first year of His birth.[38] In the second year, the Divine child began reading and writing proficiently.[39] At an early age, He lost His father. His mother single-handedly performed His '*Cūḍākarmaṇa* or *Upanayanamsaṃskāra*' at the age of five.[40]

---

36 Vidyaranya Madhava, Svami Tpasyananda (Tr), p.26.

37 *Ibid.* p.28.

38 Shastri N.S. and Ananthakrishna (Ed), V.4.1, p.28, (*prathamahā nyanaevasmagrahīa sakalavarṇamasau nijabhā*ṣikāma)

39 *Ibid.*, V.4.2, p.28, (*...dvisma eve śiśulikhitākṣarama...*)

40 *Ibid.*, V.4.15, p.29, (*upnayanaṃkila pañcamavatsare paravarayogayute sumuhūtake*) (*Cūḍākarmaṇa or the Upanayana* is one of the most important

On entering the Brahmacāryāśrama and as a part of the prescribed ceremony Ādi Śaṅkarācārya went begging for alms. In the process, He reached a poverty-stricken Brāhmaṇa's house. The house was shabby and one could make out that it was hit by extreme scarcity. The lady of the house felt utmost grief as she was unable to offer anything to the young Brahmacārī. Nevertheless, she gave a dry Āmlā fruit to Him, the only thing she possessed. Utterly moved by her distressed condition, Ādi Śaṅkarācārya prayed to Mahālakṣmī by composing the Kanakadhārāstotram.[41] Delighted with His prayers Mahālakṣmī showered gold coins upon the impoverished Brāhṃaṇa's house. Even today people recite the magical stotram to get rid of poverty, untimely death and unfortunate circumstances.

Ādi Śaṅkarācārya was about eight years old when He completed His education and earned mastery over the Vedas, Vedāṇgnas, Purāṇas, Saṃskṛta-vyākaraṛa and other texts. After Completing His education, He came back to His mother and started teaching children at His home.[42] He had now blossomed into a self-sufficient scholar. The stories related to His intelligence and wisdom had traveled to the kings and sages afar. Also, Ādi Śaṅkarācārya held boundless love and compassion for His mother and considered her as His first Guru. In order to make sure that His weak, widowed mother did not walk for miles to take a bath at the river

classic *Vedic Samskara* that marks the formal entrance of an individual into a Gurukul and his/her acceptance by a qualified Guru. The tradition differs regionally and finds mention in various ancient Vedic text. During this rite a child who has attained the age of eight years receives a sacred thread called 'Yajnopavita or Janeu' which he/she ontinues wearing across his left shoul der thereafter. Vedic texts such as the *Bodhayana Grihayasutram* encourage all representatives of society to go through the *Upanayana* Samskara without evaluating them on the basis of caste or sex. Girls were also encouraged to undergo *Upanayana Samskara* in ancient India before they started Vedic studies.)

41 *Ibid.*, (Ed), V.4.30, p.31.

42 Swami Gyananada Saraswati, p.97.

Pūrṇa[43], He prayed to the holy river to change its course and flow by the side of His house. Surprisingly, the river changed its stream.[44]

3.5. The Divine Crocodile and Śaṇkara

At the delicate age of eight years, Ādi Śaṅkarācārya had already pledged to take up Saṃnyāsa and devote His entire life towards the welfare and well-being of all. Like any other mother, Āryamba was displeased with His decision and considered it to be a mere fleeting and juvenile desire. However, Ādi Śaṅkarācārya remained unwavering towards His vow and was eager to accomplish the purpose for which He had incarnated. Despite this, His mental plight can be understood by the following verse that appears in the Śaṅkaradigvijay,

***mama na mānasmicchati saṃsṛtiṃ na punarjananī vijihāstī*।**
***na ca gururjananī tadudīkṣte tadnuśāsanmīṣdpaekṣtama*।।**[45]

(I have no yearning for worldly indulgences but my mother is not willing to let go off me. Nonetheless, she is my first Guru and therefore, I must seek her blessings before walking on the path of renunciation).

One day when Ādi Śaṅkarācārya was having a bath on the Ghāts of the Curṇa River[46], a crocodile grasped His leg and began dragging Him into the deep waters. The crocodile was none other than the Gaṇdharvasevaka Mahākāla Pralayāṇkara, who appeared as a crocodile for the sake of assisting Ādi Śaṅkarācārya in His mission.[47] The crocodile

---

43 *Purna* River/Churna river/The Big River is the largest and the longest river in the state of Kerala.

44 Shastri N.S. and Ananthakrishna, (Ed), V.5.8, p.42, (*īhitaṃ tava bhaviṣyati kālye yo hitaṃ jagat iccasi bālye*। *ityavāpya sa varaṃ taṭinītaḥ satyavāka sadanamāpa vinītaḥ*।।)

45 *Ibid.*, (Ed), V.5.60, p.46.

46 The Ghata of the curna River where the crocodile incident took place is called the Muthala Kadavu Ghata.

47 Swami Gyananada Saraswati, p.103.

portrays a crucial transformative role in the life of Ādi Śaṅkarācārya.

A crocodile is not only the vehicle of Goddess Gaṇgā and Narmadā but is also associated with the Deity Varuṇa. The worship of crocodiles is prevalent in Sanātan Dharma since time immemorial.[48]

On seeing Ādi Śaṅkarācārya drown away, His mother cried for help. However, neither she nor others were able to get Him out of the situation. Just when Ādi Śaṅkarācārya was about to drown to death, He called out,

"Mother! Please give your valuable approval for my Saṃnyāsa and this crocodile will let go of me."[49]

To save her beloved son's life and as the last alternative His mother gave her consent and astoundingly the crocodile left Ādi Śaṅkarācārya with no injuries. At that very moment, He took up Apatasaṃnyāsa[50] by reciting the Preṣamaṇtra of relinquishing all worldly pleasures.

Just as Ādi Śaṅkarācārya was preparing to leave His house and start yet another chapter of His life, His mother asked Him to return for the sake of performing her last rites. Hearing her wish, Ādi Śaṅkarācārya replied with compassion and love,

ahnyaṃba rātrisamaye samyāntare vā sañcintya
svavaśagā' vaśagāthavā māma ।
eṣyāmi tatra samyaṃ sakalaṃ vihāya viśvāsamāpnuhi
mṛtāvapi saṇskāriṣye ॥[51]

(Mother Aryaṃba! Every time you need me, you may think about me. Be it night or day, during sickness or at the time of death, I will appear before you under all conditions and will make sure that I perform your last rites).

---

48 Parpola Ashko, '*The Roots of Hinduism: Early Aryan & Indus* Civilizations', Oxford University Press, New York, 2015, p.200.

49 Shastri N.S. and Ananthakrishna, (Ed), V.5.60 - 67, p.46.

50 *Ibid.*, V.5.71, p.49, (Sanyasa during an emergency situation)

51 *Ibid.*, p.50.

As a result, at the age of eight Ādi Śaṅkarācārya left His house as a Saṃnyāsī promising His mother to return just before she leaves her material body. True to His words, He did return home for His mother's last rites and broke all social barricades attached with a Saṃnyāsī that restrict him from returning home and performing any sort of ceremony. This shows that He gave more significance to compassion and love in contrast to mindless rituals. His approach also highlights and suggests that Ādi Śaṅkarācārya was a social reformist who stood against empty and meaningless social practices.

3.6. Śaṇkara's Rendezvous with '*The Guru*'

Ādi Śaṅkarācārya at His Gurukula had heard about the magnanimity of '*Guru Govinda Bhagavatapādācārya*'. He was aware that Govinda Bhagavatapādācārya resided in the caves of Ōṃkārēśvara.[52] According to yet another version, Lord Kṛṣna appeared in Ādi Śaṅkarācārya's dream and told Him,

> ***"For someone who has an exceptional caliber like you, Govindyati who lives on the banks of river Narmadā is apt amongst all to be your Guru"***[53]

Ādi Śaṅkarācārya began walking towards the North in search of '*The One*'. He traversed various villages, humans, animals, mountains and rivers in order to reach Gokarṇa where His classmate Viṣṇuśarman joined Him and they made their way towards Ōṃkārēśvara.

The divine and beautiful Ōṃkārēśvara stands on the banks of river Narmadā and is surrounded by the Vindhyā Mountains. The place is also home to one of the twelve Jyotirliṅgams 'Ōṃkārēśvara', from which the area derives its name.

---

[52] Swami Gyananada Saraswati, p.109.

[53] *Ibid.*, p.110.

It was not only Ādi Śaṅkarācārya who zealously waited to meet His Guru. In fact, Govinda Bhagavatapādācārya was also eager to meet His disciple who was none other than Lord Śiva. It was during Govinda Bhagavatapādācārya's Tapasyā at the Bdrikāṣrama that Mahārṣi Vedavyāsa appeared before Him and advised Him to proceed towards Ōṃkārēśvara to initiate the incarnation of Lord Śiva who had appeared as Śaṅkara.[54] Consequently, Guru Govinda Bhagavatapādācārya was aware of Ādi Śaṅkarācārya's arrival.

Govinda Bhagavatapādācārya belonged to the Advaita-Vedānta tradition and was a being of realization. It is believed that sage Mahārṣi Patañjali who authored the Pātañjali Yogsūtra and Mahābhāṣyas had reincarnated as Govinda Bhagvatpādācārya.[55] It must be noted that Mahārṣi Patañjali was none other than the Ādiśeṣa or Śeṣanāga.[56] He was the direct disciple of Gauḍapādācārya. It must be noted that it is exceptionally arduous to decode the mysteries of the cosmos where a Guru may appear as an animal, tree, bird or any of these may appear as a Guru to take us at a higher physical, mental, emotional and spiritual plane.

It is recorded that as people approached the cave of Govinda Bhagavatapādācārya they sensed an incomprehensible mystic peace and serenity which was also experienced by Ādi Śaṅkarācārya. This feeling unquestionably was the result of Govinda Bhagvatapādācārya's '*saumya īśta samādhi*'.[57] In this way, not just human beings but also places, caves and cities have their aura.

On the eve of Akṣaya Navamī and during the Amrityoga Muhūrata, Ādi Śaṅkarācārya took three Parikramās of the cave and proffered Aṣṭāṇgapraṇāma before its mouth. And

---

54 Swami Gyananada Saraswati, p.115.

55 *Ibid.*, 109.

56 Vidyaranya Madhava, Svami Tpasyananda (Tr), p.47.

57 Swami Gyananada Saraswati, p.111.

so, He inaugurated the custom of circumambulation around the cave and prostrating before the same by everyone who visits it.[58]

The very next day, Ādi Śaṅkarācārya reached the cave and offered His prays. Govinda Bhagavatapādācārya could lucidly feel His divine presence. He descended from His Samādhi and called out Ādi Śaṅkarācārya's name. The moment the eight-year-old Śaṇkara entered the cave, Govinda Bhagavatapādācārya asked Him '*Who are you?*' To this Ādi Śaṅkarācārya replied by composing the Nirvāṇaṣaṭkam,[59]

manobuddhyahaṅkāracittāni nāhaṃ na ca śrotra jihve na ca
ghrāṇa netre na ca vyoma bhūmir na tejo na vāyuḥ
cidānanda rūpaḥ śivo'ham śivo'ham

(I am neither the Mana, Buddhi, Ahaṃkāra nor am I the Citta. I am neither the ear that listens, the tongue that tastes, the nose that smells nor am I the eye that sees. I am not the earth, the fire or the air; instead, I am the Supreme non-dual truth, consciousness, bliss- Śiva')

On the auspicious day of Kārtika Śukla Ekādaśī[60] Govinda Bhagavatapādācārya decided to initiate Ādi Śaṅkarācārya on to the path of Saṃnyāsa. As a result, Śaṅkara ceremoniously entered the Advaita Vedānta linage of Dandasaṃnyāsa[61] at the young age of eight years six months and six days.[62]

---

58 Shastri N.S. and Ananthakrishna,(Ed), V.5.93, p.50. (*yasya prapannaparitoṣaduho guhāyāḥ sa triḥ pradakṣiṇaparikramaṇaṃ)*

59 *'Nirvanshatkam'* is an eight verse composition of Adi Sankaracarya that He composed at the age of eight on the banks of River Narbada on the Kartika Shukla Dashmi. Nirvanshatkam highlights the non-duality of *Atman-Brahman* and is also known as *Atmashatkam.*

60 Swami Gyananada Saraswati, p.112.

61 *'Dandasanyasa'* marks the formal entrance of a seeker into the Sanyasa order. Thus, one renounces the world and becomes an

62 Swami Gyananada Saraswati, p.119.

3.7. Śaṅkara and the Non-dual Teachings of Guru Govinda Bhagavatapādācārya

Ādi Śaṅkarācārya now started staying with His Guru. In ancient India, a child not just gathered knowledge and education via texts but also absorbed various practical aspects of life by being under the guidance of a qualified Guru. As a result, Ādi Śaṅkarācārya not just assimilated the concepts of deep philosophies but also embraced the Ācāra, Vyavhāra and Vicāra of His Guru. He was grasping everything at a very fast pace.

The main teachings of Guru Govinda Bhagavatapādācārya were concentrated in the four Mahāvākyas. These Upaniṣadic teachings highlight the non-duality of Ātman and Brahman and falsify the apparent differences that exist due to the effect of Avidyā. The knowledge of the Upaniṣadic Mahāvākyas is considered as a direct means of Mukti because they enable a seeker to realize the non-dual Self and ultimately put an end to the apparent bondages. The Vedas become the source of the Four Mahāvākyas of the Vedāntic tradition which will be discussed in the subsequent chapters.

3.8. The Controlling of '*Narmadā*' by Śaṅkara

From various events of Ādi Śaṅkarācārya's life, one can infer that He was a yogi of the highest order and could control the Pañcamahābhūtas. Conversely, He made use of His Siddhis only for the sake of the well-being and welfare of all beings. It is documented that for a period of five days there was continuous rain, storm and thunder in and around Ōṃkārēśvara and thus there were calamitous floods in River Narmadā.[63] Humans, animals and birds were in extreme anguish and agony.[64] Trees and plants were being uprooted and there was devastation all around. All those who resided in Govinda Bhagavatapādācārya's Āṣrama were frightful by

---

63 Swami Gyananada Saraswati, p.115.

64 *Ibid.*, p. 116.

the sight, force and aggression of River Narmadā. While all this happened Govinda Bhagavatapādācārya was engrossed in His '*Samādhi*' and all His disciples were concerned about His safety. It was during this ruinous situation that Ādi Śaṅkarācārya took His kamandala (stoup), energized it with a Mantra and kept the same on the mouth of His Guru's cave. In next to no time Ādi Śaṅkarācārya contained the entire Narmadā River in His kamandala with the aid of His Yogasiddhi.[65] Further, in reverence of River Narmadā, He composed and sang the '*Narmadāṣṭakama*'. By doing so, He not only shielded His Guru but also saved all sentient beings from desolation. He saved the fishes, tortoise and pigs who are none but the manifestation of Lord Viṣṇu, the trees that are indeed Lord Śiva, and the Guru who is the Supreme Brahma-Viṣṇu-Maheśa.

On coming out of His Samādhi Govinda Bhagavatapādācārya was extremely pleased with Ādi Śaṅkarācārya's act of compassion. At this juncture Govinda Bhagavatapādācārya narrated to Ādi Śaṅkarācārya the prediction made by Mahārṣi Vyāsa, according to which,

vatsa taṃ śṛṇu samastavideko matsamastava bhaviṣyati
śiṣyaḥkumbha eva saritaḥ sakalaṃ yaḥ saṃhariṣyati
maholbaṇamambhaḥ||[66]

(In the future, the one who will bring the entire waters of a river into the Kamandala will be the one who will refute all non-Vedic doctrines and will protect the Vedic Dharma. He alone will be the one to explain the Brahmasūtras most appropriately).

Govinda Bhagavatapādācārya instructed Ādi Śaṅkarācārya to now progress towards the city of Kāsī where Lord Śiva will bless Him and will teach Him greater lessons

65 Shastri N. S. and Ananthakrishna,(Ed), V.5.138, p.55 (*so 'bhimantrya karakaṃ tvaramāṇastatpravāhapurataḥ praṇidhāya*| *kṛtsnamtra samaveśayadambaḥ kumbhasambhava iva svakare 'bdhim*||)

66 (i) Shastri N.S. and Ananthakrishna,(Ed), V.5.158,p. 56.
(ii) Pande Govind Chandra, p.84.

of the philosophy of non-dualism that Ādi Saṅkarācārya propagated.

3.9. Śaṇkara's Absolute Reverence for His Guru

Ādi Śaṅkarācārya's relationship with His Guru can well be appreciated by looking at His works. In countless places, Ādi Śaṅkarācārya has been described as '*the able disciple of Govinda Bhagavatapādācārya*'. It is to be noted that in the Māṇḍūkyopaniṣadkārikābhāṣya's conclusion Ādi Śaṅkarācārya bows to His beloved Guru without naming Him in accordance to the norms. It must be noted that in Indian culture the dedicated disciple doesn't utter the name of His Guru. Even in case of Śārīrakabhāṣya (Brahmasūtra bhāṣya), Ādi Śaṅkarācārya goes on to quote His Guru without taking His name and refers Him as '*The Master of the Tradition*'.[67] One can also see that in texts such as Upaniṣdkārikābhāṣya, Ādi Śaṅkarācārya claims to belong to the ancient Vedic tradition' that reached Him through and with the grace of His Guru Govinda Bhagavatapādācārya.

3.10. Śaṇkara's Arrival at the City of Kāśī

On the instructions and with the blessings of His beloved Guru, the twelve year old Ādi Śaṅkarācārya arrived at the divine city of Kāsī and resolved to stay near the Maṇikarṇikāghāta drenched in the devotion of Lord Śiva.[68] Further, It is to be noted that out of the twelve Jyotirliṅgans, the first Liṅga appeared in the city of Kāsī.[69] The beauty of this city enchanted Ādi Śaṅkarācārya to an extent that He went on to write the '*Kāśīpañcakama.*' Correspondingly, in the glory of Mother Gaṇgā who fortifies the earth, nourishes every living creature and washes away the sins of all, Ādi Śaṅkarācārya wrote the '*Gaṇgāṣṭakama*'.

---

67 Pande Govind Chandra, p.84.

68 *Ibid.*, p.87.

69 Nandakumara Prema, *Ādi Śaṅkara-Finite to the Infinite'* Chinmaya International Foundation, Ernakulam, 2013, p.45.

The magnificent city of Kāśī was taken over by non-Vedic religions. Buddhism and Jainism were thriving at a rapid pace. Buddhism in particular was engulfing the society. The city that was once the center of Vedic Dharma had become a museum of Stūpas, Vīhāras and Buddhist icons. Undesirable Tāmsic Tāṇtric practices that included human and animal sacrifices were widespread. For this reason, Ādi Śaṅkarācārya's stepping into the city was not merely to establish the Vedic Dharma but was also to unshackle the society from superstitions, unethical practices, greed, selfishness and violence.

3.11. Śaṇkara's Meeting with Padmapāda

Ādi Śaṅkarācārya garnered students, pupils, and devotees from all across the country due to His extraordinary wisdom and magnificent persona. He had a large number of willing disciples yearning to be initiated by Him. One such alacritous and enthusiastic disciple was '*Sanaṇdana*' who came from the Tamilian Cola dynasty situated on the banks of River Kāverī.[70] Sanaṃdana's ardor towards Ādi Śaṅkarācārya was laudable. It is recorded that once Ādi Śaṅkarācārya called Sanaṃdana who was across the river. In order to reach his Guru without an iota of delay, Sanaṃdana stepped onto the river Gaṇgā. Seeing Sanaṃdana's unwavering devotion towards his Guru, Mātā Gaṇgā put forth a lotus wherever he set his foot on Her. This occurrence highlights Sanaṃdana's enduring dedication towards his Guru. It was this incident because of which Ādi Śaṅkarācārya named His disciple Sanaṃdana as *Padmapādācārya.*[71] Later, Padmapādācārya authored Pañcapādikā, which was a commentary on Ādi Śaṅkarācārya's Brahmasūtrabhāṣya. A noteworthy element of this literature has been that the author Padmapādācārya elaborately throws light on the theory of 'Adhyāsa'[72] which

70 Nandakumara Prema, p.46.

71 Shastri N.S. and Ananthakrishna, (Ed), V.6.1-6.15, pp.59-60.

72 *'Adhyasa'* refers to the concept of superimposing one entity's attribute, quality, or characteristic on another. It is the erroneous projection of

was formulated by Ādi Śaṅkarācārya. Padmapādācārya also went on to write a commentary on Ādi Śaṅkarācārya's Prapañcasāra[73] and Ātmabodha. He further worked on Śivapañcākṣṛībhāṣya, wherein he goes on to expound upon the Pañcākṣaramaṅtra which is the quintessence of non-dualism (Advaita).

3.12. Śaṅkara's Epical Encounter with the Cāṇḍāla and His Four Śvānas (dogs)

The summer was phenomenal and the earth was parched. All sentient beings were striving to stay cool in the scorching heat. The swans took shelter in the clumps of lotus leaves, the fish swam to the middle of the stream, the beautiful peacocks sought refuge in the deep caverns, and the small birds rested in the shadow of the hollow tree trunks. On such a hot summer afternoon Ādi Śaṅkarācārya along with His disciples was on His way towards the Gaṇgāghāta in order to complete His daily errands. Suddenly, a Cāndạla along with His four dogs appeared before Him and stood in the middle of His way. Ādi Śaṅkarācārya and His disciples told the Cāṇḍāla and His dogs to move away from their path. Instead of getting away, the Cāṇḍāla questioned Ādi Śaṅkarācārya,

"O Great One! You preach the non-duality of Brahman-Ātman, if it is so, who do you want to remove from your way? 'The body' which is made of the same Anna that you, me, the dogs, Brahmaṇas, outcastes, and all living beings are nourished with or 'The Soul' which is all-pervading, omnipresent, omnipotent

physical body features (birth, death, skin colour, etc.) on the atman. The first mention of Adhyasa is found in the Brahmasutrabhasya of Adi Shankaracharya where He begins by explaining Adhyas and it's nature. (आहकोऽयमध्यासोनामेति। उच्चयतेस्मृतिरूप: परत्रपूर्वष्टाष्टावभास:। तंकेचित् अन्यत्रान्यधर्माध्यासइतिव दन्ति। के चित्तुयत्रयदध्यास: तद्विवेकाग्रहनिबन्धोभ्रमइति। अन्येतुयत्रयदध्यास: तस्यैवविपरीतधर्मत्वक ल्पनामाचक्षते। सर्वथापितु अन्यस्यान्धर्मावभासंतानव्यभिचरति। तथा चलोकेऽनुभव:शुक्तिकहिरजत वदवभासतेएक श्चन्द्र:सद्वितीववदिति।।)

73 Prapanchasara is a celebrated Tantrik text attributed to Shankaracharya

and shining alike in all bodies. How have you identified the boundless Self with the limited body?"[74]

Ādi Śaṅkarācārya stood speechless. Here was a Cāṇḍāla who taught Him His own philosophy and thus, He went down on His knees, folded His hands and said,

"O Supreme! You are correct. There is only one consciousness that exists in Śiva, Viṣṇu and even in the animals and the smallest of insects. I bow before you and accept you as my Guru and seek forgiveness"[75]

Suddenly, the Cāṇḍāla transformed into Lord Śiva and His accompanying four dogs transformed themselves into the divine auspicious Vedas. On seeing this utterly awe-striking event Ādi Śaṅkarācārya composed the Maniṣāpañcakam in the glory of the Cāṇḍāla and His four dogs who were Lord and the Vedas in disguise. It was at this point that Lord Śiva instructed Ādi Śaṅkarācārya in order to move towards Badrīnātha and said,

"You've recognized the essence of all life forms. You must therefore fulfill your residual tasks. The Bhāṣyas that you will write in the year named 'Jaya'[76] ***on Brahmasūtras will be admired by all. They will add to the glory of the Vedic Dharma. After you have refuted the scholars who support the non-Vedic Dharma, have re-established the authority of the Vedas, and have established the doctrine of non-dualism, you must work towards initiating Pañcāyatanapūjā, inaugurate the tradition of Tirthayātrā and finally after appointing your able disciples who will carry forward the light of non-dual wisdom towards the future generations, you must return to where you belong. My blessings are with you"***[77]

---

74 Shastri N.S. and Ananthakrishna, (Ed), V.6.20-6.32,.60-61.

75 (i) Shastri N.S. and Ananthakrishna, V.6.37, p.62.
(ii) Vidyaranya Madhava, Svami Tpasyananda (Tr), p.60.

76 Swami Gyananada Saraswati, p.122.

77 *Ibid.*, V.6.44-6.51, p.63.

3.13. Śaṇkara's Journey towards Badrīdhāma

After being instructed by Lord Śiva, Ādi Śaṅkarācārya made His way towards Badrīdhāma. He traveled on foot. Ādi Śaṅkarācārya crossed several places including parts of the present day 'Uttarākhaṇda' which were tainted with the violent and superstitious practices of animal sacrifices. Various forms of Taṇtric practices and black magic were predominant in these areas that led to the slaughter of several innocent creatures. One can only fathom the plight of the society that was smeared in ignorance. As Ādi Śaṅkarācārya passed through these regions, He established His Doctrine of non-dualism and consequently had put an end to such barbaric practices that included violence and bloodshed.

Today the distance between Kāsī and Badrīdhāma from the shortest route of National Highway-31 is 1309 km.[78] It takes approximately twenty-five hours by car to reach Badrīdhāma via this path. One can envisage the condition of roads thousands of years ago when there were no shortcuts paved out, no facilities and the pathways were strewn with pebbles, stones, hills, rivers and dense forests. Nonetheless, after crossing Haradvāra, Ṛṣikeśa, Devaprayāga, Rudraprayāga, Naṇdaprayāga, Viṣṇuprayāga, and more Śaṇkara reached the divine adobe of Badrīnātha.

The Badrī Dhāma is named after the temple of Badrīnātha which is located in the area of Camolī district of Uttarākhaṇda. The ancient Vedic texts i.e. Viṣṇupurāṇa and Skandapurāṇa make a reference to the temple with Lord Nārāyaṇa being its chief deity. Soon after reaching the Dhāma, Ādi Śaṅkarācārya selected a silent cave at the Vyāsāṣrama as an ideal place to reside.[79] He brought back

---

78 Yatra.com, '*Distance between Varanasi and Badrinath by* Road', Online, https://www.yatra.com (Accessed: April 2, 2021).

79 Swami Gyananada Saraswati, p.126.

everyone on to the path of Vedic Dharma with the help of King 'Kaṇakpāla' belonging to the Parmāra clan.[80]

One day after performing the evening worship on the banks of River Alakṇandā He went to the temple of Badrīnātha, only to find that there was no statue of Lord Nārāyaṇa at the temple and the temple was being converted into a Buddhist Vihāra and thus the statue of Lord Nārāyaṇa was thrown away in the Taptakuṇda. It is documented that He dived into the deep waters and resurfaced with the broken (Khaṇdita) statue of Lord Nārāyaṇa. Though, Śaṅkarācārya was perplexed when He saw the broken statue, however a divine oracle eradicated all His confusions,

> ***"Śaṇkara! Have no confusion. In the Yuga of Kali this broken statue will be worshiped."***[81]

Consequently, Ādi Śaṅkarācārya established the statue and the Pujāpadathi following the Vedic traditions. He further appointed a Naṃbūdirī Brahmaṇa at the temple.[82] He later established the Jotirmaṭha (also known as the Jośīmaṭha or the Uttaramnāyamaṭha)' in the town area called Jośīmaṭha.

Ādi Śaṅkarācārya decided to write and conclude the Bhāṣyas. He started by writing the Brahmasūtrabhāṣyas in a scholarly, poetic and lucid style. Next, He wrote the Upaniṣadbhāṣyas and confirmed their message of non-dualism with a simple, understandable and yet scholarly panache. He further wrote Bhāṣyas on the ten principle Upaniṣads, namely- Īśā, Kena, Kaṭha, Praṣna, Muṇḍaka, Māṇḍūkya, Taittirīya, Aitareya, Cāndogya, and Bṛhadāraṇyaka. Finally, He wrote the Bhagvadagītābhāṣya and composed the Viṣṇusahastranāma along with Sanatsujātīya and Updeśasāhasrī.

---

80 Wikipedia Contributors, 2006, '*Badrinath Temple*', https://en.wikipedia.org (Accessed April 2, 2021).

81 Swami Gyananada Saraswati., p.125.

82 For details refer to chapter-7 of this book (p. 234)

3.14. Śaṅkara's Meeting with Mahāṛṣi Vyāsa[83]

After concluding His textural works and commentaries, Ādi Śaṅkarācārya began teaching the same to His disciples. One day on the banks of the Gaṇgā He was addressing His disciples and as the session finished, a Brahmaṇa appeared before Ādi Śaṅkarācārya and probed Him by saying,

"I have heard that you have commented upon the Brahmasūtras of Vyāsa, if you are so wise let me hear you expound on at least the first Sūtra of chapter three from the same".[84]

To the above said, Ādi Śaṅkarācārya replied by saying,

Salutations! I do not claim to be wise or competent enough to be at par with Mahāṛṣi Vyāsa but since you have asked me to expound on the immaculate work, I will endeavor to do justice to the same. At the time of death, the Jīva departs from the body engulfed in the ethereal essence of the Pañcamhābhūtas"[85]

Ādi Śaṅkarācārya's response makes us conclude that the word '*Jīva*' is not limited to a human being; instead, the expression extends to all beings and establishes the oneness of all lives. Additionally, all Jīvas which include insects, trees, animals, humans, etc. are made up of Pañcamhābhūtas and at the time of death, they leave the body with the subtle essence of these elements.

Mahāṛṣi Vyāsa and Śaṅkara continued their long conversation, in which Vyāsa asked different questions and disputed Śaṅkarā. The all-wise Ādi Śaṅkarācārya on the other hand, provided appropriate and convincing replies to each inquiry posed and every refutation made. It was revealed after eight days that the Brahmaṇa was none other than

---

83 Swami Gyananada Saraswati, V.7.1-7.22, pp.71-72.

84 Svami Vrishveshwarananda, '*Brahmasutrabhashya*', Advaita Ashrama, Kolkata, V.3.1.1, pp.262-263. (*tadantarapratipattau ramhati samparişvaktaḥ; praśnaṇirūpāṇāmbhyām*)

85 Vidyaranya Madhava, Svami Tpasyananda (Tr), p.70

Mahārṣi Vyāsa. Ādi Śaṅkarācārya bowed in reverence before the Great Sage. Mahārṣi Vyāsa blessed Śaṅkarā and urged Him to live for another sixteen years in order to propagate the message of Advaita. Originally, Śaṇkarā was supposed to be alive only for a span of sixteen years.

3.15. Śāṇkara's Voyage towards Paryāga

The word '*Prayāga*' comes from the Saṃskrit roots 'pra (first)' + 'yajña (offering)' which means 'first offering'. It is believed that the first Yajña was performed in Prayāga by Lord Brahma. The word 'Prayāga' also refers to the 'joining of the holy rivers' and so, it is at '*Prayāga*' where the three holy Rivers; Gaṇgā, Yamunā, Sarasvatī come together. This conflux is known as '*Saṇgam*'. Prayāga is also referred to as the King of Pañcaprayāga (The five great rivers); Viṣṇuprayāga, Naṇdarayāga, Karṇaprayāga, Rudraprayāga and Devaprayāga.[86]

On reaching the holy city of Prayāga, Ādi Śaṅkarācārya bowed to the majesty of Mother Gaṇgā, Yamunā, and Sarasvatī. He then took a dip in the Triveṇī and on coming out heard that the great scholar Kumārila Bhaṭṭa was about to burn Himself to ashes. As a result, Śaṇkara hurried to the site only to find that the illustrious scholar had already set Himself on fire. Taking a few drops of water from His Kamaṇdala, Śaṇkara charged it with a Maṇtra and sprinkled the same on Kumārila Bhaṭṭa. With immediate effect, the fire stopped. Kumārila Bhaṭṭa was elated to see Ādi Śaṅkarācārya and instructed his disciples to worship Lord Śiva in the form of Śaṇkara. Kumārila told Ādi Śaṅkarācārya that if he had not taken the vow of ending his life, he would have written a commentary on Śaṇkara's intellectual Bhāṣyas. He further admitted to Śaṇkara that, despite his lifelong devotion to the Vedas, he had joined the Buddhist cult to lucidly and logically refute their doctrine. Even though he

86 Wikipedia Contributors, 2003, '*Allahabad*, https://en.wikipedia.org (Accessed April 2, 2021).

did so for establishing the authority of the Vedas, he had extreme guilt for being a part of the Buddhist sect. The sixteen-year-old Śaṇkara told the sixty-four-year-old Kumārila Bhaṭṭa,

> ***"O, Great Soul! You are not a sinner! I will heal you and restore your health. You must write a commentary on my bhāṣyas"***[87]

Despite this, Kumārila Bhaṭṭa refused to let go of his vow and requested Śaṇkara to go and meet his wise disciple Maṇḍana Miśra who was a great Mīmāṃsā scholar and had no faith in Nivritti Mārga.[88] He appealed to Śaṇkara for bringing his disciple on to the path of wisdom and concluded by saying,

> ***"This able disciple of mine will write a commentary on your bhāṣyas."***[89]

3.16. Śaṇkara's Momentous Debate with Scholars; Maṇḍana Miśra and Ubhaye Bhārtī

Ādi Śaṇkarācārya advanced towards Mahiṣī[90] to meet the great Karma Mīmāṃsā scholar Maṇḍana Miśra[91] who was also known as Viśvarūpa. It is recorded that he was an incarnation of Lord Brahmā. As Śaṅkara entered the village, He began asking the by-passers about the way to Maṇḍana Miśra's house. The by-passers informed Him that you can identify the house of the scholar by merely hearing the philosophical

---

87 Swami Gyananada Saraswati, p.148.

88 *Nivritti Marga;* refer to chapter 4 of this book p. 155.

89 Swami Gyananada Saraswati, p. 149.

90 *'Mahishi'* was a village located in Mithla (present day Bihar) in the Saharsa district.

91 *'Mandana Mishra'* belonged to a Maithili Brahman family. His birth name was Vishvarupa and he is said to be the incarnation of Lord Brahma. He is also known as Umveka. There are various theories regarding his origin. A few texts and scholars state that his parental house was situated in Kashmir. According to another theory, he belonged to Mithla, Bihara. Yet another story states that he was from Madhya Pradesh and a few say that he lived near Hastinapura.

conversations taking place between the parrots of the house on deep and intellectual topics related to the Vedas.[92]

After locating Maṇḍana Miśra's house Śaṇkara offered His desire to debate him. Once, Maṇḍana Miśra accepted to debate Śaṇkara, it was decided that if Ādi Śaṇkarācārya lost, He would become a householder. On the other hand, if Maṇḍana Miśra lost, he would become a Saṃnyāsī.

The task now was to find a competent judge who could be both neutral and fair. Maṇḍana Miśra delegated the task to Śaṇkara for selecting a competent and impartial judge and mediator. Śaṇkara elected Maṇḍana Miśra's wife Ubhaye Bhārtī to take up the charge. Ubhaye Bhārtī was not only a woman of substance but was a celebrated scholar. It is believed that she was an incarnation of Goddess Sarasvatī and had the knowledge of everything that could be thought.

Ādi Śaṅkarācārya with His wisdom and logic proved the non-duality of Jīva-Brahman. He also established that Mukti is possible with Jīāna alone and Karma without Jīāna is hollow. Finally, Maṇḍana Miśra lost. He was ready to become a Saṃnyāsī and the disciple of Ādi Śaṅkarācārya. However, at this juncture, Ubhaye Bhārtī objected and said,

"According to the scriptures, a married woman is the 'Ardhāṇginī' of her man. Merely by defeating my husband, you have only attained half of the total victory. Your victory will only be established if you defeat me in the debate. Till you do not debate and defeat me, my husband cannot be free from household duties and cannot take up Saṃnyāsa."

At last, Ādi Śaṅkarācārya accepted to debate Ubhaye Bhārtī. An earnest debate began between two highly accomplished scholars. Ubhaye Bhārtī was throwing all sorts of questions. She did not spare any of the Śāstras or any topic that one could think of. However, Śaṇkara answered every question in a calm and composed manner. The debate

[92] Vidyaranya Madhava, Svami Tpasyananda (Tr), pp.81-82.

between Śaṇkara and Ubhaye Bhārtī continued for seventeen days. When Ubhaye Bhārtī realized that it is impossible to defeat Ādi Śaṅkarācārya, she decided to manipulate things. Despite being aware that Śaṇkara was a Brahmacārī, who had taken up Saṃnyāsa at the age of eight, she did not hesitate in asking questions from the '*Kāmaśāstra*'. Though Maṇḍana Miśra tried to stop his wife yet she continued her questions under the pretext that '*Kāmaśāstra*' is also a Śāstra and if Ādi Śaṅkarācārya cannot answer questions related to it then He must accept His defeat. She went on to ask peculiar questions like,

O wise one! What constitutes eroticism? Which parts of the body is 'Kāma' at its plinth during sexual intercourse? Does the desire for sex remain the same during the new moon and the full moon or it varies? What about the sexual urge in young men and women?[93]

The above said questions had put Śaṇkara in an unusual predicament and He requested for a month's time. Ubhaye Bhārtī was assured that nothing would change in a month and that Ādi Śaṅkarācārya's defeat was certain. As a result, she agreed to resume the debate after a month.

Ādi Śaṅkarācārya's challenge was to not only gain knowledge in order to answer Ubhaye Bhārtī but also to ensure that His Saṃnyāsdharma was preserved. Therefore, when Śaṇkara saw King Amruka's dead body one day, He used mystic yogic siddhi to enter Amruka's body while His own body was guarded by His students in a cave. The yogic tradition refers to this complete process as 'Parakāyāpraveṣa'. It is one of the ten Siddhis mentioned by Lord Kṛṣna in the Bhāgvatapurāṇa.

After spending a month in King Amruka's body and learning everything there is to know about Kāmaśastra, Ādi Śaṅkarācārya returned in order to resume the debate with

93 Vidyaranya Madhava, Svami Tpasyananda (Tr), V. 9.58-9.72, P. 112

Ubhaye Bhārtī. He now gave all answers to her questions and she finally accepted her defeat. As per the rules of the debate, Maṇḍana Miśra accepted the path of Saṃnyāsa and became the disciple of Ādi Śaṅkarācārya.[94] Later, Śaṇkara fondly named Maṇḍana Miśra as '*Sureśvarācārya*' who authored some of the most outstanding works of all times. He wrote the celebrated commentary on Ādi Śaṅkarācārya's Bṛhadāraṇyakopaniṣadbhāṣya called the Bṛhadāraṇyakopaniṣadbhāṣyavārttika. He further penned the much-acclaimed Naiṣkarmyasiddhi, Saṃbandhavārttika and the popular Mānsollāsa. Sureśvarācārya went on to write scholarly commentaries on Ādi Śaṅkarācārya's Dakṣināmurtiaṣṭkam and Pañcikarṇam and developed the theory of Ābhāsvāda'. Even today some of his works such as Brahmasiddhi, Vibhramaviveka, Bhāvnāviveka, and Mokṣanirṇya are widely read.

3.17. Śaṇkara's Rendezvous with Hastāmalaka

Ādi Śaṅkarācārya now visited a village set near Mūkaṃikā called Śrībālī or Śrīvalī where an affluent man called 'Prabhākara' lived. He was well known because of his so-called '*crazy*' son, who behaved bizarrely, did not speak to anyone and did not listen to anybody. It was presumed that he was deaf and dumb since birth. Prabhākara brought his peculiar thirteen-year-old child to the great sage and voiced his concern. "Who are you, from where have you come, and what do you seek?" Śaṇkara asked the boy tenderly. This elicited a response from the young boy;

"O Greatest of all! Undoubtedly, I am not insentient; in fact, insentient things become sentient because of me. I am the non-dual consciousness that pervades everything. I remain untouched by the six miseries of hunger, thirst, old age, death, grief and infatuations. I am beyond birth, growth, decay, death and

---

94 One can find minute details of this debate and Adi Shankaracharya's '*Parakayapravesha*' in Madhavacharya's Shankara Digvijay

destruction. I am the ever-shining 'Ātman' that is common to all beings"[95]

The above said words reminded Ādi Śaṅkarācārya of His introduction to Guru Govinda Bhagavatapāda. Gladly, Śaṇkara accepted this young disciple who was shining with the light of wisdom and named him Hastāmalaka (the one who holds in his palm the fruit of wisdom with ease).

Hastāmalaka later recited the Hastāmalakastotra, a compilation of twelve exquisite verses of non-dualism that hold a distinguished place in the Advaitic tradition. The fact that Ādi Śaṅkarācārya Himself wrote a commentary on this masterpiece speaks volumes about its grandeur.

3.18. Śaṇkara and His Devoted Disciple 'Giri'[96]

With disciples Padmapādācārya, Sureśvarācārya and Hastāmalakācārya, Ādi Śaṅkarācārya reached Śiṇgerī the town that stands on the banks of river Tuṇgabhadra in the state of Karnataka. Here a youth named '*Giri*' began serving Śaṇkara with unsurpassed love and piety. He had little intelligence but was deeply devoted to his Guru 'Ādi Śaṅkarācārya'. He followed Śaṇkara everywhere and took close attention to His Guru's bath, clothes, food, and other necessities. His commitment was undeniable. Giri's straightforwardness was frequently mocked by others.

One day when Ādi Śaṅkarācārya was getting ready to address His disciples, Giri was away at the Tuṇgabhadra Ghāta washing His Guru's clothes. Ādi Śaṅkarācārya decided to wait for Giri and halted the class. On the other hand, Padmapādācārya requested His Guru to start the class and not wait for the dull and dim-witted Giri. Waiting for Giri according to the class was futile and time-consuming. However, Ādi Śaṅkarācārya firmly told all of His disciples

95 Swami Gyananada Saraswati, pp.170-172.

96 *Ibid.*, pp.172-173.

that the class will not commence until Giri arrived. Ādi Śaṅkarācārya went into deep Samādhi while waiting for Giri and enlightened him in fraction of seconds. The new realized Giri entered the class with a sense of gratitude. In the glory of His beloved Guru he composed one of the most magnificent hymns of all time. Hearing the unique hymn which was composed in Toṭaka meter, Ādi Śaṅkarācārya named Giri as 'Toṭakācārya' and the hymn came to be known as Toṭakāṣṭakaṃ.[97] This composition is said to be one of the most difficult, and yet the most astonishing masterpieces in the history of world literature.

Toṭakācārya continues to be an example of unwavering devotion. His narrative demonstrates that commitment, dedication, and complete surrender can lead to the earning of Guru's grace. It further indicates that the Guru is a personification of compassion who aims at the progress and welfare of His disciples.

3.19. Śaṅkara's Conquest of Bhāratvarṣa

Ādi Śaṅkarācārya's conquest of Bhāratvarṣa did not include capturing of land or defining territories; instead, included the realization of 'Self' as the Highest Principle. His conquest was not motivated by bloodshed rather it aimed at realizing unity in diversity. He never endeavored to attain the momentary; instead, He strived to let others realize the eternal behind the temporal. He promulgated the philosophy of non-dualism where all material entities i.e. humans, animals, trees and every spec of the universe are realized as the varied manifestation of the 'One Ultimate Reality'. He refuted manifoldness, diversity and any sort of dualism. His philosophy not only expounds the non-duality of all at a transcendental level but also promotes morals, ethics, co-operation and co-existence at a worldly sphere.

---

97 Swami Gyananada Saraswati, 172-173,

He traveled throughout India for establishing the authority of the Vedas and put an end to the impious act of eating meat, Taṇtrika practices and fulfilling carnal sexual desires. He reintroduced the nation to the Vedic wisdom and Sāttvic form of devotion. Śaṅkara started His spiritual conquest from Rāmeśvarama[98] and soon transformed the inner as well as the outer environment of the nation. The new Bhāratavarṣa was united. It was a place where all sentient beings existed in unity. This newfound nation respected, rivers, mountains, trees and every speck. Ādi Śaṅkarācārya had made the nation realize that variedness of names and forms was merely apparent and in essence, everyone and everything was the 'Brahman'. In this way, His spiritual conquests led to peace, harmony, mutual respect, co-existence and co-operation.

3.20. Śaṇkara's Ascendance to Sarvajñānapīṭha[99]

He walked His way to Kashmir after re-establishing Dharma and spreading the light of Advaita, and ascended the well-known 'Throne of Wisdom,'[100] also known as the Sarvajñāna Śāradāpīṭha or the seat of Goddess Śārdā which is one of the eighteen Mahāsakti Pīṭhas.[101] Only a person with perfect wisdom and realization could ascend to this throne. The Pīṭha has four doors in four directions, the southernmost of which can only be accessed by a Brahmajñānī (the one with perfect wisdom).[102] Being a

98 Swami Gyananada Saraswati, p.174.

99 *Ibid.*, pp.188-190.

100 This temple stands in the village of Sharda, in present-day Pakistan's Neelam Valley. This remarkable structure is situated 16 miles to the northwest of the 'Line of Control' in a militarily sensitive area.

101 *'Mahashaktipitha'* are the revered pilgrimages of the Shakti tradition that consider the Mother Goddess as the Highest Reality. There are a total of fifty-one Shaktipitha out of which eighteen are considered to be the Mahashaktipitha. The *'Ashtadasha Shaktipitha Stotram'* names the eighteen Mahashaktipitha along with the area where the Pithas are situated. The Sotram was composed by Adi Shankaracharya.

102 Swami Gyananada Saraswati, p.174.

Paramjñānī, Ādi Śaṅkarācārya could easily open the door. His ascension to the Sarvajñāna Shārdāpīṭha accentuates His pure, divine and taintless character.

3.21. Ādi Śaṅkarācārya's Mahāsamādhi[103]

Ādi Śaṅkarācārya walked His way into the snow-clad Himālayas and took Mahāsamādhi (477 BCE) at Kedārnātha in the thirty-second year of His life. It is documented in the Śāṇkaradigvijay that Lord Śiva's beloved bull 'Nandī' who glimmered like a camphor white swan came over to receive His Lord. As Ādi Śaṅkarācārya mounted Naṇḍī, He transformed into Lord Śiva with His matted locks. Seeing this divine sight, the Kalpaka tree showered its flowers in utmost delight. Lord Śiva soon vanquished into the snow-clad mountains at Kedārnātha never to be seen again. The last one's who saw Him walking into the snowy white Himālayas on His beloved Naṇḍī till He disappeared were His four disciples- Padmapādācārya, Sureśvarācārya, Hastāmalakācārya and Toṭakācārya.

CONCLUSION

A comprehensive review of Ādi Śaṅkarācārya's life draws attention to His magnanimous personality, lucid vision, unmatched scholarship, and compassionate character. He not only propounded a philosophy that saw all entities of the world as equal in essence but also practically made efforts to emphasize the same.

It is truly distressing that the contemporary researchers have compartmentalized His thought by referring to Him as a 'Metaphysician' while turning a blind eye towards His life, practical efforts, ethics and compassion. A few clever and ignorant academicians and scholars have further tried to manipulate His philosophy and have declared it as 'A-ethical and unfit for the world of material'. It is critical to emphasize

---

103 Vidyaranya Madhava, Swami Tapasyananda (Tr), pp.193-195

that all such allegations are unfounded, either owing to a lack of comprehension of Advaita-Vedānta Darśana or due to malicious intentions.

The life and philosophy of Ādi Śaṅkarācārya's cannot be divided or segmented. He was neither an idealist nor a skeptic like Plato or Socrates, nor was His thought restricted to any being, sect, caste, creed, nation, religion, sex or species. To be more precise, His life and philosophy were all-inclusive, all-embracing and all-incorporating. It is to be borne in mind that Ādi Śaṅkarācārya's life has been a perfect example of the inner harmonious environment which manifested as His philosophy, works and endeavors that aimed at establishing cosmic harmony. He left behind a treasure to aid future generations in attaining internal and external perfection, for the sakeh & universal harmony. As a result, separating His philosophy, works, and practical endeavors from His life and inner states is unjust. His life was a manifestation of His philosophy and His philosophy was the foundation of the life that He led. As a result, it may be argued that Ādi Śaṅkarācārya's inner state was rooted in tranquility, peace, harmony and non-duality and thus, His life, works and endeavors were merely a reflection of the same.

He did not aim at concord, coherence and non-dualism to exist only amongst humans. That again is a very limited view of His philosophy and life. He aimed at wholesome accord and synchronization. No doubt He preached and instructed the human race for obvious reasons because only humans tend to waver from the path of Dharma and humans alone can strike a balance by following the same. A great soul who Himself existed in non-duality cannot see men, women, animals, trees and the entire cosmos as distinct and in compartments. One can very well infer from His life and philosophy that He held no special preference towards humans rather His compassion was all-encompassing. If one insists that Ādi Śaṅkarācārya fostered special preference towards the human race, he is refuting the very philosophy of non-dualism. The moment there emerges even an iota of division, disparity, hate or preference towards any entity of the cosmos, at that very moment the entire Advaita Vedānta philosophy collapses.

The forthcoming chapter will discuss Ādi Śaṅkarācārya's philosophy in view of environmental harmony which must be seen in continuation with the life that He has led and not in seclusion of the same.

Oṁ Sākṣācchaṅkararūpabhṛte Namaḥ

(I bow before Śaṅkara who is a manifestation of the Supreme Brahman 'Śiva')

4.
Ādi Śaṅkarācārya's Philosophy: A Prelude to Environmentalism.

There is no discipline of philosophy more widespread and susceptible to misunderstanding as Advaita Vedānta. To understand Advaita Vedānta accurately, we must first understand the dissimilarities in intellectual and spiritual attitudes that exist between Indian and Western philosophies. Indian sages have expounded upon philosophies that they have lived and experienced. Their ethics have been rooted in their metaphysics. The intimacy between ethics and metaphysics has nowhere been stressed as firmly as in the case of Advaita Vedānta whose philosophical framework has manifested as the determining principle of personal, social, moral, religious, and spiritual life in India. The philosophy that exists inseparably with Mokṣa as the highest value cannot be anything but 'Ethical'.

Ethics being a normative science that examines human ends goes on to establish standards based on which human conduct is appraised. The appraisal of human demeanor is fundamental to the topic of human good. As a result, ethics and metaphysics are linked.

It is not important to ponder over the question of whether Advaita Vedānta announces certain codes of conduct or not. The central concern is whether or not it is possible to deduce logical codes of existence from its metaphysics. The metaphysics of Advaita Vedānta can unquestionably be used to derive ethical codes of being and reverence for all lives.

The philosophy considers the non-dual 'Brahman' to be the Highest Good and this becomes a subject of much criticism amongst scholars and philosophers. Further, Ādi Śaṅkarācārya is criticized for laying too much stress upon Jñāna and disregarding Karma and Bhakti. He has also been condemned for overtly focusing upon asceticism and giving up cranial human desires. It should be ucidly understood that all of these hostilities have developed as a result of ignorance in comprehending the central message of Advaita Vedānta philosophy, due to restricted information of the same, or merely to manipulate it deliberately.

Ādi Śaṅkarācārya is not only one of the most logical, sharp and outstanding philosophers that any country has ever produced in the history of the world but is also the most misinterpreted one. However, here the issue is not with His writings or His philosophy instead the concern lies with the way people have misunderstood His life, works and thought.

Ādi Śaṅkarācārya's writings and Bhāṣyas have been extremely lucid, flexible, all-enveloping and had no ambiguity. It must be noted that most confusion that people have faced is due to the misinterpretation of the concept of 'Māyā' which is one of the central ideas of His philosophy. Further, He has been labeled as the proponent of 'Māyāvāda'. It must be clearly understood that Ādi Śaṅkarācārya advocated the all-ready existing philosophy of the Brahmasūtras, Upaniṣads and the Bhagvadagītā. In various places, He refers to His own expositions as Upaniṣadaṁśāstram. The reason why Ādi Śaṅkarācārya's elucidations hold a paramount position is due to the impeccable logic that He makes use of to demolish inverse stances and establish the Advaitic position.

Ādi Śaṅkarācārya without a doubt appreciates the world of names and forms which has a limited existence. At no point has He negated the world like the 'Sky Flower'. In this regard, Prof. Hiriyanna aptly states,

"Psychologically the theory is realistic, the illusionary objects have a reality but are less real when compared to the objects of the world and the worldly objects are less real when compared to that which is really real 'Brahman', while for all practical purposes the things of the world are 'Satya', Brahman is 'Satyasya Satyam."[1]

Along these lines, the unsympathetic critics of Ādi Śaṅkarācārya who assert that His philosophy is sheer imaginative speculation and has no practical purpose fall flat. Ādi Śaṅkarācārya's philosophy is in no way futile rather it gives the much-needed understanding of one's life and the world. It allows us to take charge of our impulses and decorates us with values, ethics and morals of the highest kind. To appreciate Ādi Śaṅkarācārya's ethics one has to lucidly understand His Pārmārthika, Vyāvhārika and Pratibhāśika standpoints.

As far as free will is concerned, the question is not whether a person has free will or not. The question is that how this free will is preconditioned for moral responsibility and advances for an ethical life in general. Consequently, a moral agent must have both- 'The Freedom of Will' and 'The Freedom of Choice'. The critics of Ādi Śaṅkarācārya contend that- 'If the freedom of will is completely denied, the ethics of 'Ought to be, ought to do, ought not to be and ought not to do' will be reduced to meaninglessness. It is to be cognized that the problem of free will is recognized by a non-dualist like Ādi Śaṅkarācārya. He acknowledges the entire phenomenal world that appears to be distinct and has its roots in Avidyā. Dualism and variedness are a bi-product of Adhyāsa and therefore injunctions like '*you ought*

1 M. Hiriyanna, '*Outlines of Indian Philosophy*', Motilal Banarsidas Publications, Delhi, 1932, p.346.

to be good' or *'you ought not to be evil'* become hollow for a realized one. As a result, freedom can be understood as both,

- ***choosing and acting in one's own accord positively.***
- ***absence of compulsion negatively.***

With the above backdrop, this chapter will not only make efforts to view Advaita Vedānta in terms of environmental harmony but will also endeavor to address a variety of other questions that are raised against it.

It is important to recall what has been stated in chapter-2 of this book. The book uses the rampant word 'Environment' with the connotation as expounded by the Vedic texts and not as understood by the Western world. The word 'Environment' is to be further comprehended as totality, all-inclusive, all-embracing, all-comprehensive, Absolute and Ultimate. It connotes to the Highest Principle in the material world called 'God or Īśvara' and the Highest of Reality at the transcendental level known as 'Brahman'. It is a symbol of the internal, external and cosmic states of all lives and further defines the Svabhāva, Dharma, and inherent worth of each entity.

Even though this chapter is a prelude to Ādi Śaṅkarācārya's timeless philosophy, the guiding light for us must not be Ādi Śaṅkarācārya merely as a scholar, meta-physicist, logician or as a philosopher, rather it is important to see Him as an illumined Sage who aimed at the reconstruction of the society and endeavored to make everyone realize the non-duality of all existences for the sake of Lokasaṁatā and Sarvabhūtahita because Śaṅkara is indeed the one who means the welfare of all lives (*śaṅkaram lokaśaṅkaram*).

4.1. Meaning of Advaita Vedānta Darśana

Before we ensue further and look at 'Environment' in view of Ādi Śaṅkarācārya's philosophy it is important to understand the very meaning of 'Advaita Vedānta Darśana'. The word 'Advaita' is made of Saṃskṛta prefix 'A' which suggests 'not or non' and the word 'Dvaita' which suggests 'Two'. As a result, the word 'Advaita' means non-dual or not-two. 'Advaita' is that in which there is no two-fold-ness, dichotomy, or dyad. It ascertains non-duality by the negation of duality. The Ultimate Brahman so supremely exists that one cannot even imagine it in terms of numbers. The phrase 'Vedānta' (*vedanāma antaḥ vedāntaḥ*) on the other hand, alludes to the physical end of the Vedas and the beginning of the Upanishads. Thus, the Upaniṣads are also referred to as Vedānta. The word 'Vedānta' is made of two Saṃskṛta words 'Veda' which means 'Wisdom' and 'Anta' which refers to 'conclusion'. Therefore, Vedānta is the concluding portion of the Vedas which underscores non-duality. Finally, the word Darśana is casually translated as philosophy. While the word philosophy means 'Love for wisdom'. The word 'Darśana' is derived from the Saṃskṛta word 'Dṛs' which means the 'Vision of Truth'. 'Advaita Vedānta Darśana' therefore implies 'The non-dual concluding vision of truth'. With this non-dual understanding, all other pursuits of knowledge come to rest and it is only by knowing this (non-dualism) that one can know everything else. In other words, 'Advaita Vedānta Darśana' is the culmination of the Vedic wisdom.

4.2. Brahman-The Ultimate Principle

When we talk about 'ethics,' we frequently presume diversity. Ādi Śaṅkarācārya, on the other hand, argues that diversity is only apparent and not ultimately real. Many people have criticized Ādi Śaṅkarācārya and His philosophy as being A-ethical, A-theist and consequently not appropriate for the world. Regrettably, this is a very fallacious interpretation of Advaita Vedānta. Most philosophers and researchers have overlooked the fact that Ādi Śaṅkarācārya comes to evaluate the world based on the ultimate reality of the 'Brahman' and not vice-versa as has been deduced.

Ādi Śaṅkarācārya accentuates on the idea of an Absolute Principle called 'Brahman' which is also referred to as the 'Ātman'. This Ātman is all-pervading, omnipotent, omniscient, and the whole of creation is contained in this Universal Spirit. This Brahman, says the Bṛhadāraṇyakopaniṣad has two forms- Nirguṇa and Saguṇa,

dve vāva brahmaṇo rūpe-murtaṃ caivāmūrtaṃ ca।
martyaṃ cāmṛtaṃ ca, sthitaṃ ca yacca, sacca, tyacca॥[2]
(Unquestionably there exist two essential Brahman the formed and the formless, the mortal and the immortal, the stationary and the moving, the true and the apparent.)

Brahman becomes the non-dual quintessence of all entities (humans, animals, birds, trees, plants, rivers, mountains and so on) and establishes unity, equality, and oneness of the entire creation, which appears to be fragmented. Ādi Śaṅkarācārya propagates that there is only one Universal Spirit that envelops all apparent variedness of the cosmos. It indwells, pervades and further becomes the cosmic entities of names and forms. In this respect, the Bhagvadgītā, Upaniṣads and the Vedas repetitively stress upon 'Sarvabrahmavāda (all is the Brahman)' which is evident from the following verses,

eko vaśī sarvabhūtāntarātmā ekam rūpam bahudhā yaḥ karoti।[3]
(He indwells all beings as the very Self and He alone becomes manifold)

sarvam khalu idam brahma।[4]
(All is the Brahman)

The nature of Brahman is said to be Sat-cit-ānanda (being-consciousness-bliss).[5] This nature is present in the

2 Swami Mdhavananda, '*Brihdarnayakopnishad with Commentaries of Shankaracharya*', Advaita Ashrama, Himalayas, 1950. p.329. (V.2.3.2)

3 *Ibid.*, p.840-841. (V.5.12.1)

4 *Ibid.*, p.466-467. (V.3.4.1)

5 Deshmukh Srikrihna, (Tr & Com), '*Aproksanubhuti*', Motilal Banarsidas, Delhi, 2019. p.37. (V.24, *brahmaivāhaṁ samaḥ śāntaḥ saccidānandalakṣṇāḥ। nāhaṁ deho hyasadrūpo jñānamityucyate budhaiḥ॥*)

minutest of insects and in the massiveness of the cosmos. The Brahman is the Sākṣī or the silent witness and is the knower of all (Sarvajñātā). However, it is beyond the realms of logic and intellect, therefore it can only be realized. It sans any gulfs and all objects of the world are pervaded and indwelled by it. It is self-proved (Svayamsiddha), unborn (Anādi), eternal (Ananta), self-illuminated (Savayamprakāśita), and non-dual (Advaita). The assumptions of "I am a human", "He is a dog," "I am more powerful than the weaker beings," "I must kill animals who are different from me," and "I must cut down trees to capture the land" are all statements of an ignorant and unwise being caught-up in the cobweb of perceptible forms in which the Brahman appears. He has the logical sight to see the discrepancies but lacks the spiritual vision to see non-duality.

As the human race continues to abolish the flora and fauna, they fail to realize that they are not only destroying forms that have a specific role to play within the material world but are impairing their very own survival. It is to be carefully understood that all beings of the world are interconnected, interwoven, and interdependent upon each other for survival. These sentient beings are the Ultimate Brahman established in peace. As a result, says the Māṇḍūkyopniṣad,

ṣāntam śivamadvaitam[6]

(That auspicious non-dual Brahman (Śiva) is all peaceful)

It must also be noted that the seeming variedness of the cosmos falls under the umbrella of limitations of Deśa-pariccheda (limited by place), Kāla-pariccheda (limited by time), Vastu-pariccheda (limited by forms). However, Brahman remains beyond boundaries and disunions. Satya or Reality cannot be multifaceted. There cannot rein many truths or many realities and so, the 'Absolute Truth' exists

---

6 Joshi, Bimali, Trivedi, '*112 Upanishads, Vol-1, Mandukyopnishad*', Parimal Publications, Delhi, 2013. p.63. (V.7, *Mandukyopnishad*)

as non-dual. The Brahman (Ātman) is beyond words, thoughts, descriptions and intellect. The word 'Brahman' and 'Ātman' are used merely for intellectual comprehension. Despite this, no words can remotely define that 'Ultimate', leave alone explaining it completely. The only way to know 'It' is through experiencing 'It' (Anubhūti). Therefore, a being who realizes the Ultimate Brahman rises above the peculiarities of mine-your, man-animal, this-that and other poles of opposites. He acquires a vision to see the permanent Brahman in the temporary world of names and forms and understands these divisions as verily the 'Self' which is indeed division-less. In this regards says the Īśāvāsyopniṣad,

***yastusarvāṇi bhutānātmanyevānupaṣyati,* ।**
***sarva-bhūteṣū cātmānam tato na vijugupsate* ॥[7]**
(He who looks at all beings as the Self and the Self as all beings knows that 'Unknown'. He in whom all beings appear as the non-dual 'Self' goes beyond Moha (attachment) and Śoka (Dukkha))

It is for this reason that the realized ones remain established in Dharma and virtues like non-violence, compassion, sharing, amity and brotherhood. Universal fellowship becomes the very nature of a realized one. He rises above Rāga-Dveṣa and all beings remain uniform before him.

In case, Ādi Śaṅkarācārya's only aim was metaphysics or intellectual explorations the concept of Nirguṇabrahman would have been quite adequate. However, Nirguṇabrahman is appropriate for those who, over a period of many births have reached a stage of concluding that 'All is the Brahman'. The same is not suitable for a common man who is dealing with mundane errands, responsibilities of a family, pains, dejections, sorrows, failures and confusions related to birth, death, right, wrong and life. A mundane man needs a Higher Being who becomes his protector, comrade, guide, mentor and leads him to 'Mokṣa' through the path of virtue and

7 Joshi, Bimali, Trivedi, pp.2-3, (V.6, *Ishavasyopnishad*)

wisdom. It is here that Ādi Śaṅkarācārya brings in the concept of Saguṇabrahman or Īśvara which is the key-note of His metaphysics and ethics. As a result, the concept of an all-powerful, all-pervasive 'Īśvara' has a great physical, emotional, psychological, ethical and spiritual significance in Advaita Vedānta. Hence, Ādi Śaṅkarācārya states in His Bhāṣyas,

'From śrutatvāccha it can be concluded that the all-knowing Brahman is the first cause of the world. The Upaniṣads speak of Brahman as Saguṇabrahman and Nirguṇabrahman. Wherever Brahman appears with attributes, it is to be worshiped'[8]

ekoham bahusyām[9]
(I am one and I will become countless)

teṣāṃ khalv eṣāṃ bhūtānāṃ trīṇy eva bījāni
bhavanty āṇḍajaṃ jīvajam udbhijjam iti[10]।
hantāham imās tisro devatā anena
jīvenātmanānupraviśya nāma-rūpe vyākaravāṇīti[11]॥
(Of all these living beings, there are only three origins: beings born from eggs, beings born from living beings and beings born from seeds. Let 'Me' now enter into these by means of this living Self and let 'Me' be the apparent names and forms)

yaḥ pṛthivyāṃ tiṣṭan pṛthivyā antaro, yaṃ pṛthivī
na veda yasya pṛthivī śarīraṃ yaḥ pṛthivīm antaro
yamayati eṣa ta ātmāntaryāmy amṛtaḥ[12]
(He who inhabits the earth, but whom the earth does not know, whose body is the earth and who controls the earth from within, is the 'Internal Ruler', your own immortal 'Self'.)

---

8 Swami Vishveshwarananda, '*Brahmasutrabhashya*', Advaita Ashrama, Kolkata, 2014. pp.36-37. (S.1.1.11, *śrutatvācca*।).

9 Jha Ganganatha, *The Chandogyaupanishad with Shankara Bhashya*', Oriental Book Agency, Puna, 1942.

10 *Ibid.*, pp.309-313. (V.6.3.1)

11 *Ibid.*, pp.313-314. (V.6.3.3)

12 Swami Shantananda Saraswati, '*Brihdarnayakopnishad Based on Shankara's Commentary*', Advaita Ashrama, Himalayas, 2019. p.104. (V.3.7.3)

vāsudevaḥ sarvamiti[13]
(Everything is indeed the Vasudeva)

sarvalokamaheśvaram, suhridam sarvabhutanāma[14]
(As Maheśvara I'm the 'One' residing in the hearts of all beings)

mattaḥ parataraṁ nānyat kiñchid asti dhanañjaya।
mayi sarvam idaṁ protaṁ sūtre maṇi-gaṇā iva॥[15]
(None but 'Me' is the cause. I am the string in which all beings are strung as the jewels).

ekam sat viprāḥ bahudā vadanti[16]
(He is the 'Only Truth' known by the wise as many)

The verses above emphasize that the Divine not only penetrates all beings but also takes on the form of the apparent cosmos. Furthermore, the great Advitin Svāmī Rāmakṛṣna Paramhaṃsa emphasizes this thought in His teachings when He states,

'jitra jīva tatra śiva'[17]
(Wherever there is life, there exists Śiva)

In this perspective, one may appreciate India's culture, wherein the earth, water, fire, sky, air and space, as well as all kinds of creatures, birds, reptiles, insects, mountains, caverns, dwellings, machines and even the deceased beings, are revered as the "Ultimate Divine." While all of these names and forms exist within the confines of space and time, they are all the eternal and limitless 'Truth' that we aspire to realize.

---

13 Shankaracharya, '*Shrimadhagvadagitabhashya*', Manav Prabodhan Pranyasa, Bikaner, Rajasthan, 2016, p.122. (V.7.19,)

14 Goendka Harikrishna, '*Shrimadbhagvadgita Shankarabhashya*', Gita Press, Gorakhpur, 2019. p.166. (V.5.29,)

15 Shankaracharya, '*Shrimadhagvadagitabhashya*', p.118. (V.7.7)

16 *Shtapathbrahman*, (V.10.6.3)

17 Wikipedia contributors, 2020 '*Teachings of Ramakrishna*', Wikipedia, Online, https: //en.wikipedia.org/wiki/Teachings_of_Ramakrishna, (Accessd on 11 April 2021)

Īśvara: ***The Highest Reality of the Material World–*** When Ādi Śaṅkarācārya speaks of the Saguṇabrahman and Nirguṇabrahman, He is not referring to two distinct Realities instead He is referring to the same Reality from two distinct viewpoints- 'The Absolute and The Empirical'. From an Absolute point of view, Brahman alone exists. However, from an empirical point of view 'It' exists as the Īśvara. For this reason, Īśvara becomes a practical necessity to realize the Ultimate Brahman. Hence, the Ultimate that exists in the Vyāvahārika Jagat as the Īśvara is the same that exists as the Supreme Brahman at the Pārmārthika level. While we consider that the various forms in which the Brahman appears have no permanent existence, we have to also take into account that this is true only from an Absolutistic point of view. However, this does not mean that at an empirical level the concept of God has no value in Advaita-Vedānta. Since the concept of Īśvara is the nearest to understanding the Brahman in the material world, Īśvara becomes the 'Highest Reality' of the cosmos and is of the highest value. Īśvara is the Ultimate abode of ethics, virtues, truth, compassion, love, wisdom and the highest good. Consequently, Īśvara or God has immense significance in the Advaita-Vedānta philosophy. Just as a child has to come into the world through his mother's womb, likewise one has to go through the Saguṇabrahman to realize the Nirguṇabrahman.

Non-dualism does not negate the appearance of dualism. A scientist who appreciates optics and dispersion of light will be aware that the sky is colorless, yet he will continue to see and enjoy the various colors that appear in the sky with the awareness that the sky, in reality, has no color of its own. Similarly, a wise being will see the formless Brahman as the very dog, the tree, the river, the sage and the Īśvara. He will be aware that ultimately, all temporary names and forms are rooted in the permanent and the permanent alone exists as the 'Final Truth'.

Svāmī Rāmakṛṣna Paramhaṃsa despite being a non-dualist continued worshiping Mahākālī throughout His life. Ramaṇa Mahāṛṣi despite being an Advaita Vedāntin continued worshiping Śiva as the Ultimate Self and Ādi Śaṅkarācārya continued worshiping the Supreme in varied forms. Thus, God or Īśvara is of immense importance practically, philosophically and to realize the 'Self' ultimately.

4.3. Jagat-The Material World

Advaita Vedānta grasps the world as apparently real. This must not direct us to the conclusion that the world is useless or unreal. Instead, one must try to understand real, unreal and apparently real at a deeper level. While 'Real' is that which remains perpetual, constant, and unaltered eternally, 'Unreal' is like the sky flower, the horns of a rabbit, or the son of a barren woman. However, 'Apparently Real' is that which is neither real nor unreal, like the rope-snake analogy where the snake is real until one gains the knowledge of it being the rope. Therefore, 'Real' is the Highest Truth (Parmārthika), 'Unreal' comes under dreams and illusions (Pratibhāṣka) and 'Apparently Real' is the world of names and forms that has ephemeral reality, is subject to birth, death, change and decay (Vyāvhārika).

Advaita Vedānta has various theories that explain the relationship between the world and Brahman. They prove that the internal, external, cosmic environment and all apparent entities of the material world are nothing but the Highest Reality. A few such theories are,

- **Sarvabrahmavāda**: All is the Brahman.
- **Jalataraṇgavāda**: The world is rooted in the Brahman just as waves are rooted in the ocean.
- **Īśvarakārṇvāvāda:** God is the cause of the entire world.
- **Vastūprabhāvavāda**: World is the shining glory of Brahman.

It is due to the conditionings of Avidyā that one analyses the non-dual Brahman with the lenses of duality and considers dualism to be real and concluding. Due to Avidyā, one considers the dog, the untouchable, the woman as being distinct from him, fostering a sense of inferiority or abhorrence towards them. One also develops attachment in the name of love towards a few under the powerful influence of Avidyā. Trapped in ignorance he sees the temporary forms but is incapable of seeing the permanent Brahman behind them. This dualism becomes the bedrock of violence, racism, religious hate, exploitation of the environment, cruelty towards animals, crimes and a whole gamut of personal, social, political and universal unrest. In this regard it will be apt to quote the crux of chapter eleven of the Bhagvadagītā Śāṅkarabhāṣya, when Arjuna sees the Viśvarūpa of Lord Kṛṣna, he is awe struck and says,

"I see all the Gods, all living beings in You. I see Brahmā sitting on the lotus. I see Śiva. I see all the sages and all serpents as your very body. I see all directions in You. I see countless varied faces, arms, and stomachs that are Yours. I am unable to understand the form of the universe, which has no start, no middle, and no end. You are imperishable; the whole of creation is You. You alone are the protector of the eternal order; you sustain all living beings. O! Greatest of all, I tremble with fear seeing the whole cosmos as You. I see in You the flowing rivers and oceans. In You, I see all living beings. You are Vāyu, Agni, Jala, Yamrāja, Caṅdra and the seed of all living creatures. O! Lord, You pervade everything and thus, You are everything. You are the moving and the non-moving beings. Having seen all Your forms, I am elated with joy and yet I tremble"[18]

Along these lines, it can be reckoned that the veil of duality of the world is fallacious because the whole of cosmos is rooted in the non-dual Brahman. Therefore, Ādi Śaṅkarācārya refers to this fallacious veil of manifoldness as

---

18 Shankaracharya, '*Shrimadbhagvadgitabhashya*', pp.162-186. (Ch-11, *Vishvarupadarshanayoga*),

'Mithyā' when He says '***Brahma Satyam, Jagan Mithyā***'. He merely negates the duality of the world and not the world itself as most scholars have misinterpreted. Ādi Śaṅkarācārya most certainly accepts the world as 'Vyāvhārika Sattā'. In this respect states the Taittṣryaopniṣad,

yato va imāni bhutāni jāyante[19]
(It is that (Brahman) from which these beings are born)

Further, most people consider that the gist of Ādi Śaṅkarācārya's philosophy is,

'brahm satyaṃ jagat mithyā'[20]
(Brahman alone is real while the world is unreal)

As one tries to decrypt the above said, it is crucial to recognize that, no doubt Ādi Śaṅkarācārya expounds on '*Brahma Satyam Jagan Mithyā*', but He also goes on to explicates upon '*Sarvam Khalu Idam Brahm (All is the Brahman)*[21]' and so which one will be counted as the 'Very Thought' of Ādi Śaṅkarācārya? As a result, complete negation of the objective world like the child of a barren woman is a bizarre deduction. He never contravenes the objective world as the '*horns of a rabbit*'. In this respect, Ādi Śaṅkarācārya says,

dṛṣṭ jñānamayim kṛtva pasyedbrahmamayam jagat[22] ।
(Seeing the Brahman in the entirety of the world is the noblest vision)

The realization of the Self leads to a state where all names and forms drop off their individual identity and shine as the

---

19 Swami Nikhilananda, '*The Upanishad-Taittirya and Chandogy Based on Shankara's Commentary, Vol. IV*', Harper Brother Publishers, New York, p.67. (V.3.1.1)

20 (i) *Vivekachudamani* (*V.20, brahma satyam jaganmithyā jīvo brahmaiva nāparaḥ । anena vedyam sacchāstram iti vedāntaḍiṇḍimaḥ*).
(ii) Shastri. S.N, 2019 '*Brahmajñānavalimālā*', Online, Shastra.com, https://www.shastras.com/adi-sankara/brahma-jnanavali-mala/ (V.2) (Accessed on 11 April 2021)

21 Swami Nikhilananda, p.206. (V.3.14.1)

22 Deshmukha Shrikrishna, p.150. (V.116)

'Brahman'. Therefore, instead of referring to Advaita Vedānta as 'Māyāvāda', it will fairly be appropriate to refer to it as '*Sarvabrahmavāda*', where the whole of cosmos is not reduced to being illusionary but is elevated as the Highest Reality. The world is far from being non-existent or void. This can be understood if we pay attention to Ādi Śaṅkarācārya's rejection of the Buddhist theory of non-existence of external objects in the regal Brahmasūtrabhāṣya where He states that,

"We cannot say that the objects of the world are non-existent. Because these objects are experienced, they cannot simply be void"[23]

Even if one argues in favor of the negation of the material world, he has to acknowledge the world in order to negate it. It is to be realized that one cannot deny the sky flower, son of a barren woman, or horns of a rabbit. It is also worth noting that if the world were illusionary, Ādi Śaṅkarācārya would not have declared the three levels of Reality, namely; Parmārthika, Vyāvahārika and Pratibhāṣika. Even in the case of Pratibhāṣika, which includes illusions, hallucinations, and dreams, it can be said that their existence is real till the time they last. British philosopher Francis Herbert Bradley in this regard puts it aptly when he says,

"at each stage is involved the principle of that which is higher and every stage is therefore true. But on the other hand, it is taken for itself and measured by its own idea; each level has its own truth, it meets its own claims and is proved false by that which lies beyond. The doctrine of degrees of truth and reality is an answer to our problems. Everything is essential and yet nothing is worthless in comparison to the other. Nothing is perfect and yet everything contains vital perfection. Therefore, appearance is an error but not every error is an illusion"[24]

---

23 Swami Vishveshwarananda, pp.196-197 (S.2.2.26 *Nābhāvaḥ Uplabdheḥ*II)

24 F.H. Bradley, '*Appearance and Reality*', Oxford Press, London, 1966, pp.430-431.

It is also important to take into consideration the life led by realized beings of the Advaita Vedānta order. Ādi Śaṅkarācārya, Svāmī Vivekānanda, Svāmī Cinmayānanda, Svāmī Dayānanda Sarasvatī and many more have led a life of perfection. They elected to dedicate their lives to the welfare and the well-being of all beings. Despite being realized they never disregarded the world and made uninterrupted efforts in order to maintain peace, harmony and non-violence with the dint of love, compassion and wisdom of non-duality. This argument can also be proved by paying consideration to Ādi Śaṅkarācārya's approach to the world. Despite being a non-dualist of the highest order He admired various forms in which Brahman appears. If He did negate the world then He would not have written hymns in the glory of Kāśī, Gaṇgā, Yamunā and more.

As we decipher Ādi Śaṅkarācārya's philosophy, it becomes necessary to examine His life thoroughly. After closely examining His life and works, one may infer that He neither denies the reality of the world nor refutes the tangible distinctions that exist within it for smooth operation. Nevertheless, He strongly negates the final reality of diversity and dualism. He denies the ultimate reality of dualism as 'Mithyā' and says that the non-dual principle 'Brahman' is the only reality that is all-pervading and exists as the temporary names and forms. He finally concludes that 'Jīva' is non-dual from the 'Brahman'. Therefore, when He wrote the Gaṇgāṣtakama and described the glory of Mother Gaṇga, He not only was all praises for Her worldly, transitory and altering form that nourishes all beings but was also established in the reality that behind the Divine form was the all-encompassing Brahman. The same applies to all entities of the cosmos. Consequently, we have to acknowledge the value, worth and truth of every existence which ultimately is the Highest non-dual 'One'.

Ādi Śaṅkarācārya's philosophy untangles the dilemma associated with plurality without contradicting the non-duality and absoluteness of the Brahman, which becomes the cause and conclusion of the entire world. The world is limited and exists as neither real nor unreal. Nonetheless, it is through this world that one can realize the 'Ultimate Essence'. Therefore, the world has a pragmatic reality and holds good until the time one apprehends it as the Brahman. Once a being has realized the world as the Brahman, he sees the Self in all and all in the Self and thus it is the 'Self' that alone exists.

A person who has been tainted by ignorance will regard the world of duality as being Ultimately Real. A Bhakta who with the dint of submission understands that the universe is non-dual at its core but is yet to realize the same will treat everything as the 'Divine'. A philosopher will try to see the world through the lenses of logic and metaphysics and may or may not deny the reality of the world. A scientist could consider the world to be only 'Material.' A realized sage, on the other hand, will embrace all of the aforementioned viewpoints because he will see them as merging into the Supreme Brahman. Therefore, the pluralistic vision of the world is merely an error of perception and correction of error means freedom from plurality. Only from a transcendental perspective, where 'Brahman' is the Highest Reality, is the world unreal and not otherwise.

It is also important to remember that our senses only provide us a limited perspective of the world. Everything we see, hear, taste, smell and touch are far more than what we comprehend. Sensory data is used to describe the internal and external organs of a living creature. Any being, on the other hand, is far more than the physical components that make him or her. All objects of the world are not known to us completely, we only see a very limited portion of their being. Therefore, to reduce these entities to being mere material is a pretty fallacious understanding. Sense data can never be taken as a valid source of knowledge because relying upon sense data can lead us to fallacies. Merely by looking at the shining sand in the sun, one may fallaciously conclude it to be water. Likewise, a moving tree may appear to be a thief at night. Further, Ādi Śaṅkarācārya refers to the world as,

- **Anirvacanīya**: It is that which is indescribable.
- **Sadasadvilakṣṇa**: It is that which is neither real nor unreal. The individual entities of the cosmos last only till the time Avidyā lasts and are revealed as the Ultimate Brahman once Jñāna dawns.
- **Māyā**: It is that power which hides the reality (Āvaraṇaśakti) and reveals that which is not (Vikśepaśakti).
- **Avidyā:** It is that which is not known completely because one can only see a limited portion of the world through the senses.

From the foregoing, it is apparent that Ādi Śaṅkarācārya never refers to the world as 'Void or Imaginary.' Therefore, what is apparently real is certainly not worthless and what is useful may not be utterly real. The universe of seeming diversity in all its forms is unquestionably conducive to the realization of the Ultimate Principle. The Vyāvahārika becomes the means to realize the Pārmārthika, just as one thorn is needed in order to get rid of another thorn. Therefore, it is only through material that one can transcend material and realize the immaterial.

Ādi Śaṅkarācārya's view has always created ripples of controversy and appreciation since time immemorial and this will continue in the future depending upon one's understanding of His unique philosophy. Ādi Śaṅkarācārya's Vyāvahārika emphasizes the need for religion, culture, ethics, and morals. A Darśana that considers Mokṣa as the ultimate Puruṣārtha is bound to stress upon the above said in order to realize its goal. So, Vyāvahārika becomes the ground for morals, ethics, compassion, love, co-existence, co-operation, Sahvāsa, Sahbhoga and Sahkāra in order to step-up the ladder.

The above said argument that talks of the whole creation as a means to realize the Ultimate Reality is in support of Ādi Śaṅkarācārya's thought. Therefore, it may be deduced that whether the world is real or illusionary is a judgment or axiology based on the individual's insight. With this thought, Dvaita, Viśiṣṭādvaita, and Bhedābheda are the numerous insights, evaluations and levels of the world in course of an enquirer's quest that finally merge into Advaita (non-duality).

4.4. Jīva-The Individual Soul

caitanyasyaikarūpatvadbhedo yukto na karhicit ।
jīvatvaṁ ca mṛṣā jñeyaṁ rajjvaṁ sarpagraho yathā ॥[25]
(undivided consciousness alone exists. it is imprudent and delusional to see the jīva exist as isolated from the self just as it is incorrect to perceive the snake as separate from the rope).

Advaita Vedānta Darśna considers Jīva or the individual soul as infinite and non-dual with the Brahman. It is critical to note that the term 'Jīva' does not exclusively refer to human beings; rather, 'It' refers to all living entities who go through the cycle of birth, development, old age, transformation and death. In short, 'Jīva' is the 'Individual Self.' In this respect, Ādi Śaṅkarācārya states,

brahmaṇaḥ sarvabhūtāni jāyete parmātmanaḥ ।
tasmādetāni brahmaiva bhavantītyavadhārayate[26] ॥
(All living beings sprout from the Brahman. Hence, one should know all as the Brahman)

He affirms that Jīvas are many with their respective bodies i.e. human, animal, bird, tree, etc. This can be explained by the example of Ghata-Ākāśa (pot-space) analogy. If there are ten pots, each one contains Ākāśa, which is constrained by form, time, and space. This Ākāśa is identical to the Ākāśa found outside of the Ghata. Thus, the belief that Ākāśa is limited in the Ghata is a fallacy; the fact is that Ākāśa is non-dual and all-pervasive both within and outside the Ghata. In

---

25 Deshmukha Shrikrishna, p.65. (V.43)

26 *Ibid.*, p.80. (V.49,)

the same breadth, Ādi Śaṅkarācārya in Bhagvadagītābhāṣya states,

sarvabhūtastham ātmānaṁ sarvabhutāni cātmani |
īṣate yogayuktātmā sarvatra sama-darśanaḥ ||[27]
(The one who attains inner equanimity and vision of non-duality sees the Self in all beings and all beings in the Self).

At the highest level, 'Jīva' is the Nirguṇabrahman and remains birth-less, death-less, age-less, beyond transformation, time and space. However, the 'Jīva' ties itself down into the chains of Karmas and experiences transmigration and rebirth due to the effect of Avidyā. Until and unless the Jīva doesn't realize its true nature of being the 'Ultimate Brahman' it remains in a state of individuality, duality and rebirth. Its journey continues from body to body and from one life to the other. Therefore, Ādi Śaṅkarācārya makes it clear,

"He who sees manifoldness in 'It' goes from death to death "[28]

The enlightened beings, saints and sages have always held the authority of the Upaniṣads to be paramount. The Upaniṣadvācyas talk of the non-duality of Brahman and Jīva. On the basis of the same, Ādi Śaṅkarācārya establishes the non-duality of Jīva-Brahman and declares,

śrutyā nirāritaṁ nūnaṁ nānātvaṁ svamukhena hi |
kathaṁ bhāso bhāvedanyaḥ sthite cādvayakāraṇe[29] ||
(Upaniṣad (Śruti) exterminate manifoldness of the world with their profound verses. Brahman is non-dual and the one alone. How can then the world be different from it?)

The Jīva is the agent and the enjoyer, it acquires merits and demerits. As long as the Jīvas, over a period of various births do not put an end to the dualities by conquering

---

27 Shankaracharya, '*Shrimadbhagvadgitabhashya*', p.109. (V.6.29)

28 Swami Vishveshwarananda, p.28. (S.1.1.4) (also see *Kaṭha Upaniṣad* 2.4.11).

29 Deshmukha Shrikrishna, p.78. (V.47)

Avidyā they will continue to suffer in various names and forms, across varied births. Hence, it becomes our duty, responsibility and Dharma to assist other beings in climbing up the ladder and attaining Mukti from the cycle of birth and death because in their liberation lies our own liberation. Ādi Śaṅkarācārya clearly states in the Bṛhadārṇyakopaniṣadbhāṣya,

'When all Avidyā vanishes, the knower attains Sarvātmanbhāva (I am in all, all are in me) where he sees nothing else, hears nothing else, understands nothing else but the 'Brahman'. For him, the 'Self' is the all-pervading principle. This wisdom extends also to dreams, and he experiences 'sarvo smīti manyate (I am all this)'. Therefore, even if one experiences difference that is equivalent to a hair's tip (Bālāgramātramapi), it is nescience.'[30]

From the above said, it may be concluded that Jīva is non-dual from the Brahman and it is Brahman alone that appears as the varied individual Jīvas and the world of material. Hence, when a man sees distinction and kills animals for the sake of amusement, fashion, food and pleasure, or when he ruins nature in the name of technological progressions he falls prey to duality. Sadly, this duality is untrue because the whole of creation is the non-dual Self. In this context says the Bhagvadgītā Śāṅkarabhāṣya,

vidyāvinayasampanne brāhmaṇe gavi hastini ।
śuni caiva śvapāke ca paṇḍitāḥ samadarśinaḥ ॥[31]
mattaḥ parataraṁ nānyat kiñcid asti ।[32]
(The wise one sees me with equanimity in a learned, in a cow, in an elephant, in a dog and in an outcaste. Not even the tiniest of creature exists as distinct from me)

---

30 Swami Madhavananda, '*Brihdarnayakopnishad with Commentaries of Shankara*', Advaita Ashrama, Himalayas, 1950, pp.658-660. (V.4.3.20)

31 Shankaracharya, '*Shrimadbhagvadgitabhashya*', p.95. (V.5.18)

32 *Ibid.*, p.118. (V7.7)

4.5. Māyā: The Power through which the Infinite appears as Finite

In the popular work Vivekacurāmaṇi, Ādi Śaṅkarācārya talks about Māyā and says,

avyaktanāmnī parameśaśakth anādyavidyā triguṇātmikā parā kāryānumeyā sudhiyaiva māyā yayā jagatsarvamida prasūyate sannāpyasannāpyubhayātmikā no bhinnāpyabhinnāpyubhayātmikā no sāṅgāpyanaṅg hyubhayātmikā no mahādbhutā'nirvacanīyarūpā[33]

(The un-manifest power of Īśvara that is beginning-less and triguṇātmaka is superior to its effects. Only the one with a clear intellect can infer 'Māyā' that projects the whole of the universe. It is neither real nor is it unreal, nor is it both, nor different, nor same, it has no parts nor is it the whole. It is just wonderfully 'Indescribable (Anirvacanīya)').

The concept of Māyā holds a prime position in the Advaita Vedānta Darśana. While Sāyaṇācārya[34] points out that in the Ṛgveda it refers to both Prajñā (wisdom) and Kapaṭa, (deception) Yāska[35] in his Nighaṇtu describes it as 'Intelligence'.[36] Māyā has also been expressed as the power of delusion, illusion, or magic. However, Ṛgveda defines it as,

anekarūpagrahaṇasāmarthyam[37]

(Māyā is the mysterious power through which 'The One' becomes many).

---

33 Sri Shankaracharya Pranipatchaitanya (Tr), Dhiman Satinder(Ed) '*Vivekachudamani*', Chinmaya Mission Foundation, Tamil Nadu, 2012, pp.29-31. (V.108-109)

34 Sayanacharya is more commonly known as 'Sāyaṅa'. He was a Mīmāṁsā scholar belonging to the Vijaynagar empire.

35 Yaska is the 4th century Sanskrit Grammarian and is the author of the Nirukta.

36 Balasubramaniam. R, '*Concept of Mukti in Advaita Vedanta*', Madras University, 1981, p.305.

37 *Rigveda,* (V: 3.53.8 and V: I.47.18: *rūpam rūpam maghavā bobhaviti māyāḥ kṛṇvānastanavam parisvām triryaddivaḥ parimurtam jagat svairmitrairaṇtrūpā ṛtāvā,).*

Often people forget that Ādi Śaṅkarācārya in the Brahmaūtrabhāṣya also calls the projected world that has unimaginable beauty and wondrous beings as,

'mansāpyacintyaracanārūpa'[38]
(Unequalled magnificent workmanship)

Ādi Śaṅkarācārya sees the world as a profound mystery when He refers to the same as 'Atigambhīrambhāvyāthatamyam'.[39] From this, one can deduce that the projected world is certainly not dismissed by Ādi Śaṅkarācārya as 'A City in the Sky'. Therefore, it is important to understand the concept of Māyā in the most appropriate manner as the 'Power of Īśvara.' This makes Māyā no less than God. Without Māyā God will cease to be. However, it is to be comprehended that God alone is the holder of Māyā. In regards with the same, Svāmī Vivekānanda the Neo-vedāntist states,

"The concept of Māyā must not be seen as the theory of the explanation of the world. It is simply a factual statement of the paradoxes of thoughts, actions and also of the vicissitudes of nature around"[40]

From the above, it may be concluded that Māyā is that power through which the infinite becomes finite, the nameless assumes names and the formless takes forms. It is through Māyā that the Brahman appears as Śiva, Viṣṇu and Brahmā. Māyā gives us an opportunity to worship 'The One' who is beyond worship. Further, it is because of the grace of Māyā that we can experience the formless Brahman as the green beautiful tree, the playful puppy, the flowing Gaṇgā, the tasteful food, the hot sun and the magnificent Himālayas.

---

38 Swami Vishveshwarananda, pp.21-22, (V.1.1.2, *sambhāvitatmaḥ śilpibhirmanasāpyālocayitumaśakyam [beyond the imagination of the most able architecs]*).

39 *Ibid.*, p.143. (V.2.1.2)

40 Swami Vivekananda, '*Jnanayoga, Vol-II*', Ramakrishna Vivekananda Centre, New York, 1982, pp.39-44.

Māyā, which is the power of Īśvara is nothing but His grace that makes us experience Him as the 'Very World'. In the Bhagvadgītā, Ādi Śaṅkarācārya states,

> ***The Supreme indwells in the hearts of all beings and due to His power called Māyā, He makes these entities wander as though they are entities seated on a material machine made of material energy.***[41]

It is desirable to recognize Māyā as the cause and Adhyāsa along with Avidyā as the effects. In the introduction of His well-known Brahmasūtrabhāṣya, Ādi Śaṅkarācārya discusses Adyāsa in great detail. In brief, Adhyāsa is the superimposition of the attributes of one object on the other. It becomes the reason for divisions and dualities. The Jīva superimposes on itself the attributes of matter. As a result, the Jīva limits its being and entangles itself in the cobweb of pain and suffering. He considers the forms such as man, woman, animal, tree as being ultimately real. Based upon his misconception he develops Rāga (like, attachment) and Dveṣa (dislike, hate, jealousy) towards these apparent distinctions. Rāga and Dveṣa become the cause of Karma that lead to merits and demerits. This further binds a person. A 'Baddha (bound)' fails to realize Divinity amongst all and further goes on exploiting these various names and forms while binding himself in the unforgiving shackles of Karma. Therefore, all acts of a human arise due to superimposition. He sees the forms but misses the Divinity in them. This superimposition compels humans to overpower nature, demolish forests, contaminate the five great elements and further make them swell with pride. Fear, pain, misery, hate, violence, jealousy, exploitation, greed, possessiveness, thefts, murders, rapes and all other evils have their roots in dualism. Only when 'I' consider 'you' as a separate existence will 'I'

---

41 Shankaracharya, '*Shrimadbhagvadgitabhashya*', p.263 (V.18.61, *īśvaraḥ sarvabhūtānāṃ hṛddeśerjuna tiṣthati। bhrāmayan sarvabhūtāni yantrārūdhāni। māyayā*॥).

exploit 'you', 'possess you', 'be violent towards you or hurt you'.

Adhyāsa makes humans kill animals for the sake of momentary pleasure of the tongue. This superimposition of the mind alone makes us feel "I am hungry for a chicken burger", "I am the owner of this land and all dogs who sit here must be killed", "My company must cut down the forests to make profits". Likewise, one superimposes the attributes of senses and says that "I am deaf", "I love sweets" or "It is very hot".

Superimposition becomes the cause of damaging the environment and its sentient beings. This superimposition alone led to the mass killing of forty thousand dogs in Kerala in 2015,[42] this alone led to the polluting of the Holy River Gaṇga, deforestation, global warming, the tigress Avni murder case,[43] and other evils of the world. This superimposition makes us see a beautiful divine calf as a commodity to be eaten away. This superimposition makes us ignore the importance of crocodiles, snakes and buffaloes in the cosmos and promotes us to purchase brands that kill these sentient beings in order to manufacture boots, purses and belts made out of their skin. This superimposition made a man rape seven cows at a cow shelter in 2019[44] and made four men rape a dog and cut off his genitals leading him to death in Mumbai.[45] All these cases highlight the fact that due to ignorance of considering duality as ultimately real and with the desire to feed the greed of senses, these criminals were unable to see the divinity behind all the forms that they chose to hurt and exploit.

42 K.Jayalakshmi, '*Cull of 40,000 Dogs in Kerala*', International Business Times, 2015.

43 Mengle. S. Gautama, '*Tigress Avni Shot Dead in Fake Encounter*', The Hindu, 2018.

44 Sengar Shweta, '*Man Arrested For Raping Seven Cows at a Shelter in Ayodhya*', India Times, 2019.

45 Gupta Kritika, '*Mumbai Male Dog Brutally Gang Raped by four, Dies After Fighting for His Life*', India Times, 2018.

The word 'Avidyā' in Advaita Vedānta is a technical term that refers to 'Ignorance' of the nature of 'Self' and seeing the world of duality as real. It is translated, as 'Nescience' and is generally understood as 'defect or error'. However, Avidyā is all-powerful and gives birth to Upādhis (limiting adjuncts). These lead to Nāmarūpa, Karma and further become the cause of Janam, Maraṇa, Dukkha, Vyādhi and so on. Avidyā becomes the cause of the Vyāvahārika experience of the individual souls. Further, it is the cause of Adhyāsa and Ādi Śaṅkarācārya identifies Avidyā with Adhyāsa and says,

"Adhyāsa itself is Avidyā"[46]

Therefore, 'Adhyāsa (Superimposition)' is that in which the superimposed is apparent. However, that on which superimposition is made remains true and changeless. Just as a being who suffers from an eye disease called 'diplopia' sees two moons, a man who suffers from Avidyā sees duality. This duality is a disease that leads to further pain and suffering. Avidyā is un-manifest during deep sleep, therefore there is no Adhyāsa. However, it manifests as plurality during dreams and it completely manifests as the diverse universe in case of the waking state. While Avidyā may explain the multifarious cosmos, the same remains a mystery and is itself inexplicable. Hence, questions like when did Avidyā come and when will it go are themselves statements of Avidyā, since time is seen a component of ignorance in Advaita Vedānta. It thus is eternal and unborn. Ādi Śaṅkarācārya in this regard avers,

"It is beginning-less, end-less, natural and unreal; it creates a sense of agency and is experienced by all"[47]

Therefore, at an intellectual level, there is no solution to the dilemma of Avidyā because the existence of Avidyā is

46 Swami Vishveshwarananda, Adhyasa, pp.7-10.

47 *Ibid*, p.11.

neither real nor unreal. However, when we rise above logic and hold on to our experience and intuition, the presence of Avidyā vanishes and everything shines as the very Brahman. A person who has seen everything as the Brahman in his deepest spiritual state awakens as the 'Realised One'. Like any other being, he also sees distinctions but he remains established in the truth that the dog is the Brahman, the tree is the Brahman, the Self is the Brahman and everything seen and unseen is nothing but the Brahman. In this context, Ādi Śaṅkarācārya states,

rajjvajñānatkṣaṇenaiva yadvadrajjurhi sarpiṇī।
bhāti tadvaccitiḥ sakṣādviśvākāreṇa kevalā॥[48]

(The illusion of snake is possible only due to the ignorance of the rope. Likewise, the duality of forms is possible only when one is ignorant about the 'Pure Consciousness' that alone exists).

Therefore, all beings of the world are divine. They sprout from the Brahman and hence are referred to as 'Sat'. Sentient beings such as humans, animals, birds, insects and trees have Cidābhāsa (reflected consciousness), subtle and gross body whereas insentient beings like stones, pebbles and mountains have a gross-physical body. However, whether the being is sentient or insentient; it is the very Brahman,

brahmaiva sarvanāmāni rūpāṇi vividhāni ca।
karmāṇyapi smagrāṇi bibhārtiti śrutirjagou॥[49]

(śruti declares that it is Brahman that manifests through all names and forms, all actions are also the Brahman)

4.6. Dharma: The Cosmic Order

It becomes imperative to understand 'Dharma' in the right context before we delve deeper into the various aspects of Advaita Vedānta philosophy. Dharma is the seed that becomes the immortal tree of values, ethics, responsibilities and virtues. In Advaita Vedānta realization of one's true

48 Deshmukha Shrikrishna, p.70. (V.44)

49 *Ibid.*, p.82. (V.50)

nature is said to be the highest of good. Whatever is moral is 'True'. It is for this reason that there exists no defined line between ethics and metaphysics in Advaita Vedānta. Not just Advaita Vedānta, in fact, all schools of Indian philosophy that may differ in metaphysical concepts finally agree that realization and morality are interwoven. Dharma, therefore, is both moral and real.

The word 'Dharma' comes from the Saṃskṛt word 'Dhr' which means sustenance, upholding, or uplifting. Therefore, epistemologically 'Dharma' is that which harmoniously upholds, enriches and sustains the whole of cosmos and its sentient beings. 'Dharma' becomes one of the most central concepts of the Advaita Vedānta Darśana. It is Dharma alone, which becomes the bedrock of Ādi Śaṅkarācārya's sublime ethics. In order to truly comprehend the meaning of the word 'Dharma' it becomes imperative to delve into the seven meanings, in which it is recognized,

1. Dharma as Svabhāva of an Entity: In this context 'Dharma' signifies the very nature of all objects of the cosmos. It is the essential property, nature, or disposition of a thing or a being. It is Dharma due to which something is born, sustained, regulated, transformed and perished. Therefore, the Dharma of a river is to flow. Fluidity is the very nature of all water bodies. Hence, Dharma is the Svabhāva of an object or being and the Svabhāva of an object or being is its very Dharma.

2. Dharma as Cosmic Order or Ṛta: In this context Dharma refers to the natural law that makes the whole cosmos operate in a certain way. Dharma understood in the sense of 'Moral Cosmic Order' has its roots in the Ṛg Vedic 'Ṛta' which highlights the unitary order in the physical and ethical spheres. Thus, here Dharma means the cosmic natural laws which are ethical, moral and just in the operation of the universe. It becomes imperative for a human to abide by these cosmic laws and thus preserve himself by preserving others. It is to be realized that the whole cosmos is interwoven and in the welfare of all beings lies our own welfare. In this way, Dharma is that ground on which the seeds of respect, caring, sharing and veneration germinate. These lead us to the fruit of self-realization. In this case, Dharma is the order of the cosmos or the universal law.

3. Dharma as Duty and Responsibility: Dharma is also understood as 'Duty' which ought to be carried out. In Indian culture, no documentation or contract was ever needed in order to bind someone for the sake of performing a duty. Duty has been considered a natural Dharma and not as a forced obligation. Thus, Mātṛdharma, Pitṛdharma, Ardhāṅginīdharma, Patidharma, Mānavdharma and more are regarded as natural duties.

The moment a man brings in a cow, it is regarded as a Mother who fosters the entire family and is also fostered in return. The entire family which includes the 'Mother Cow' lives together (Sahvāsa), works together (Sahkāra) and enjoys the fruits of their hard work together (Sahbhoga). While the cow, as Mother, fulfills her duties and responsibilities towards the family, the family also diligently performs their responsibilities and duties towards the Mother Cow. This co-existence, co-operation, and co-dependency exists as 'Dharma.' Further, if it is the Dharma (duty) of a tree to provide shade, fruits and medicines to all the beings, it also becomes the Dharma (responsibility) of humans to protect the tree, nurture it and revere it. Consequently, Dharma is a natural sense of duty and responsibility.

India is a land that has never spoken of rights. When one talks of rights, there is a sense of demand. However, when one talks of duties and responsibilities towards other lives, there is a sense of reverence. It is therefore important that humans realize their duties as 'Dharma' towards themselves, their families, environment, animals, nation and the cosmos. When duties are carried out with reverence as Dharma instead of being carried out as a cumbersome task in order to earn rights for selfish benefits, it will lead to holistic harmony and peace.

4. Dharma as a Social Norm: In the sense of social norm 'Dharma' includes all rules, regulations, social, political, environmental laws that help the society in leading a life of moral, legal, customary, traditional, cultural, religious and environmental concord. In this context, it becomes the Dharma of a citizen to respect and regard the rules of the king, Prime Minister, or the President of a country. It is one's Dharma to be honest towards one's family, partner, nation, all beings and the cosmos. It is one's Dharma to perform morning ablutions, consider a guest as the very God, serve the needy, respect the animals and revere nature as the Mother. Thus, in this regard Dharma acts as the social order for the maintenance of accord, peace and joy.

5. Dharma as Puruṣārtha: In this framework, Dharma refers to that which a human aims at or that which is sought. It refers to the moral and ethical pursuit of a human or may be of any being. Though the Puruṣārtha are meant for humans yet the four Puruṣārtha of Dharma, Artha, Kāma, and Mokṣa can very well apply to all beings of the world. The first Puruṣārtha 'Dharma' applies to all lives. It is due to Dharma that a being is conceived as a human, dog, tree, or river. Dharma alone grants them their Svabhāva. Dharma defines their roles in the cosmos and society. The second Puruṣārtha 'Artha' needs to be reinterpreted not merely as 'money or wealth' but as that which nourishes and protects a being and assists it in executing, maintaining and abiding by its Dharma. No doubt, in the case of humans this can superficially be understood as the 'power to purchase.' It is through money that a human can sustain himself, his family, get a shelter, earn his bread and carry out his duties. However, in the case of other beings e.g. a tree, Artha will be understood as the land in which the seed is sowed, the water, manure, medicines that nourish it and make it capable of executing its Dharma in the scheme of the cosmos. Likewise, for any animal also it means nourishment, protection, and the capability to execute and uphold its Dharma. The third Puruṣārtha 'Kāma' in the case of humans refers to the mental, physical, emotional desires. This is certainly not different from that of other beings. All animals, plants and birds desire love, appreciation and care. Even mountains and rivers require the same amount of love and care. For a goat, a dog, or a hen, merely food and shelter are not enough; they also need love, companionship, and care in order to move up the spiritual ladder.

Sir Jagdish Chandra Bose not just believed but also proved that plants have life, are conscious and feel pain, pleasure and fear. In 1902, he wrote a research paper called '*Responses in the Living and Non-Living*' in which he mentioned that,

'plants grew more quickly when exposed to nice music and gentle whispers, and poorly when exposed to harsh music and loud speech, they become depressed when exposed to polluted air and darkening skies. Plants could feel pleasure and they could feel pain.'[50]

The fourth Puruṣārtha 'Mokṣa' is the highest aim of not just humans but of all beings. All entities take birth and die, they are transmigrated and finally, they rise up the ladder with each birth. Their end aim is no different from that of a human. It is for this reason that many Ṛṣīs and Munis have seen themselves as animals, reptiles and birds in their past lives. Though with each birth we assume varied names and forms yet our aim remains the realization of 'Self' as the Non-dual Reality.

6. Dharma as Religion: Dharma also refers to religion, i.e. Hinduism, Jainism, Buddhism and so on. In India,

---

50 Pal Sanchari, '*J C Bose: The Little Known Story of How India's First Biophysicist Proved Plants Have Life*', The Better India, Bangalore, 2016,

philosophical wisdom expresses itself through the body of religion. It is through religion that the people of India put philosophies into practice. Religion in India has its roots in 'Darśana' but it extends to morality, ethics, spirituality, culture, social dos-don'ts and much more. To be precise, in India religion, philosophy, and life itself are inseparable. In context to this book, environment and animals are the very Self and they exist as the base of religion. Thus, worshiping a cow, a river, a pīpala tree, Mother Earth, the five great elements and every speck of the universe becomes an important part of the Vedic religion.

7. Dharma as Virtue: In this perspective, Dharma is considered as a virtue or the highest moral good. Therefore, acts such as feeding animals, watering plants, providing medical aid to injured beings, serving others with a vision of non-duality, helping others without the desire to gain anything in return, truthfulness, honesty, kindness, compassion are considered not merely as revered virtues but are considered as Dharma.

The above said are the seven different connotations in which Dharma has been understood. However, the above said do not limit the meaning of Dharma.

Ādi Śaṅkarācārya defines 'Dharma' as that 'which is observed by people belonging to varied Varṇas and Āśramas and becomes the means of Abhyudaya and Niśreyas'.[51] 'Abhyudaya' refers to the prosperities attained in the world by following Dharma whereas 'Niśreyas' refers to Mokṣa. Thus, Dharma refers to the various cardinal virtues associated with various Āśramas and Varṇas. Let's have a look as to how Dharma as duties was prescribed for the society in order to maintain peace and harmony holistically,

---

[51] Goindka Shriharikrishna Das, '*Shrimadbhagvadgitabhashya*', 2019, Introduction.

1. **Sādharanadharma**[52]**:** These are 'The General Codes or Universal Duties' that are meant to be followed and apply to the entire human society. These include,

a) **Ahiṃsā** or non-violence in thoughts, speech and actions to any living being (human, animal, plant, bird, or other sentient entities).

b) **Satya** refers to truthfulness in thoughts, words and actions towards oneself, society, sentient beings, environment, and otherwise.

c) **Asteya** or non-stealing refers to the non-theft of anyone's property in thoughts, words, and actions. It promotes respecting and non-stealing of not only another human's property but also refers to the non-stealing of nature's bounties or non-stealing of any animal's life, organs, and freedom. Sadly, today human beings have ignored this virtue and are stealing away the plenteousness of nature. They steal away an animal's right to live for the sake of its skin, its organs, and its fur. They fail to realize that they are indulging in theft by stealing the abundances of other sentient beings without their will.

d) **Iṅdriyanigreha** or controlling the senses that motivate us to see, hear, taste, touch, and smell things of sensual pleasure. It is to satisfy these five thieves that a being kills a tiger, hampers the purity of a river, rapes a woman and indulges in murders.

e) **Śauca** or cleanliness refers to purity not merely on a physical plane but also in terms of Antaḥkarṇa. It is the internal dirt that we hold on to which leads to polluting the external environment.[53]

---

52 Kumar Surendra,'*Manusmriti*', Aarsh Sahitya Prachar Trust, Delhi, 2017, p.856 (V.10.63, *ahiṁsā satyamsteyaṁ śaucamindriyanigreḥ* । *etaṁ sāmāmsikaṁ dharma caturvarṇyebravinmnuḥ*॥).

53 Sridhar N, '*Samanya Dhama and Spirituality*', Prabuddha Bharat, Kolkata, 2015, p.120.

2. Varṇāśramadharma[54]: Varṇa must not be understood as social segregation rather it stands for a logical and scientific manner in which a society is arranged for the welfare and well-being of all lives. It does not divide the society into classes nor does it generate any hierarchy instead it classifies the kind of people that exist in a society in accordance with the dominating Guṇa and nature. These are specific duties and are prescribed in accordance to one's dominating Guṇa; Sattva, Rajas, Tamas. Let's have a look at these four Varṇas with the right understanding,

a) **Brahmaṇa** are those who are predominantly Sattvic and must live, think, speak and act accordingly. Their actions must be installed in wisdom, patience, calmness, kindness, compassion, self-sacrifice, welfare and well-being of all lives.

b) **Kṣatriyas** are those who have partially dominant Sattva-Rajas. Their actions are recommended to be rooted in charity, decision-making, knowledge and physical strength for the sake of protecting the weak and safeguarding their interest and well-being.

c) **Vaiśyas** are those who are Rajas-Tamas dominant. They keep the economy rolling by indulging in acts that generate wealth. The Vaiśyas are expected to share their wealth for the welfare of all living beings.

d) **Śūdras** are those who are purely dominated by Tamas. They take care of laghūdyoga and serve the society and all living beings by adding to the value and glory of it.

3. Āśramadharma: In this case for holistic growth and cosmic welfare, human life is divided into four stages,

a) **Brahmacārya,** where the life of a human is dedicated to the study of texts in order to learn the sublime

---

54 Shankaracharya, '*Shrimadbhagvadgitabhashya*', p.256 (V.18.41, *brāhmaṇa-kṣatriyaviśām śūdrāṇām ca parantapa* । *karmāṇi pravibhaktāni svabhāva-prabhavairguṇai*॥)

teachings of compassion, kindness and Sarvabhūtāhita. This is also a stage when one prepares himself in order to earn and develop skills, knowledge, information and realization towards his duties and responsibilities.

b) **Gṛhastha** is that stage of human life where he works for the well-being of all. He sustains his family, serves the society and works for the interest of all lives. He makes use of Artha and Kāma based upon Dharma. He performs the five daily Mahāyajñas namely: Brahmayajña-recitation of Vedas. Devayajña-offerings made to the Divine/Guru. Pitṛyajña-offerings made to the deceased ancestors. Bhūtayajña-offerings made to animals, birds and other sentient creatures. Manuṣyayajña-offerings made to lesser fortunate human beings.

c) **Vānaprastha** is that stage of human life when he hands over his possessions to his heirs or donates them and goes into seclusion to prepare himself for the final stage. At this stage one gives up Artha and Kāma and continues to be established in Dharma. This is a stage of meditation and contemplation.

d) **Saṃyāsa**, is the final stage. At this stage, a human gives up all mental, emotional, and physical attachments and remains established in the righteousness of Dharma with the aim of attaining Mokṣa. He is rooted in equanimity and withdraws from all worldly acts at a mental, emotional and physical level. At such a stage one remains free from likes and dislikes. Such a being has no desire to exploit anyone or harm any life.

In terms of environment and animals Sādharanadharma, Varnāśramadharma and Āśramadharma promote compassion, non-violence, kindness and wellness of all life forms. It concentrates on uplifting every being without being biased towards any.

4.7. The Paths of Pravṛtti and Nivṛtti Dharma

It is imperative to understand that Advaita Vedānta cannot be cataloged as either a pure religion or a dry philosophy. Instead, it strikes a remarkable balance between religion which is its very body and the highest vision of truth which becomes its soul. It paves a subtle bridge between material and trans-material, ethical and trans-ethical, religious and trans-religious, empirical and trans-empirical. Advaita Vedānta works holistically. It aims at relieving beings not merely on the worldly sphere but also at the very root and finally leading them to the highest realization. One can certainly not expound upon Ādi Śaṅkarācārya's ethics without highlighting His conception of religion, values and morality under the head of Pravṛtti Dharma (Karma, Bhakti) and Nivṛtti Dharma (Jñāna) in the introduction of His celebrated Bhagvadgītābhāṣya,

talrackaḥ dvividho hivedoktoḥ dharmaḥ; pravṭtilakṣanḥ nivṛttilakṣanaḥ ca।
jagataḥ sthiti kāraṇamprāṇinām̐ sāṣad abhyudaya niḥśyasa hetuḥ॥[55]
(Dharma that has been expounded in the Vedas is two-fold in nature: outwardly it is known as Pravṛtti Dharma which is action-oriented and inwardly it is referred to as Nivṛtti Dharma which is contemplation oriented. Dharma also brings about stability in the cosmos by ensuring Abhyudayaḥ which is necessary for social and economic well-being and Niśreyas which is meant for the realization of the Highest Principle).

Both Pravṛtti Dharma and Nivṛtti Dharma occupy an extremely important place in understanding and interpreting Ādi Śaṅkarācārya's timeless philosophy. While Pravṛtti Dharma leads to the purity of mind, Nivṛtti Dharma becomes the direct means of realizing Mokṣa. Ādi Śaṅkarācārya in this regard states,

The Dharma of action must be performed as worship to Īśvara. It must be performed with a disinterested frame of mind and should be free from any sort of attachment. This will not only

---

[55] Shankaracharya, '*Shrimadbhagvadgitabhashya*', Introduction

bring about prosperity but will also lead to purity of mind. It is through this that one becomes eligible for Jñānaniṣṭhā (Self-knowledge). This alone becomes the cause of wisdom and is the means to Mokṣa.[56]

From the above, it can be concluded that Pravṛtti Dharma constitutes of the following,

- **Phalābhisandhi Varjitaḥ (Karmayoga):** actions done without attachment to the fruits.
- **Īśvarapaṇabudhyā Anuṣṭhiyamānaḥ (Bhaktiyoga):** actions done as worship of Īśvara.

1. Karmayoga-The Path of Disinterested Action

The word 'Karma' generally and technically refers to,

- 'Action' (Kriyata iti karma vyāpāramātram)
- Prints left behind by our actions or our doings.
- The unforgiving 'Law of Karma'.
- The ritualistic actions prescribed by the Vedas.

Ādi Śaṅkarācārya Himself uses the word 'Karma' in the Bhagvadgītābhāṣya in varied contexts[57] and gives a precise meaning to the same. He suggests that when any action is performed in the mode of ego it is said to be 'Karma' that binds down a person and makes him reap the good or bad fruits of his action. However, when an action is performed in the mode of disinterestedness, it is said to be 'Akarma'. Therefore, when Ādi Śaṅkarācārya suggests that a realized person has 'No Actions', He means that his actions are not

---

56 Shankaracharya, '*Shrimadbhagvadgitabhashya*', Introduction.

57 *Ibid.*, pp.79, 86, 216. (V.4.18: *karmaṇyakarma yaḥ paśhyed akarmaṇi ca karma yaḥ* । *sa buddhimān manuṣyeṣu sa yuktaḥ kṛitsnakarmakṛite*॥ V.4.36: *api ced asi pāpebhyaḥ sarvebhyaḥ pāpakṛittamaḥ*। *sarvaṁ jñāna plavenaiva vṛijinaṁ santari ṣyasi* ॥ V.4.37:*yathaidhānsi samiddhógnir bhasmasāt kurute-rjuna*। *jñānāgniḥ sarvakarmāṇi bhasmasāt kurute tathā*॥ V.15.2: *adhaśh cordhvaṁ prasṛitās tasya śhākhā-guṇapravṛiddhā viṣayapravālāḥ*। *adhaśca mūlāny anusantatāni karmānubandhīni manuṣya loke*॥)

installed in ego, are devoid of any personal gains, and are thus beyond any fruits whatsoever.[58] Hence, Ādi Śaṅkarācārya's concept of physical performance of Karma is based upon one's internal states and motives.

When one goes on to feed a dog or preserve a tree with the desire to attain social appreciation or gather publicity, the action is said to be installed in ignorance. Likewise, when a man feeds thousands of cows merely for the sake of proving and showing off his financial power, status and goodness, he is performing the act of charity in ignorance. The act outwardly may appear to be of great generosity. However, internally the act is performed with a desire to gain something and thus it binds a person down and makes him reap fruits of pain and pleasure.

It is inappropriate to consider the physical performance of actions as 'Karma' and physical inactivity as 'Akarma'. Actions are mental, physical and verbal. One remains the performer of action till he considers himself as the agent. The moment he realizes that he is not the agent and there is a 'Higher Being' who is the doer, the realized one has no actions and therefore has no fruits. Before one becomes qualified in order to enquire into the nature of the Self one is required to undergo the discipline of Karma. It becomes imperative for a person to perform actions that are conducive and assist him in his journey in realizing the Self. It has to be understood clearly that without the performance of actions that promote purity of mind neither Phalabhogavirāga is possible nor is Mokṣa attainable. Karma becomes indispensable because of its purifying virtue. The urge to act arises from the desire to attain happiness. Thus, selfishness is the cause of all actions.[59] Here, it is important to note that- **Ahaṁkāra** (ego) and **Phalābhisaṅdhi** (attachment to

---

58 Shankaracharya, '*Shrimadbhagvadgitabhashya*', p.35 (V.2.2, *kutastvā kaśmalam-idaṁ viṣame samupasthitaṁ*। *anāryajuṣtam asvargyaṁakītikaram arjuna*॥)

59 *Ibid*, pp.117-118 (V.7.4-7.5)

the fruits) become the seed of selfishness. Under the control of desires, a being acts in three ways,

- **Kriyābuddhi**-This is my action.
- **Kārakbuddhi**-I am the doer of this act.
- **Phalabuddhi**-Since I am doing this act, I must get this fruit.

All the above-said actions arise due to the veil of Avidyā. Therefore, Karma is a product of Avidyā. In this regard, Ādi Śaṅkarācārya declares,

"Before Jñāna, Avidyā manifests as Karma, Kāraka and Phala. It is perceived by Pramāṇabuddhi and becomes the cause of action. Thus, all acts are performed in a state of Avidyā and are Kāmyakarmas that bind a being to reap the fruits. None can evade this whatsoever"[60]

If all good and bad actions performed tie us down and make us reap the fruits, then what is it that one should exactly do? The answer lies in 'Karmayoga'. Every act done with a sense of ego is morally evil even though it may appear to be good. All human acts are done either due to 'Rāga or Dveśa'.[61] These become the seed of desire and all that is born out of desire is evil. Selfish desires need immediate satisfaction. In order to attain immediate gratification, one becomes blind to the future consequences and considers it as the most urgent need. This is a classic case of what the human race is doing to nature because of its unending greed and ignorance. For the sake of physical beautification, animals become a subject of lab research in order to produce promising cosmetics. Merely because the land is needed to build state-of-the-art malls, cinema halls, and homes, construction companies not just cut down forests but also destine thousands of animals to a life without shelter, food,

---

60 Shankaracharya, '*Shrimadbhagvadgitabhashya*', pp.93-94 (V.5.14)

61 *Ibid.*, p.70 (V.3.34, *indriyasyendriyasyārthe rāgadveṣau vyavasthitau । tayorna vaśamāgacchet tau hyasya paripanthinau॥*)

and water. These companies for the sake of making quick profits play with flora and fauna in the most heartless manner. Also, killing an animal merely to attain liberation is a heinous act carried out in the name of religion and rituals. Therefore, all the above-mentioned acts are born out of greed to look beautiful, incur profits, or attain liberation in the name of religion. These are acts that are rooted in desire that needs instant fulfillment and disregard potential penalties. Such acts of gluttony and desire become a hindrance in realizing the Self. They bind a being to the Saṁsāra and entangle him in the cycle of birth-death-rebirth, making him constantly experience pain and pleasure that sprouts from Avidyā. As a result, ego-generated actions must be abandoned. Nevertheless, this in no way suggests that one becomes complacent, lazy and refuses to act. On the other hand, one must perform actions for the welfare of all, installed in **Niśkāmabhāva** and without mental clinging by following the path of Karmayoga. In this regard, the Bhagvadgītā suggests that,

mokṣa karmaiva yogah, karmayogah[62]
(It is merely Karmayoga that leads to Mokṣa)

In order to train the mind to be detached from the fruit of action the process of self-negating through the disinterested performance of action is prescribed by Ādi Śaṅkarācārya. Hence, in compositions like 'Nirvāṇśatkama' and 'Daśaśloki' when Ādi Śaṅkarācārya uses self-negation as a technique, He is only trying to break the association of 'I and Mine' with the world of belongings. Such compositions in no way refute the world, they only refute the I-ness and My-ness that make us associate with the world, make us believe that we are the doer, and bind us to the fruit of actions.

62 Shankaracharya, '*Shrimadbhagvadgitabhashya*', p.59 (V.3.3, *loke'smin dvividhā niṣthā purā proktā mayānagha jnānayogena sāṇkhyānāṁ karmayogena yogināṁ* ||)

A person may be impelled to ask as to what kind of actions are to be performed with a disinterested frame of mind? Here, Karmayoga becomes instrumental and Ādi Śaṅkarācārya considers purified actions as a means to attain Cittaśuddhi. Karmayoga also becomes a preliminary moral discipline and training for a Sādhaka. The actions prescribed for a Karmayogi are that of Svadharma (*śvabhāvajam karma*).[63] Ādi Śaṅkarācārya suggests that one must be installed in Svadharma in accordance to one's Āśrama and Varṇa.[64] Therefore, it is important to understand that everyone is not meant to do everything. Following the path of Varṇavyavasthā, each being of the society falls under one of the four Varṇa and is supposed to accordingly perform his duty so that there may exist peace, harmony and wellness in the society. If Brahmins continues to spread the light of wisdom, the whole society will be well educated, wise and free from defects such as illiteracy, destruction of the environment, and intellectual invasion. The society will have hygiene, sanitation, holding women, children and animals in high esteem. Their acts will also lead to social progress in terms of scientific research and discovery. Likewise, if Kṣatriyas continue to be physical protectors, there will be preservation of notional art, architecture, culture, physical property and religion from any foreign invasion. Further, if Vaṣyas continue to carry out commercial activities virtuously, humans, animals, nature and the whole of the country will prosper. There will be economic harmony and financial joy within the country. On similar lines, if the śūdra continue to take care of serving the society with utmost devotion, wellness will prevail throughout. As a result, when each being is installed in self-duty and self-action (Svadharma and Svakarma) all will live together in harmony (Sahvāsa), work together in

63 Shankaracharya, '*Shrimadbhagvadgitabhashya*', p.256 (V.18.41, *brāhmaṇa-kcatriyaviśām śūdrāṇām ca parantapa* । *karmāṇi pravibhaktāni svabhāva-prabhavair guṇaiḥ*।)

64 *Ibid.*, pp.264-265 (V.18.66, *sarva dharmān parityajya mām ekam śaraṇam vraja*। *aham tvā sarvapāpebhyo mokṣayiṣyāmi mā śucaḥ*।।)

peace (Sahkāra) and will enjoy the fruits of combined efforts (Sahbhoga).

It is imperative to not only execute one's own duty and responsibility in the scheme of cosmos but also assist others in the execution of their duties without interfering in their Dharma. In regards to Karmayoga, Svāmī Vivekānanda pronounces,

> ***"Sacrifice in the spirit of utmost renunciation is the climax of Karmayoga"***[65]

Therefore, when we indulge in deforestation we not only interfere in the Dharma of the forest, individual plants, and animal life but we also promote carbon dioxide emission, soil erosion, habitat destruction of various bio-lives, loss of bio-diversity and more.

Ādi Śaṅkarācārya stresses that action alone cannot lead to the Ultimate realization, though it certainly purifies the mind and makes it fit enough for the awareness of Brahman-Ātman identity. Therefore, Karmaphalatyāga, or renunciation of the fruit of action for the sake of Sarvabhūtahita is highly recommended and appreciated. An action becomes a duty only when one renounces the fruit attached to it. Here, one must broaden his vision in understanding 'Karmaphalatyāga'. The same in no way means that one should forgo his own interest. It only means that one must stop claiming them as exclusively his own, should be free from mental clinging and must remain in equanimity at all times. The Fruit of an action is not always that which gratifies the desire-ridden ego. A person may widen his interests towards the society, country, environment, sentient beings and thus he will be working for the welfare of his own widened Self. Karmaphalatyāga becomes essential in leading a person on to the path of Self-

---

65 Swami Vivekananda, '*The Complete Works of Swami Vivekananda Vol. I*', Vedanta Press, USA, 1947 pp.84-85.

realization. Also, it is merely through Karmaphalatyāga for the sake of cosmic welfare that an aspirant carves out a concrete spiritual identity with the whole of the cosmos. This point is highlighted in the Bhagvadgītā when Śrī Kṛṣna tells Arjuna to act for the welfare of all by citing His own and Rājā Janak's example because in the welfare of all lies one's own welfare. This attitude arises when all divisions eradicate and one is installed in the Self.[66]

From the above, one can conclude that when a being is on the path of Pravṛtti Dharma, he is suggested to act in a disinterested manner and in accordance with Varṇāśramadharma, he is expected to foster ethics, morals and virtues of the highest order. Unfortunately, people have chosen to ignore Ādi Śaṅkarācārya's ideas related to the same and have misunderstood His timeless philosophy. However, Ādi Śaṅkarācārya's philosophy and works are impregnated with virtues that ultimately lead to the realization of the non-dual Self through the path that is paved for the welfare of the environment and well-being of the entire cosmos.

2. Bhaktiyoga-The Path of Complete Surrender

Bhakti is an overwhelming emotion of 'Love' that is associated with the heart. Humans, animals, birds, plants and all living beings are governed by this powerful emotion. In Advaita Vedānta for the protection, promotion and propagation of Dharma, Īśvara appears over and over again. In this way, Advaita Vedānta Darśana provides enough opportunity for the seeker to engage in Bhakti (love). The overflowing love for Īśvara bestows the devotee with a unified vision of truth where he sees everything, all beings, varied events, good-bad, pain-pleasure as rooted in the Īśvara. Flora-fauna and all phenomena of Nature become the very manifestation of Īśvara that needs to be approached with devotion.

---

66 Shankaracharya, '*Shrimadbhagvadgitabhashya*', pp.65-66 (V.3.20-3.24)

The doctrine of Vibhūtis of the Bhagvadgītā makes it extremely casy to view Prakṛti's bounties as the declaration of Īśvara's divine grace. Thus, a devotee would joyfully worship everything as either God or as everything attached to God. Hence, worshiping the snake, the bull, the Gaṇga, the city of Kāśī and even worshiping the poisonous Dhattūrā is seen as an act of worshiping Lord Śiva. A devotee loves to eat white butter and finds the city of Mathurā as heaven because his beloved little Kṛṣna was born here. A devotee bows to the fish, pig, tortoise and other beings for his revered Viṣṇu appeared in these forms. Love and Bhakti are beyond questions, logic and intellect. In the case of Bhakti, your relationship with 'One' leads to your connection with all. Advaita Vedānta considers two kinds of worships,

- **Saguṇopāsanā** (worship of Brahman with qualities as Īśvara)
- **Nirguṇopāsanā** (worship of Brahman without qualities).

The object of Saguṇopāsanā is the realization of Īśvara and His Vibūtis. The devotee worships the Ultimate in a certain form such as the stone, the tree, Śiva, Viṣṇu, or Devī. He is free to choose any form that may appeal to his mind and induces in him overflowing devotion. For the same Ādi Śaṅkarācārya introduced the concept of Pañcadevopāsanā that aims at not merely choosing one's beloved Īśta but it also leads to reverence for all other forms. Let's see how Pañcadevopāsanā eradicates all kinds of divisions and leads a person to appreciate all forms in which the Divine appears,

- Though the devotee has immense love and Bhakti towards his chief Deity yet he worships the other four Devas. He prays to them that his devotion towards his chief Deity should be strengthened by their grace.
- 'Pañcadevopāsanā' may also be seen as reverence to 'One Ultimate' who appears as the five Devas. Just as five fingers are rooted in one palm, likewise, Śiva, Gaṇeśa, Nārāyaṇa, Devī, and Surya are also rooted in the

Brahman. Thus, a devotee fosters no special preference towards any form and worships them as 'The One'.

However, Ādi Śaṅkarācārya is of the view that the worship of Īśvara can help a being in progressing on the path of realization and act as the bedrock for Jñānayoga but it cannot itself lead to the realization of the Ultimate.

Those who are devoted to the worship of Brahman without qualities (Nirguṇopāsanā) are the ones who have given up all desires, who are installed in non-duality and who consider all living beings as the non-dual Brahman.[67] These Saṃnyāsīs may be considered as equal to those who are on the path of Jñāna. There exist four kinds of following devotees[68] that one may come across,

1. **Ārtas** are devotees who turn to Īśvara because of extreme pain and disillusionment faced in the world of material.
2. **Arthārtis** are devotees who approach Īśvara for the sake of gaining favors and rewards.
3. **Jijñāsus** are devotees who advance towards Īśvara for the sake of intellectual satisfaction.
4. **Jñānis** are devotees who are the absolute lover of Īśvara. The Bhagvadgītā announce the Jñānis to be the very form of Lord.[69] These devotees don't turn towards God because they are disillusioned by the world or have any sort of suffering. They seek no pleasures nor desire any rewards. These devotees also have no intellectual desires. Their love goes beyond the material, the physical and the intellectual. Such devotees love God merely because they knows no other way. Tirumūlar, Appar, Mīrābāī are various examples of such Jñānis. Such beings see their

67 Shankaracharya, '*Shrimadbhagvadgitabhashya*', pp.187-188(V.12.3, *ye tva kṣaram anirdeśyam avyaktaṁ paryupāsate* I *sarvatragamacintyaṁ ca kūṭa-stham acalaṁ dhruvaṁ*I).

68 *Ibid*, p.121 (V.7.16, *caturvidhā bhajante māṁ janāḥ sukṛtinórjuna*I *ārto jijñāsur arthārthī jñānī ca bharatarṣabha*II).

69 *Ibid.*, p.122 (V.7.18, *udārāḥ sarva evaite jñānī tva tmaiva me matam* I *āsthitaḥ sa hi yuktātmā mām evānutta māṁ gatim* II)

beloved God in all beings of the cosmos and all beings in their beloved God.[70] This devotee is installed in the highest form of worship. Just as there exist different devotees, there also exist various stages of devotion (Bhakti),[71] which are,

1. **Devotee feels that his beloved Īśvara is exclusively his/her**: Rāvaṇa is an appropriate example of this devotion. At this stage, duality exists and one sees God and His creation as separate and thus the dog, the man, the tree are not revered as Īśvara but are seen as merely His creations.
2. **Devotee feels that he/she belongs to his beloved Īśvara**: Mīrābāī is a suitable example of this devotion where she completely surrenderes to Lord Kṛṣna. At this stage, all pains-pleasures, good-bad, variedness of forms are seen as the will of the Lord and are accepted as His supreme desire. There is complete surrender at this stage and the whole creation is revered as the Īśvara.
3. **Devotee becomes one with the Īśvara**. At this stage, the devotee does not lose his identity instead; he expands his identity and becomes the Īśvara himself. This can be understood by the drop-ocean analogy where the drop of water expands its identity and becomes one with the ocean. At this stage, there exists no duality. The entire creation that appears as distinct is nothing but the Divine himself who through His Līlā appears as the tree, the donkey, the horse, and the swan. The devotee gains the vision to decode the mystery of variedness and understands that in reality, all is indeed the 'Divine Self'.

Initially, the path of Bhakti can be extremely tough. However, with the dint of patience and consistency there

---

70 Shankaracharya, '*Shrimadbhagvadgitabhashya*', V.9.29, pp.146-147 (*samo'haṁ sarva-bhūteṣu na me dveṣyósti na priyaḥ*। *ye bhajanti tu māṁ bhaktyā mayi te teṣu cāpy aham*॥)

71 *Ibid.*, p.77 (V.4.11, *ye yathā māṁ prapadyante taṁs tatháiva bhajāmyaham*। *mama vartmānuvartante manuṣyāḥ pārtha sarvaśaḥ*॥

arrives a situation when Lord Himself starts talking to His devotee despite being non-different from him. In all his endeavors, God will assist him, protect him and will automatically pave a path that leads to the final destination.[72] In devotion, slowly but steadily God reveals Himself in every creation of the world by bestowing His devotee with Buddhiyoga and Divyadṛṣti. It is due to unconditional love and unselfish devotion that a devotee gains God's utmost grace (Anukaṃpā). By this grace the darkness of Ajñāna is dispelled and there is dawn of Bhaktijñāna where the entire cosmos shines as the 'Very Self'. Thus, Bhakti aims at the realisation of our non-dual, infinite nature.

Although we are finite, yet we seek the infinite because in essence, we are 'Unlimited'. Had we been finite by nature, we would have been satisfied with ourselves but we are not. Moreover, we cannot be both finite and infinite at the same time.[73] Therefore, our real nature is that of infinitude on the grounds of the following points,

1. The experience of finitude is nullified by the experience of infinitude. On the other hand, infinitude cannot be nullified by any other experience whatsoever. Those who have had a realization have never behaved ordinarily for they are established in perfection. Therefore, he who knows the Brahman becomes the Brahman.[74]
2. The very fact that we constantly wish to drop off our finitude and be established in infinitude points towards our real nature as infinite and eternal truth, consciousness and delight (Sat-cit-ānanda)

The highest form of Bhakti bestows the devotee with two gifts without which Jñānayoga can never be attained, they are,

---

72 Shankaracharya, '*Shrimadbhagvadgitabhashya*', p.144 (V.9.22, *ananyāś cintayanto māṁye janāḥ paryupāsate\teṣāṁ nityābhiyuktānāṁ yogakṣemaṁ vahāmy aham॥*)

73 Swami Vishveshwarananda, pp.73-74 (S.1.2.20, *śārīraścaubhyepi hi bhedenainamdhīyate॥*) (S.1.2.21, *viśeṣanabhedvyapadeśābhāṁ netrau॥*)

74 *Ibid.*, S.1.2.20 and S.1.2.21, 1.1.4, pp.28 (also see Mundakopnishad 3.2.9)

1. Cittaśuddhi (purity of mind): Cittaśuddhi removes the dirt of selfishness, greed, and anti-social tendencies such as hurting other beings, destruction of the environment, harming national properties and various other acts of violence. It further allows us to see all beings in the light of non-duality, love, wisdom, compassion and kindness. It is impossible to love God without loving all beings for they are indeed the Divine that we seek. They are the very body of Īśvara. As announces the Bhagvadgītā,

***yaccāpi sarva-bhūtānāṁbījaṁ tad aham arjuna*।**
***na tad asti vinā yat syānmayā bhūtaṁ carācaram*[75]॥**
(I am the very seed of all beings! There is no moving or stationary being that exists outside of Me. All are indeed My forms).

Therefore, a Jñāni holds no enmity towards any creature (nirvairaḥ sarvabhūteṣu) and bows to the dog, the tree, the earth and the whole of creation as his beloved Īśvara.[76] Along these lines, he who has realized the whole cosmos as the very Lord has reached the pinnacle of his Bhakti.

2.Cittaekāgratā (Supreme concentration): When a devotee realises the glory of Lord he is endowed with Cittaekāgratā.[77] The enlightened devotee is now aware that the entire creation is a manifestation of the Divine. He worships his Lord with single pointed concentration (bhāvasamanvitāḥ).[78] The more intense the Bhakti the more easily all forms melt away and one realises the whole creation as the Supreme Spirit. Cittaekāgratā plays an important role as one is elevated to Jñānayoga. Thus, Bhaktiyoga becomes the ground for Jñānayoga in Advaita Vedānta Darśana.

---

75 Shankaracharya, '*Shrimadbhagvadbhashya*', p.161. (V.10.39)

76 *Ibid.*, p.186 (V.11.55, *matkarmakṛn matparamo madbhaktaḥ saṅgavarjitaḥ*। *nirvairaḥ sarvabhūteṣu yaḥ sa māṁ eti pāṇḍava*।)

77 *Ibid*, p.151 (V.10.7, *etāṁ vibhūtiṁ yogaṁ ca mama yo vetti tattvataḥ*। *so vikalpena yogena yujyate nātra samśayaḥ*।)

78 *Ibid.*, p.151 (V.10.8, *ahaṁ sarvasya prabhavo mattaḥ sarvaṁ pravartate*। *iti matvā bhajante māṁ budhā bhāva samanvitāḥ*।)

Ādi Śaṅkarācārya shines as a Jñānayogi in His commentaries, a Karmayogi in His life and a Bhaktiyogi in His compositions. He is an amalgamation of all three Yogas. Those who share an intimate bond with their beloved Lord are recommended to follow the path of Bhaktiyoga and surrender in the feet of Īśvara. By doing so, all acts of the devotee will be in the service of God and thus the devotee will have neither actions nor their corresponding fruits.

The reason why Bhakti appears in the Bhagvadgītā in the mid of Karma and Jñāna is because Bhakti acts as a bridge between action and wisdom, between material and immaterial and between ethics and trans-ethics. It is merely through Bhakti that material can be realized as Divine and finally all material names and forms can melt into the light of Jñāna where everything shines as the Brahman. While Ādi Śaṅkarācārya does not accept Bhakti as an independent means to Mokṣa, He considers the same as essential in being led to the path of Jñāna.

From the above one can conclude that Bhakti holds a prominent place in Advaita Vedānta. Through devotion, one can attain environmental harmony and cosmic wellness. No doubt, Jñāna becomes the direct means of liberation but Karma and Bhakti become important milestones that lead to Jñāna. At the highest point of Bhakti, the devotee is enlightened and the darkness of duality disappears. He sees his beloved Īśvara in the whole of the cosmos and is thus free from any sort of likes and dislikes. When he treats an injured calf, he treats his beloved Kṛṣna not just with medicines but with devotion and love of Sudāmā. When he feeds a hungry dog, he feeds his beloved Śiva not merely with food but with the surrender and joy of Naṇḍī. He not just nourishes a tree with water but nourishes it with his maternal dedication just as Pārvatī nourishes Gaṇeśa.

3. Nivṛtti Dharma-The Path of Wisdom The word 'Nivṛtti' connotes to 'Withdrawal From' and 'Turning To'. Hence, it means withdrawal from worldly acts and turning within. The word is used in terms of ethics. Therefore, Nivṛttidharma means the ethics of Nivṛtti. It also refers to the path of Saṃnyāsa (renunciation).[79] In yet another context, it also means 'The Path of Eternal Wisdom (Jñānayoga)' that leads to renunciation in action (Karmasaṃnyāsayoga).[80] Ādi Śaṅkarācārya in His Bhāṣya on Bhagvadgītā defines the same as,

nivṛttilakṣanam dharmam jñāna vairāgya lakṣanam[81]
(nivṛttidharma points towards wisdom and dispassion)

When one attains the highest spiritual state, one is naturally established in Jñāna, Vairāgya and Saṃnyāsa that become the essence of Nivṛttidharma.

Pravṛttidharma becomes the ethical pre-requisite for Nivṛttidharma. Again, it becomes essential to understand that Pravṛtti and Nivṛtti Dharma have been separated merely for scholarly interpretation. Just as there exists no fine line between childhood, youth, old age and all the stages merge into each other. Likewise, Pravṛtti and Nivṛtti Dharma are two stages of the same path.

The essence of Nivṛttidharma lies in Jñānayoga, which is technically referred to as Brahmaniṣthā or Samyagdarśananiṣthā where everyone and everything shine as the Brahman. However, Ādi Śaṅkarācārya's Jñānayoga has been a subject of much criticism. Most people have developed a misconception that at the stage of Samyagdarśananiṣthā a person is supposed to lead a life of seclusion and passivity in the mid of some forest and cut off all ties with the world. A few even go on to define this stage as the stage of 'Action-less Brahman'. Before one jumps to

---

79 Shankaracharya, '*Shrimadbhagvadgitabhashya*', p.252 (V.18.30, *pravṛttiṁ ca nivṛttiṁ ca kāryākārye bhayābhaye। bandhaṁ mokṣaṁ ca yā vetti buddhiḥ sā pārtha sāttvikī*।)

80 Goendka Shri Harikrishnadasa, (Introduction, *sarvakarmasanuyāsa pūrvakāt ātmanjñāniṣtharūpāt dharmādbhavati*)

81 *Ibid.*

such conclusions one must refer to the life lived by Ādi Śaṅkarācārya and all other realized beings of the Advaita Vedānta tradition and rectify their view of Jñānayoga.

Ādi Śaṅkarācārya never adopted a complaisant attitude instead, He was extremely active and thus He touched every nook and corner of India not just physically but also mentally and spiritually. He flowed through the country just like the Gaṇgā, which doesn't stop anywhere and wherever it goes it fosters and nurtures all beings and purifies all lives. He did not retire to the forest nor did He live in seclusion instead He elected to live as a Saṃnyāsī within the society and decided to transform it and the transformation was such that even today He exists as the unifying spirit of India. He never entertained bogus, unscientific, empty, and ritualistic ideas instead, He was moved by love, compassion and duty which is evident when He returned to perform the last rights of His mother. He defied all phony restrictions associated with a Saṃnyāsī that restrict him to be a part of social ceremonies.[82] However, He did not remain passive towards the Adharma that was prevailing in the society and re-established the Vedic Dharma, established the four Maṭhas, gave birth to the Daśnāmisaṁpradāya, wrote Bhāṣyas, compiled hymns and the Prakraṇagranṭhas. He participated in discussions and out of compassion stopped Kumārila Bhatt from burning himself to ashes.[83] His unmatched compassion is evident when He refers to the Cāndala and his for dogs as Śiva and the four Vedas.[84] Whether the Cāṇḍāla and the four dogs were Śiva and the Vedas in disguise or whether Ādi Śaṅkarācārya knew that all beings cannot be anything other than Śiva are two versions that have the same message. Thus, the scholars and researchers need to connect with Ādi Śaṅkarācārya in order to understand His profound life and vision. Mere metaphysical, logical, and argumentative

82 Vidaranya Madhava, Svami Tapasyananda (Tr), pp.154-155.

83 *Ibid.*,p.77.

84 *Ibid.*,pp.60-62.

deductions cannot help in understanding the soul of Advaita Vedānta instead; they will be mere intellectual speculation.

At the same time, our interpretation of Jñānayoga largely depends upon how we interpret the word 'Jñāna'. The word literally means 'Wisdom'. It is different from the experiential knowledge of the Brahman which Ādi Śaṅkarācārya, refers to as 'Vijñāna'.[85] Jñāna is the intellectual understanding of the nature of Ātman from the scriptures as well as from the Guru.[86] In brief, Jñāna is the conviction that in spirit one is action-less, pure, and that which is the non-dual essence of all living beings. Therefore, when the intellectual knowledge gained from the texts and a qualified Guru is applied in one's life practically, it is said to be Jñānayoga. Ādi Śaṅkarācārya in this context states,

> ***"Jñānayoga is the transformation of wisdom into practice by the controlling of senses"***[87]

4.8. Saṃnyāsa- A Life Installed in Wisdom

Saṃnyāsa is the path of wisdom that leads to natural perfection. It is not a state of renouncing things or developing aversion towards them rather, it is a state of being established in the Brahman. It is a state where one accepts everyone and is flowing with love for each life in the spirit of detachment. Consequently, a Saṃnyāsī works for the upliftment of all beings with a vision of everything being 'The Self'.

In order to understand the concept of Saṃnyāsa, one must understand Vividisaṁnyāsa and Vidvadsaṃnyāsa. The former refers to formal Saṃnyāsa that one usually takes on

---

85 Shankaracharya, '*Shrimadbhagvadgitabhashya*', pp.72-73 (V.3.41, *vijñānanam viśeṣatastadanubhavaḥ*)

86 *Ibid.*, (*jñānanam śāstrata ācaryataśca ātmādinām avabodaḥ*)

87 *Ibid*, p.220 (V.15.11, *yatanto yoginaścai manpaśyanty ātmany avasthitam*। *yatantó 'py akṛtātmāno nainaṁ paśyanty acetasaḥ*।)

in the fourth Āśrama. However, the later Saṃnyāsa is mental and refers to the inner transformation. This Saṃnyāsa is not dependent upon any external factor and Ādi Śaṅkarācārya is more concerned with this kind of Saṃnyāsa than the formal Saṃnyāsa.[88] When a person is established in mental renunciation, he may not go in for a formal Saṃnyāsa and yet he may live a life of a Saṃnyāsi who works for collective peace and harmony. The Bhagvadgītā talks about this Saṃnyāsī in the following verse,

jñeyaḥ sa nityasannyāsī yo na dveṣṭi na kāṅkṣati ।
nirdvandvo hi mahābāho sukhaṁ bandhāt pramucyate ॥[89]
sāṅkhyayogau pṛthagbālāḥ pravadanti na paṇḍitāḥ ।
ekam api āsthitaḥ samyagubhayor vindate phalam ॥[90]
sannyāsas tu mahābāho duḥkham āptum ayogataḥ ।
yogayukto munir brahma na cireṇādhigacchati ॥[91]
yogayukto viśuddhātmāvijitātmā jitendriyaḥ ।
sarvabhūtātmabhūtātmākurvann api na lipyate ॥[92]

(The one who holds no animosity towards any being, the one who sans all expectations, the one who is free from all dualities is indeed a Saṃnyāsī. He is free from all actions that bind him. Only those smeared in ignorance consider Saṃnyāsa to be distinct from Karmayoga. The wise ones state that he who submits to any of these attains the non-dual Highest Truth. Oh, Mighty Arjuna! Without Karmayoga and Saṃnyāsa it is extremely difficult to attain the Highest State. However, the one installed in yoga eventually attains the Highest Reality 'Brahman'. He who has controlled his body, whose senses have been conquered and whose inner states have been purified, whose soul has become non-dual with the soul of all living beings, such a being performs his actions for the sake of Lokasaṃgraha and yet remains unattached to them)

---

88 Svami Madhavananda (Tr & Com), p.487-491 (V.3.5.1)

89 Shankaracharya, '*Shrimadbhagvadgitabhashya*', p.90 (V.5.3).

90 *Ibid.*, p.90 (V.5.4).

91 *Ibid.*, pp.90-91 (V.5.6).

92 *Ibid.*, p.91 (V.5.7).

From the above, one can understand that Jñānayoga along with Saṃnyāsa is the most desirable. However, it is important to understand what kind of Saṃnyāsa and actions are considered necessary. Here, Saṃnyāsa means Vairāgya/ or detachment from worldly enjoyments. It is giving up of worldly dualities and not giving up the world as such. It is important to realize that it is due to dualities that one gets stuck in the cobweb of pleasures and pains. Giving up these dualities means attainment of Vairāgya. It is further important to contemplate upon what kind of actions are desirable for a Saṃnyāsī. Here, only actions of attachment are to be given up and not acting in its literal sense is to be abandoned. Hence, when a Saṃnyāsī approaches a man, woman, child, tree, bird, or animal for the sake of serving them, he fosters no preference or aversion towards any form, and thus he is installed in detachment, non-discrimination and a vision of non-duality. Further, when he gives food, water, or medicines to any of these, he is free from the 'Kartābhāva (doership)' and has no actions left. As stated before 'No Action' does not mean uninterested action, instead, it means eagerly performing disinterested actions. Disinterested actions are carried out without any attachment or personal interest though one is enthusiastic in serving the 'Living Brahman'. Such a being has no craving for wealth, relationships, or fame. However, the Saṃnyāsī works towards creating the wealth of harmony and is aware of the non-dual relationship that all beings of the world share. A Saṃnyāsī is the abode of Dharma, virtues, morals and ethics. The Bhagvadgīta enlists the following virtues[93] that a Saṃnyāsī fosters,

---

93 Shankaracharya, '*Shrimadbhagvadgitabhashya*', pp.224-225 (V.16.1-16.3, *abhayaṁ sattva saṁśuddhir jñānayogavyavasthitiḥ। dānaṁca damaśca yajñaśca svādhyāyas tapa ārjavam॥ ahiṁsā satyam akrodhas tyāgaḥ śāntir apaiśunam। dayā bhūteṣv aloluptvaṁ mārdavaṁ hīr acāpalam॥ tejaḥ kṣamā dhṛtiḥ śaucam adroho nātimānitā। bhavanti sampadaṁ daivīm abhijātasya bhārata॥*)

- *Fearless (nirbhaya)*
- *Internally Pure (śuddhaṃtaḥkaraṇa)*
- *Enlightened (brahmajñānī)*
- *Charitable (dānī)*
- *Exercises self-control (dama)*
- *Self-sacrificing (tyāgī)*
- *Studies the Vedas (svadhyāyī)*
- *Devoid of passion for honor (yaśasatṛṣṇāmukta)*
- *Simple and sober (saral)*
- *Non-violent (ahiṃsaka)*
- *Truthful (satyavādī)*
- *Renouncer (utsargī)*
- *Tranquil (susthiraṃ)*
- *Free from anger (krodharahita)*
- *Peace-loving (śāṃtipriyā)*
- *Abhors fault finding(niṃdā apremī)*
- *Compassion for all beings (sarvabhūtakaruṇāmaye)*
- *Free from greed (lobhrahita)*
- *Holds reverence for the Śāstras (śāstrapriya)*
- *Gentle (sajjan, komal)*
- *Endowed with brilliance (tejasvī)*
- *Forgiving (ṣamānvita)*
- *Fortitude (dhairyaśīla),*
- *Appreciates cleanliness (śuddhipriyā),*
- *Taintless (drohrahita),*
- *Not-boastful (ahaṁkārarahita),*
- *Austere(tigmāṃśu),*
- *Pure in mind, body and soul (viśuddha),*
- *Modest, steady and determined (śālīna, acala, manasvina)*

The above-said virtues have an essential bearing on ethics and morals in terms of an individual and a society. A person who is decorated with the above-mentioned virtues cannot be anything but installed in Dharma and can look forward to 'Mokṣa'.

Ādi Śaṅkarācārya in the Bhagvadgītā bhāṣya interprets Karmasaṃnyāsa as renunciation in action and not renunciation of action.[94] Thus, a being who is installed in Vairāgya and gives up actions of attachment is said to be on the path of Saṃnyāsa. At this stage, a Saṃnyāsī doesn't stop performing actions instead he performs them while being installed in Jñāna because at this stage Karma merges into Jñāna and it is Jñāna that alone exists. As a result, Karma does not lose its identity; instead, it exists in the realm of Jñāna.

4.9. Mokṣa-The Final Realisation

Advaita Vedānta has a unique way of looking at liberation. At the outset, it propagates that the Self is never in bondage and is 'Nityamukta (eternally liberated).' However, due to identification with the temporary adjuncts the Jīva considers itself as distinct from the Brahman, limited in identity and in bondage. In the second place, liberation is not something outside of us or in some place called 'Heaven' that is attainable at a future date. The very desire of attainment of someplace called 'Heaven' is a state of bondage in view of Advaita Vedānta. On the other hand, liberation is attainable in this very lifetime and while having a body.[95] This conception is known as 'Jīvanmukti'. In other words, the realization of oneself as the non-dual Ultimate Principle while one is alive is said to be a state of Jīvanmukti. Jīvanmukta has a clear understanding that Mokṣa is not from the world but through and along with it.

The life of a Jīvanmukta becomes an ideal for the society. The enlightened man must leave behind his footsteps for others to follow. He must motivate and assist others to walk on the same path. Henceforth, extending care towards fellow beings, service towards old and sick animals, birds, or

---

94 Shankaracharya, '*Shrimadbhagvadgitabhashya*', pp.92-93 (V.5.11, *kāyena manasā buddhyā kevalair indriyair api। yoginaḥ karma kurvanti saṇgaṁ tyaktvātmaśuddhaye॥*)

95 Swami Vishveshwarananda, pp.25-30 (S.1.1.4, *sindhaṃ jñvitopi viduśa aśarīratvam*)

humans and protecting the environment is not incompatible with the teachings of Ādi Śaṅkarācārya but are rather desirable. This ideal has also been advocated by various other Advitins like Svāmī Vivekānanda, Lokmānya Tilak, Mahātmā Gāṇdhī, Svāmī Ramaṇa Mahāṛṣi and more.

A Jīvanmukta, At this stage, is aware of his nature and needs no reminder of the same. Therefore, now he needs no Vedas, scriptures, or any sort of Pūjavidhi to remind him of his being the Brahman. At this stage, all forms of animals, birds, and the very environment are elevated to the level of the 'Self /Brahman'. This wisdom is natural to him just as life itself. This thought may be explained with an example of a person who has tasted sugar. He need not be reminded that the sugar is sweet. Likewise, the realized one needs no reminder that he must revere and preserve all beings. Here, the words 'Revered' and 'Preserved' are being used for the sake of communicating an idea. However, at this stage, such words are annulled and a pearl of spontaneous, unbroken wisdom where all is the 'Self' dawns. Technically 'Jīvanmukti' refers to the dawn of non-dual wisdom even while a being has a body, mind and intellect. It is commendable that even while a being lives, he rises above dualities of pain-pleasure, like-dislike, man-animal.

A common person may ask that do the realized ones have no pain when they fall, are they above diseases and do they have no upheavals if they are insulted? If they do feel all the above-said, then how are they any better than an unrealized being? This query is natural but here the answer lies in understanding that 'pain is inevitable while suffering is optional.' The realized one also experiences fever, cold and pain but remains stationed in the awareness that all of these are merely the experiences of the body and not of the Ātman. However, an unrealized being associates with these experiences and considers them as his own because he considers the body to be the only Self. When hungry, a realized one will understand that the body is hungry and will eat food as medicine without any passions. On the contrary, an unrealized being will consider this hunger as real and final. He will eat in the mode of passion for the sake of satisfying his taste buds but sadly, passion and greed are beyond satisfaction. One's identification with the body becomes the cause of misery and leads to the destruction of environment internally and externally. When we associate with the physical body and try to satisfy its greed we become prone to internal diseases i.e., blood pressure, hypertension, diabetes, cancer and a hoard of other ailments. At an external level, our association with this temporary body leads us to deforestation, using animals for experimentation, non-vegetarianism, climate change, global warming, leather trade, population explosion, acid rain, genetic modification of crops, unnatural crossing of animal species, urban sprawl, ozone layer depletion, ocean acidification, polar ice caps and the list is endless. When one identifies oneself with the body, he unwisely tries to do all that which gives pleasure to it even at the cost of killing other beings and destroying Nature. When he elects to do so, he forgets that the whole cosmos is interwoven and harming anything will eventually harm him. It is considering the body as ultimately real and bowing down to its desires that pose a problem and becomes the ground of diseases, disharmony, wars, crimes, discriminations and environmental chaos. On the contrary, a wise one is aware that all needs are that of the body and not of the Self. He destroys nothing for there is nothing other than him that exists. Therefore, even though the wise one experiences pain, pleasures, distinctions and sees variedness of forms, he is aware that all of this is fleeting and all of this is merely apparent.

Now arises another question in the mind of a layman that if the wise one has realized all, how can he say things like 'Do not Harm the Trees', 'Today is Monday', 'It Is Very Late'? How can he talk in terms of form, time and place when he doesn't identify with any? The explanation lies in the fact that firstly, such references of form, time, space, and name are used for the ease of making others understand the context in which a thought is being communicated. Secondly, the explanation lies in technically what is known in Vedānta as Bādhita-ahaṃkāra. Ahaṃkāra co-exists with Mana, Buddhi, and Citta and persists as a part of the Antāḥkarṇa. In the case of a Jīvanmukta, this Ahaṃkāra that has been falsified and is called 'Bādhita-ahaṃkāra'. The concept of Bādhita-ahaṃkāra can be understood by the example of a burnt rope. A burnt rope has superficially apparent plating but cannot be used to bind anything and has no use. Likewise, Bādhita-ahaṃkāra exists in a Jīvanmukta yet it is of no use and cannot bind him. Therefore, when a Jīvanmukta says 'I am going, 'we will study tomorrow' and 'do not hurt any animal' he is not bound by place, time, or forms rather he is aware of the momentariness of all these and uses his Bādhita-ahaṃkāra as an ornament to interact with the world while he exists as an Udāsin (unattached to limitations). Thus says Ādi Śaṅkarācārya that,

yasminsarvāṇi bhūtāni hyātmatvena vijāntaḥ ।
na vai tasya bhāvenmoho na ca śokódvitīyātaḥ ॥[96]
(He who sees the Self in all beings has no delusion or sorrow due to the absence of duality)

From the above, it can be cognized that considering a wise being as inert, stone-like, crude, or uncaring, is merely going astray with one's uncontrolled imagination due to lack of comprehension of Advaita Vedānta Darśana. Instead, a wise one is installed in love that sans attachment. Here it becomes imperative to understand the difference between love and attachment. While attachment is binding, momentary and thinks of what can be derived from others. Love is installed in freedom, is eternal and thinks of the well-being of all. At this stage, the love of a being is not limited to any specific person or object instead it extends to all life

96 Deshmukha Shrikrishna, p.88. (V.54)

forms, it expands from 'Aham (I)' to 'Sarvam (all).' In this regard, Ādi Śaṅkarācārya states,

"Just as an individual in the state of deep sleep sees no diversity, likewise the one established in wisdom sees no diversity in the waking state even though he perceives such diversity. Such a being may perform actions yet remains inactive. Such a one is the knower of Brahman."[97]

The above-said statement also throws light on the performance of action installed in inaction. As discussed before 'Sarvakarmsaṃnyāsa' is a state of renunciation in action and not renunciation of action. The wise one remains detached towards the fruits of actions and sans Kartābhāva. Thus, such a being will be free from any joy or disappointment attached to the fruit of his actions installed in wisdom. At no point, Sarvakarmsaṃnyāsa should be interpreted as a state of not performing actions. Instead, Sarvakarmsaṃnyāsa refers to the performance of disinterested actions in the most eager manner for the welfare and prosperity of all lives. A being of this kind will automatically work for the preservation of environment and all sentient beings. He will strive hard to maintain the purity of rivers and oceans and will make efforts to preserve the forests. However, he will not do all of this with a sense of ego or for the attainment of any fruit. He will do all of this merely because of his very nature.

Many people think that because a Jīvanmukta remains unaffected by merits and demerits of action he has the free will to act as he may wish (Yathāiṣṭācarṇa). Thus, the question arises that will a Jīvanmukta act in an unrighteous, undisciplined, and anti-social manner? Here, one needs to understand that a Jīvanmukta attained the stage of Jīvanmukti by walking on the path of values and once he

---

[97] Mayeda Sengaku, '*Updeshsahasri*', Motilal Banarsidass, Delhi, 2006, p.124 (V.10.13, *susuptavaj jāgrati yo na pasyati dvayaṃ ca pasyannapi cadvayatah*। *tathā ca kurvannapi niskriyasca yah sa ātmavinānya itīha niscayaḥ*।)

attains Jīvanmukti he realizes his essence as the Brahman, which is all peaceful (*ṣāntam śivadvaitam*).[98] Because the Jīvanmukta is established in Dharma, he is bestowed with an all-pervading self-vision. The Jīvanmukta will alone be the one who harms and the one who is harmed. While eating if the tooth hurts the tongue, one won't go ahead and get the tooth removed. Thus, even those who harm the Jīvanmukta will be seen by him as his very Self. In this regard, Ādi Śaṅkarācārya's beloved disciple Sureśvarācārya in his well-known work Naiṣkarmayasiddhi states,

"virtues such as non-enmity make a spontaneous appearance without effort in case of him who has attained wisdom"[99]

Therefore, virtues such as compassion, non-enmity, non-violence, kindness are natural to a Jīvanmukta just as Rāga and Tāla are natural to an accomplished singer. The question of a Jīvanmukta being 'Adharmic' is itself pointless. Advaita Vedāntic point of view sees categorical imperatives such as 'Love Thy Neighbour', 'Thou Shalt Not Steal' and 'Thou Shalt Not Kill' as statements that are applicable for those enveloped in Avidyā. These imperatives do not apply to a Jīvanmukta who is the epitome of wisdom, love and compassion. Therefore, a Jīvanmukta is above duty and whatever he does for the welfare of all is because of his very essential 'Brahman Nature'.

The Sañcitakarma or collective karmas of the Jīvanmukta are exhausted the moment he realizes the Self. The Prārabdhakarma or those actions that have already sprouted, come to an end only once they give the fruits. The Āgāmikarmas also end with the dawn of wisdom. Hence,

---

98 Joshi, Bimali, Trivedi, p.63. (V.7)

99 Sureshvaracharya, Shastri Krishna Pandita, '*Nishkarmayasiddhi*', Achutyagranthamala Karyalaya, Varanasi, 2013, pp.167-168 (V.4.69-4.70, *uttpannātmaprabodhasya tvadveṣtatvadyo guṇāḥ। ayetanto bhavantyasa na tu sādhanarūpiṇaḥ।। imaṁ granthamupāditsuram-ānitvādisādhanaḥ। yatntaḥ syāna durvritaḥ pratyagdharmānugohayam*।।)

after the exertion of Prārabdhakarma Jīvanmukta perishes away in body. His Antāḥkarṇa merges with the Tanmātras (subtle elements) completely.

It is to be noted that the realized ones who have a mission to fulfill are born and reborn. Despite many births, such realized ones are not affected by Avidyā and remain at bay from the boundations of Karmas. Śrī Kṛṣna, Rāma, Buddha, Ādi Śaṅkarācārya come under this category and are Jīvanmukta who appear as and when the need arises.

The Jīvanmukta is eternally free from all bondages and decides to drop off his body. This dropping of the body in its gross and subtle form is known as 'Videhamukti'. The difference between Jīvanmukti and Videhamukti is merely for intellectual understanding and is important to those who are not realized. However, for the one who has realized himself, as the Brahman, Jīvanmukti-Videhamukti, birth-death, etc. make no difference. This can be understood by the example of a cow who is worshiped and a garland is put around her neck. The cow remains oblivious of the garland and soon when the garland dries up and falls, she remains unconcerned about it. Likewise, the body and extinction of the body have no significance for the Jīvanmukta at the highest level. However, at a mundane sphere, 'The Body' becomes his instrument to serve all beings, to set an example, and for the establishment of Dharma.

4.10. Sarvabhūtāhiteratāḥ and Loksaṃgraha: The Delight in the Welfare of All Beings

Sarvabhūtāhiteratāḥ[100] (delight in the welfare of all beings) is propounded by Ādi Śaṅkarācārya in the Bhagvadgītābhāṣya as a unique trait of the Jīvanmukta that must not be ignored. Sarvabhūāhiteratāḥ not only becomes the grounds for developing consciousness towards the

[100] Shankaracharya, '*Shrimadbhagvadgitabhashya*', p.97 (V.5.25, *labhante brahmanirvāṇam ṛṣayaḥ kṣīṇakalmaṣāḥ*। *chinnadvaidhā yatātmānaḥ sarvabhūtahiteratāḥ*॥).

environment and animals but also becomes the bedrock for cosmic peace, concord, comradeship, and fellowship. A Jīvanmukta works tirelessly for the welfare of the cosmos and this proves that he is not passive.[101] Further, Śrī Kṛṣna explains to Arjun the importance of working for the welfare of all by a being of realization.[102] In this context, He points out the case of Rājā Janaka and others who perform actions as,

1. **The realized ones:** who act while being established in inaction as their very nature and in order to set an example for others to follow.

2. **The unrealized ones:** who act in order to attain purity of mind and further attain the above-said state.

While the actions of Sarvabhutahita and Loksaṃgraha of a realized one can be an ideal for others, such actions performed by the unrealized ones can lead them to the path of realization. The word 'Lokasaṃgraha'[103] is used by Ādi Śaṅkarācārya with the connotation of '*preventing the world form getting degenerated.*' If the Jīvanmukta decides not to work for the welfare of all beings, he will fail to set an example. Therefore, common people will continue to lead a life smeared in violence, tarnishing the bounties of Mother Earth, gratifying their greed and will remain ignorant towards Svadharma and Svakarma. As a result, the society will be pushed into the darkness of chaos, evil and inhumanity. Like an Avatara, a Jīvanmukta acts for the sake of re-establishing Dharma, protecting the innocent, setting an example for future generations, and bringing the ignorant on the path of compassion and righteousness. For the sake of Lokasaṃgraha and the well-being of a nation, all humans, animals, and natural resources are needed. Not only do

---

[101] Shankaracharya, '*Shrimadbhagvadgitabhashya*', p.79-80 (V.4.19, *yasya sarve samārambhāḥ kāmsaṅkalpavarjitāḥ। jñānaagnidagdhakarmāṇaṁ tam āhuḥ paṇditaṁ budhāḥ*)

[102] *Ibid.*, p.65 (3.20, *karmaṇaiva hi saṁsiddhim āsthitā janakādayaḥ। lokasaṅgrahamevāpi sampaśyan kartum arhasi।*)

[103] *Ibid.*

humans contribute to the progress of a nation but Nature in general, animals and even the tiniest of beings have their role to play. Therefore, welfare is always collective and never in compartments. In this regard, Mahātmā Gāṇdhī states,

***"The greatness of a nation and its progress can be judged by how it treats its animals"*[104]**

When we concentrate on merely 'Specifics' and show disregard to all other creatures, we sway from the path of 'Lokasṃgraha'. We may pacify ourselves that we are working for the welfare of all. However, in reality, we work for ourselves and the human race with which we identify in terms of similarity of form. Our acts installed in dualism manifest as volcanoes, earthquakes, famine, nuclear wars, the cult of machines and destruction of the whole ecosystem. On our path of development, if we take every creature along and see our progress in the progress of others, it will be the application of 'Lokasṃgraha' in its truest sense.

Sarvabhūtahita and Loksaṃgraha must not be confused with acts of helping the world or making it perfect. A Jīvanmukta is aware that the cosmos doesn't need his assistance. Whatever he does is merely for the 'Self' because at that stage 'Self' alone exists and a person assists others in realizing the same Self. Therefore, Sarvabhūtahita and Loksaṃgraha are in favor of environmental harmony and reverence for animals. A remarkable statement made by Ādi Śaṅkarācārya in His commentary on the Bhagvadgītā proves the above said,

***'ātmaupamyena sarveṣu bhūteṣu sukham dukham vā samameva paśyati'*[105]**

(The realized one sees the pains and pleasures of all beings as his own)

---

[104] Thakur S. Bhart (Ed), "*The Future of Leadership: Addressing Global Issues Complex*", Palgrave, Mcmillan, USA, p.120.

[105] Shankaracharya, '*Shrimadbhagvadgitabhashya*', p.261 (V.18.54, *brahma-bhūtaḥ prasannātmā na śocati na kāndṣti*। *samaḥ sarveṣu bhūteṣu madbhaktim labhate parām*॥)

Unselfish and altruistic acts are known as Lokasaṃgraha that are meant for the welfare of all lives. In chapter three, verse 21-26 of the Bhagvadgītā Bhāṣya, Ādi Śaṅkarācārya declares it mandatory to perform actions which are meant for the sake of Lokasaṃgraha. Such actions lead to the purity of mind. Ādi Śaṅkarācārya advocates acting for the welfare of all creatures and explains the word 'Lokasaṃgraha' as,

"lokasya unmārga dravriti nivāraṇam"[106]
(Preventing the world from walking on the path of evil)

From the above, it is clear that Lokasaṃgraha is meant for Sarvabhūtahita. For a being of realization, Sarvabhūtahita becomes his very nature. However, for a seeker, Sarvabhūtahita requires conscious effort. Further, even people who belong to various Varṇas and Āśramas are required to cultivate ethics, morals and virtues such as being honest, being kind, protecting the environment and so on. No doubt, Ādi Śaṅkarācārya nowhere specifically talks of environmental ethics if someone sees 'Environment' with the contemporary understanding of the same. It is important to understand that,

- Ādi Śaṅkarācārya sees no division in the Self.
- The present-day chaos was not prevailing then.

However, Ādi Śaṅkarācārya's philosophy needs to be used mindfully, judiciously and diligently, in order to tackle environmental disharmony from which many other issues crop up. In the Bhagvadgītā Bhāṣya, Ādi Śaṅkarācārya also accepts Tapa, Yagya and Dāna as obligatory actions that must be performed in order to attain a state of purity. Therefore, he who has a burning desire for liberation must be installed in Ahiṃsā (non-violence), Dayā (compassion), Śama (tranquility), Dama (control of senses) and more.

---

106 Shankaracharya, '*Shrimadbhagvadgitabhashya*', p.65. (V.18.54)

It will be interesting to note that the whole credit of conceiving Ahiṃsā as a positive quality has been credited to Mahātamā Gāṇdhī. However, it was Ādi Śaṅkarācārya who interpreted 'Sarvabhūtāhiterati' as Ahiṃsā when he states,

'sarvabhūteratāḥ sarveṣāma bhūtānāma hita anukuiye ratāḥ ahiṃsaka ityartha'.[107]
(The well-being and welfare of all living beings is rooted in non-violence)

Therefore, for Ādi Śaṅkarācārya working for the well-being and welfare of others itself is Ahiṃsā because when you work for the welfare of something or someone as the Self, you would not exploit it, hurt it or kill it. In addition, one cannot overlook the importance that Ādi Śaṅkarācārya attaches to 'Dayā', a quality that one must cultivate towards all beings. In regards with 'Dayā, He states that,

'kṛpā dhūteṣu dukhiteṣu'[108]
(Extending kindness to those in pain)

Ādi Śaṅkarācārya, therefore, states that compassion and kindness towards all beings is an essential quality to be fostered. When Ādi Śaṅkarācārya talks about compassion, kindness, non-violence, nowhere does He limit it to merely human beings instead he talks of all beings. If he did limit the same to merely human beings, the entire philosophy of Advaita Vedānta would have crumbled. The above-said statement of Ādi Śaṅkarācārya contains the essence of all philanthropic activities.

When one feels the pain of the earth that is being exploited and the pleasure of the peacock who dances as his own pain and pleasure, he takes his first step to realizing the non-dual, ultimate Brahman.

---

[107] Shankaracharya, '*Shrimadbhagvadgitabhashya*', p. 187 (V.12.4)

[108] *Ibid*, p.224 (V.16.2, *ahimsā satyam akrodhas tyāgaḥ śāntir apaiśunam*। *dayā bhūteṣv aloluptvaṁ mārdavamhīr acāpalam*।।)

CONCLUSION

The closeness between ethics and metaphysics has been densely accentuated in the case of Advaita Vedānta. The philosophy of Ekātmavāda finds expression in India's individual, social, ethical, religious and spiritual life. With Mokṣa being the conclusion, Advaita Vedānta cannot be anything but 'Ethical'. It is to be discretely understood that if Advaita Vedānta merely spoke of humans and had ignored other forms in which the Brahman manifests, the entire theory of Ekātmavāda would have crashed. Further, to conclude that the entire world is an illusion is again misinterpreting the philosophy of Sarvabrahmavāda. Ādi Saṅkarācārya's philosophy, works and enterprises would have been futile if the entire world was non-existent. Why would He put in efforts for the sake of an illusionary world is a question to be pondered over. It becomes desirous to understand that the world is comparatively less real than the Highest Reality (Brahman), just as dreams are less real than the world that we experience in our awakened state. Though the world is prone to constant change, it is temporary in existence and is limited by space, time, names and forms yet it cannot be discarded as unreal or as the horns of a rabbit.

Advaita Vedānta refuses to deal with 'Ethics' as a list of codes of conduct for the realized ones. It in no way enforces a realized being to 'do' or 'not to do' something. The reason why we do not find codes of conduct in Advaita Vedāntic works for a person who has realized the Self is not because it is inconsequential but because the same is the ground of a person's very existence. There exists a large body of Advaita Vedāntic literature that deals with ethics. The Saṁhitā, Brāhmaṇa, Dharmaśāstra, Purāṇa and Itihāsa are bejeweled with virtues and morals. Thus, Advaita Vedāntic works take into account common morality for granted and do not remain indifferent towards it. It must be borne in mind that the philosophy of Advaita Vedānta will lose its very foundations if ethics and morals are not gone through in the process of realizing the Highest Good-Brahman. Consequently, Advaita Vedānta aims at establishing a person in wisdom, love, non-duality and Highest Reality. The one who is established in these will automatically have his actions rooted in cosmic welfare, well-being, amity and peace. The philosophy focuses on the permanent internal illumination that manifests as acts of universal concord rather than focusing on actions that are external, transitory, robotic and arise due to the fear of commands of '*ought to and ought not to*'.

In this way, one can derive logical codes of existences from Advaita Vedāntic metaphysics. It is often said that half knowledge is extremely dangerous. Scholars, philosophers and the common man repeatedly turn a blind eye to the fact that Ādi Śaṅkarācārya acknowledges the world of names and forms as,

- **Temporarily real.**
- **Division-less whole that appears diverse.**
- **More real than the dreams and less real than the Highest Reality-Brahman.**
- **Indescribable.**

At no point, Ādi Śaṅkarācārya negates the world like the son of a barren woman. Therefore, the indifferent opponents of Ādi Śaṅkarācārya who proclaim that His philosophy is utterly imaginative supposition and has no practical application lose their grounds. Ādi Śaṅkarācārya's philosophy is certainly far from being vain. On the contrary, it decorates one's life with consideration, reverence, prudence and ethics. It sanctions us to be in charge of our whims and beautifies us with values and morals of the highest kind. In order to comprehend Ādi Śaṅkarācārya's ethics one has to logically, coherently and clearly understand His Pārmārthika, Vyāvhārika and Pratibhāśika positions.

Ādi Śaṅkarācārya certainly goes on to recognize the problem of free will as the all-inclusive phenomenal world that seems to be varied and has its roots in Avidyā. Dualism is an outcome of Adhyāsa. For this reason, commands like 'you ought to be good' or 'you ought not to be evil' for a realized being become hollow in view of Advaita Vedānta.

As ethics in view of Advaita Vedānta are highlighted, they also form the base of comprehensive environmental harmony. Since Advaita Vedānta is a wholesome and divisionless philosophy it cannot have a discriminating view towards the different forms in which the Brahman appears. Thus, the beauty of this philosophy lies in its universal, organic and non-dualistic approach towards all entities of the cosmos that are pervaded, in-dwelled and rooted in the Highest Reality.

At no point do internal, external and cosmic environments, stand distinct. More importantly, all entities, i.e. Humans, animals, birds, trees, insects, rivers, five elements are equal in essence and installed in harmony. Unfortunately, the environmental disharmony is a result of the distortion of man's internal environmental states that lead to cosmic turbulences, havocs, upheavals, and disorders.

From the reasons presented in the above-said chapter, it can be lucidly concluded that environmental harmony is not in opposition with the philosophy of Advaita Vedānta. The upcoming chapter will throw light upon Ādi Śaṅkarācārya's spiritual diciplines in view of environmental harmony.

Oṁ Advaitasthāpanācāryāye Namaḥ

(I bow before Śaṅkara who established the glory of Non-dualism)

5.

Ādi Śaṅkarācārya's Ādhyātmika Sādhanā for Universal Harmony

The methodical discipline needed to realize the Highest Wisdom is referred to as 'Sādhanā.' It is a journey in which the seeker gradually purifies himself and is established in the Ultimate Reality. In Advaita Vedānta the Sādhnā particularly aims at realizing the 'Self'. All beings are recognized as the 'Highest Reality' as a result of this awareness. Thus, Advaita Sādhanā aims at methodical discipline in which one develops the vision to see the permanent behind the temporary names and forms. Gradually, it so happens that all the apparent names and forms melt into the Self and finally the all-pervasive 'Self' remains. Therefore, the present chapter will throw light upon the various methods given by Ādi Śaṅkarācārya that slowly but surely lead to the realization of the 'Self (Brahman)'.

5.1. The Four-fold Means: Sādhanacatuṣṭya

Out of compassion for all, Ādi Śaṅkarācārya bestowed a four-fold means upon humankind to realize the 'Non-dual Truth'. As one moves ahead on the spiritual path the four pre-requisites known as Sādhanacatuṣṭya[1] become

---

[1] (i) Shri Shankaracharya, Swami Madhavananda (Tr & Com), '*Vivekachudamani*', Advaita Ashram, Himalayas, 1921, p.8, (V.19, *adau nityānityavastuvivekaḥ parigrayete। ihāmutraphalabhogavirāgasta dantaram। śamādiṣatkasampattimumukṣutvamiti sphutam)।*

(ii) Swami Vireshwarananda (Tr & Com), '*Brahmasutrabhashya*', Advaita Ashram, Kolkata, 2014, pp.19-20 (S.1.1.1, *nityānityavastuvivekaḥ ihāmutrabhogavairāgaḥ śamādamādisā dhanasampatmumukṣutvamca)*

increasingly essential. Śaṅkara highlights the same in His ace Prakhraṇgraṇthas; 'Vivekacūḍāmaṇi, Aparokṣānubhūti and Balabodhasaṃgrah'. Although, these are to be practiced by humans yet their benefit extends to all lives. It is to be taken note of that the following four are to be practiced as a whole yet the chapter will dwell into each individually in order to lucidly understand them.

1. Viveka[2]: This is the ability to discriminate between the real and unreal, the permanent and the temporary. Our physical sight can fall prey to errors but the vision of truth makes us see beyond the material forms. While the sight sees a tree that can be uprooted, the goat that can be eaten for pleasure or the horse that can be kicked, it is the vision of discrimination that allows us to see all these names and forms merging into the Brahman, which is the very source of all lives. It is through Viveka that we develop a vision to see the permanent behind the temporary. Therefore, a Vivekī realizes that all temporary names and forms that have limited existence in the apparent world are in their essence Permanent and Ultimate. Viveka fosters in one's heart reverence for all lives because the realized one goes beyond 'Sight' that merely sees the limited and develops 'Vision' that realizes the permanent.

2. Vairāgya: This refers to a lack of passion for physical pleasures. Dispassion should not be mistaken for hostility or hate towards the material world. A person on the path to enlightenment cannot have either likes or dislikes. Dispassion implies that a person is no longer reliant on material objects for pleasure since he has realized that he alone is the summit of eternal joy. A being on the path of realization will have compassion, love, and kindness for all living beings because all these are synonymous with wisdom. A wise one will neither be attached to any of the beings nor to any of the objects of

2 Deshmukha Shrikrishna (Tr & Com), '*Aproksanubhuti*', Motilal Banarsidas, Delhi, 2019, p.11 (V.5, *nityamātmasvarūpaṃ hi dṛśyaṃ tadvipari tagam। evaṃ yo niścayaḥ samyagviveko vastunaḥ sa vaie*)

the world. He will not try to seek any joy out of them because he knows that no object or being of the universe can give him lasting happiness. Such a being may dedicatedly serve animals and humans for years, but their death will not jolt him for he knows that nothing has been lost. Such a being sees death in the light of wisdom. He knows that nothing is destroyed for everything is the Brahman. Nonetheless, dispassion does not make a seeker arid, coarse, or apathetic; rather, it causes him to cherish the eternal while being disinterested towards the ephemeral.

3. Ṣaṭasāṁpatti: These are the six virtuous behavioral traits that are to be fostered. These traits are essential in the attainment of the Highest Truth. The six virtues to be cultivated are,

a) Śama[3]: It means control of the mind. Here, the mind refers to 'Manas.' Mind is strange. It can be the cause of bondage or of liberation. It can be destructive or be the source of harmony. Today we are witnessing the horrors of climate alteration, global warming, epidemics, destruction of plates and animal life. Such a situation has arrived due to the veracity of our minds. Along these lines, it is suggested that we constraint our minds. Further, the purity of it can be maintained by the practice of Dhyāna,[4] Pūjā, Japa and Bhajana. The mind is fine-tuned via such activities, and the senses can no longer govern the same or bind us to act according to their whims. The controlled mind abandons the urge to exploit nature, its bounties, or kill animals for the sake of sensory gratification. The pure mind assists us in realizing our true nature. As a result, 'Śama' is the discipline of swimming through the waves of thoughts that occur as a result of past Vāsanās. Those with a strong willpower may

3 Deshmukha Shrikrishna (Tr & Com), *Ibid*, p.13 (V.6, *sadaiva vāsanātyāgaḥśamóyamitiśabditaḥ*। *nigraho bāhyavṛttīnāṃ daṁo ityabhidhīyate*॥)

4 *Ibid*, p.156-157 (V.123, *brahmaivāsmīti sadvṛttya nirālambatayā sthitiḥ*। *dhyānaśabdena vikhyātāparmānandadāyinī*॥)

easily do this while others require the use of 'Dama' to attain the samc.

b) Dama[5]: It is that through which one masters the five Jñānendriyas and the five Karmaendriyas. A lack of Dama can create havoc and the same is evident if we look around. Today, people have no control over their sight that motivates them to watch pornography and make it a billion-dollar market. It is watching such things that disturb the mind to an extent that crimes like animal rapes, children molestation and women sexual abuse take place. Today, we have no restraint over our tongues and therefore all animals that were the ornaments of Mother Earth end up decorating our dinner plats and become our meal. From eating snails, bats, birds to dogs, pigs, and cows, the human race has surpassed the term 'Inhumanity'. Without second thoughts, man has enslaved himself to the pleasure of the tongue. Likewise, we have submitted to loud Tāmasic music that excites us internally and adds to sound pollution externally. We want the coolness of the air for our comfort and so we resort to air-conditioners, which heat up the planet and lead to global warming. However, if we let our senses take control of us, soon we will be engulfed in the talons of dipping health, destroyed peace of mind, robbed bounties of the Mother Earth, broken relationships and a very ugly world that we will architect for ourselves. The only way we can deal with all of this is through the spiritual Sādhanā of 'Dama'. One has to be constantly vigilant of any Tamas or sloth that may get an opportunity to creep in. The senses must be engaged in the service of all beings. The eyes must be trained to appreciate beauty in all existences, and the tongue must be taught that food should not be consumed for the sake of pleasure, rather as medicine to alleviate hunger. Our Karmendriyas should be made to work for the prosperity and well-being of all sentient beings. Additionally, knowledge

5 Deshmukha Shrikrishna (Tr & Com), p.13(V.6, *sadaiva vāsanātyāgaḥ śamóyamiti śabditaḥ nigraho bāhyavṛttīnāṃ dama ityabhidḥiyate)*

of Dama will make Śama effortless. As a result, Dama must be undertaken with zeal, integrity and sincerity.

c) Uparati[6]: This refers to a state of being where one withdraws oneself from the external and is established in the 'Self'. At this stage, a person is no more touched by opposites like pain-pleasure, good-bad, mine-yours, man-animal. He embraces everything and everyone as the 'Very Self'. Spiritual training and intellectual quest lead to the attainment of this stage. Uparati bestows us with stability and balance in our everyday tasks, which helps us to lead a life installed in wisdom that remains untouched by any sort of dualities and their corresponding effects. At this stage, we do not attach Upādhis (limiting adjunct)[7] to ourselves and to others and thus we are completely free from any Rāga-Dveṣa (likes-aversions). At this juncture the vision of a person goes through a tremendous transformation but that in no way means that the one on the path of realization or the one who is realized will no more experience the world. The trees will still appear green to him, and the rainwater will equally soak him but now the tree and the rainwater will be the 'The One' that appears as many. At this point, a being completely gives up Karma installed in passion. Giving up of Karma in no way implies that now, he will not act if something undesirable happens before him. He surely will act but the reasons will no longer be the same as before. He will act in a completely detached manner, to uphold the spirit of Dharma, to maintain justice and to set an example. None but Lord Kṛṣna can be a better paragon of the same. He

---

6 Deshmukha Shrikrishna (Tr & Com), p.16 (V.7, *viṣayebhyaḥ parāvṛttiḥ paramoparatirhi sā sahanaṃ sarvaduḥkhānāṃ titikṣā sā śubhāmatā*).

7 The term '*Upadhi*' has a variety of meanings, including title, degree, quality, peculiarity, appearance, attribute, nickname, and so on. The word Upadhi, in Vedanta is used with the connotation of 'limiting adjunct.' In Sanskrit Upādhi is defined as उपसमिपे स्थित्वा स्वीयान् गुणान् अन्यत्र आदधाति (being near something causes it to transfer its property to something else, for example, a crystal kept on a blue fabric appears blue.)

was, Nityaśuddha, Nityabuddha, Nityamukta and yet He acted in order to uphold Dharma and provide justice to those who were weak. Ādi Śaṅkarācārya Himself is an example of how Karmas have to be performed for the well-being and welfare of all despite being in the spirit of detachment for the sake of upholding the spirit of Dharma.

d) Titikṣā[8] **:** It means forbearance, tolerance, and patience. Titikṣā is the fostering of an attitude that is rooted in equanimity while the arrows of pain, harsh times, harsh words, harsh actions and hate are shot at a person. Regardless of such occurrences and people who may cause insult and suffering, The seeker in no way develops a feeling of dislike, hate or harm towards anyone. This attitude should not be misinterpreted as passivity. This only means that a person will certainly act in a way that assists others to be established in Dharma and will continue to do so without developing any negativity towards anyone. Let us understand this through an example of how a person behaves under the influence of alcohol. He is abusive, undesirable and even anti-social at times. However, a realized being or the seeker will not develop any sort of hate towards the drunkard because it is not he who is acting in an undesirable manner but it is the alcohol, which is making him act in this way. Likewise, a being under the influence of Avidyā may act in the most heinous manner but a wise being will assist the other in getting rid of Avidyā rather than developing hate against him. Such a man who sees all beings with equanimity will not only assist human beings to move up the spiritual ladder but will assist animals, trees and all lives to evolve spiritually.

e) Śraddhā[9]**:** The same means 'Faith'. Faith can move mountains and it also becomes the bedrock of our lives. Thus, faith is seen as a virtue installed in the *Guru* (who is the

---

8 Deshmukha Shrikrishna (Tr & Com), p.16 (V.7).

9 *Ibid*, p.17 (V.8, *nigamācāryavākyeṣu bhaktiḥ śraddheti viśrutā*)

dispeller of darkness), in the *Vedas* (that are wisdom themselves) and in *Dharma* (which is the ethical and moral code of the universe). Therefore, Śraddhā becomes the ground on which the above-mentioned four virtues can be cultivated.

f) **Samādhāna**[10]**:** It alludes to a single-pointed focus on the non-dual 'Self,' by knowing which everything else can be known. It is via this that we can find answers to all our questions, solve all of our problems, and break free from the shackles of dualism.

4. Mumukṣutva[11]**:** It's a yearning to understand our ever-liberated nature. In Advaita Vedānta the Ātman is forever free and nothing can bind it. Therefore, at the core humans, animals, birds, and plants are eternally liberated. All creatures, however, consider themselves bound and limited because they mistakenly associate themselves with transient names, forms, relationships and the Saṃsāra. Thus, Mumukṣutva refers to the blazing desire to break free from all shackles that seem to bind us and recognize our ever-liberated nature of Sat-cit-ānanda. Once the wave knows that it is non-different from the ocean it will not only become the ocean but will establish non-duality with all other apparent waves that are also the ocean. It must be lucidly comprehended that, once the wave is instituted in the ocean, it will no longer remain a temporary, fleeting wave. Its identity will expand. Likewise, once a being realizes that he is the non-dual Brahman, he will be established in Self-sameness that is the essence of the cosmos. Therefore, the permanent, all-knowing, omniscient, omnipotent, and all-pervasive Brahman shall shine through all transitory names and forms.

---

10 Deshmukha Shrikrishna (Tr & Com), p.17 (V.8, (*cittaikāgryaṃ tu sallakṣ ye samādhānamiti smṛtam*)

11 *Ibid*, p.19 (V.9, *saṃsārabandhanirmuktiḥ kathaṃ syānme dayānidhe iti yā sudṛḍhā buddhirvaktavyā sā mumukṣutā*)

5.2. The Practicality of Ṣravaṇa, Manana, Nididhayāsna and Niṣṭhā

It's fascinating to observe how in ancient India a seeker was gradually led to the path of realization. For the same, teachings and lessons were usually intertwined with a method that makes the entire process of learning, simple, relatable, easy to remember, effortless to retain and practically applicable. Thus, the seeker moved on after basic preparation in search of a competent Guru. Under the kind guidance of a qualified Guru, he took on the path of listening (Ṣravaṇa), reflection (Mnana), and contemplation (Nididhyāsana) as a method of realizing the Ultimate Self. All of this is applied to and through the 'Four Mahāvākyas' which remain interconnected by a process. This process provides a logical sequence that furnishes us with a road map of our progress through Ṣravaṇa, Manana, Nididhayāsna and Niṣṭhā. The process is as follows,

1. The student approaches the Guru with the burning desire to understand the Highest Reality. The Guru begins with defining the Truth as *'Prajñānam Brahma'* (The Consciousness is Brahman)'. Since this Vākya gives a general definition of Brahman, it is said to be the statement of definition or the 'Lakṣṇavākya'. Now the student hears (Ṣravaṇa)[12] it and reflects upon the same but is also surrounded with various doubts because till now he has always considered the Ultimate Truth to be separate from himself (Parokṣa).[13] Therefore, the confused and doubtful student reproaches the Guru in order to get further clarity.

2. The Guru tells the student that there is 'No other to be sought' except himself. Thus, the Guru declares to the student the teaching of 'Tat Tvam Asi' (That Thou Art)'.

---

[12] *Shravana* refers to the student's careful listening of the non-duality of Jīva-Brahman (*jiva brahma eikya*) as propounded by his Guru.

[13] *Paroksha* is the distinction between the subjective concept and the objective reality.

Since this Mahāvākya instructs a student to 'Seek Himself' it is known as the statement of instruction or 'Upadeśavākya'. The student at this stage contemplates (Manana) upon the teaching of non-dualism that the Guru gave him through the Vākya.[14]

3. The student is now enriched with the wisdom of the non-duality of Ātman and Brahman. The student repeatedly meditates in order to contemplate and rise above the false notions of the Self as 'Triśarīra,[15] Pañcakośa,[16] Pañcamahābhūta, Pañcakarmaindriya,[17] Pañcajñānendriya,[18] and Antaḥkaraṇa'.[19] After deep contemplation, the student has the direct realization of 'Ahaṃ Brahmāsmi (I am the Brahman).' Since this Mahāvākya leads to the experience of realization, it is said to be an 'Anubhavāvākya'. This is a stage of Nididhyāsana.[20]

4. After the student realizes the nature of the Highest Reality, the Guru advises the student to forever be established in the Supreme wisdom of 'Ayamātma Brahma' (The Ātman is Brahman). The last Mahāvākya is the statement of perpetual practice and is therefore called the

---

14 *Manana* refers to the stage of reflection on the teachings given by the Guru

15 *Trisharira* in Advaita Vedanta referes to; Kāraṅaśarīra (causal body), Sukṣmaśarīra (subtle body) and Sthūlaśarīra (gross body)

16 *Panchakosha* in Advaita Vedanta referes to; Annamayakosha (food sheath), Prāṅamayakośa (vital breadth sheath), Manomayakosha (mind sheath), Vijnanamayakosha (intellect sheath), Ānandamayakosha (bliss sheath)

17 *Panchakarmaindriya* in Advaita Vedānta referes to; Mouth (organ of speech), Hand (organ of grasp and work), Feet (organ of movement), Anus(organ of excretion) and Genital (organ of reproduction)

18 *Panchjnanendriya* in Advaita Vedānta referes to; Eyes (sight), Ears (sound), Nose(smell), Tongue(taste) and Skin(touch)

19 *Antahkarha* in Advaita Vedānta referes to; Mann (thought), Buddhi (understanding), Ahanākara (feelings of identification and attachment), Citt (storage of samskaras)

20 *Nididhyasana,* the stage of meditation on the Ultimate Truth

'Anusaṁdhānavākya'. Holding on to this Vākya by the virtue of Niṣṭhā assists the student in never losing sight of his realization of truth despite being in the world of material flux.

An example of how Nididhyāsana is important along with Śravaṇa and Manana can be illustrated by the example of the game of chess. In this popular Indian game, it is difficult to defeat the king as long as his defense mechanism i.e. the queen, bishops, elephants, soldiers and horses are not defeated. Likewise, it is impossible to overcome Avidyā as long as its defense mechanisms i.e. sense of doer-ship, enjoyer-ship and their by-products, which are pride, hate, like, jealousy, anger and greed exist towards even the tiniest of creatures. As a result, Advaita Vedānta Darśana prescribes Nididhyāsana' for the elimination of Viparītabhāvanā (contrary notions). It is Viparītabhāvanā Alone that makes us kind towards humans and abhor animals or makes us exploit them as objects of experimentation, amusement and otherwise. Over a period of many lives, Viparītabhāvanā becomes Dṛḍhavāsanās (strong habitual tendencies). Habits are very difficult to overcome. A person despite being a doctor and knowing the harmful effects of drinking, smoking and non-vegetarianism will continue to indulge in them due to his habit. A person who drags his feet and walks will continue to do so despite knowing that it is not a good habit. Even if he makes a resolve to not drag his feet, he will soon forget the same. Such is the powerful effect of Vāsanās that overpower wisdom and resolve. The only way to overcome these Vāsanās is by making conscious and deliberate efforts to ingrain habits that directly refute our 'Vāsanās', i.e. if one is in the habit of sleeping late, he has to make conscious attempt to sleep and rise early. Similarly, the habit of polluting our water sources, tossing trash on the streets, and plucking leaves and flowers for no cause must be overcome by cultivating non-distructive behavior until one attains the Highest Wisdom and is free from such habitual tendencies.

It is easy to suggest that one should perceive animals, birds, plants and the whole of cosmos as your own 'Self' but is this applicable? In the much-celebrated work Ātmabodha, Ādi Śaṅkarācārya refers to seeing duality as a disease and considers the thought 'Aham Brahmāsmi' as the medicine,

evaṃ nirantarābhyastā brahaivāsmrīti vāsanā।
haratyavidyāvikṣepannroganivā rasāyanam॥[21]

(The continuous practice on the thought 'I am the Brahman' acts as a medicine that puts an end to the disease of duality.)

Fears, hostility, and contempt towards animals and other beings, the desire to dominate Nature, and the urge to destroy the earth may all be attributed to considering dualism as fundamentally true. Duality is necessary for functioning in the physical world, but it is not ultimately real. This disease of dualism can be treated by continuously reminding oneself that 'I am the Brahman' until this thought manifests as the final realization.

It must be understood clearly that the process of Ṣravaṇa, Manana, Nididhyāsana and Niṣṭhā is a single body. The four do not exist in isolation; rather they merge into one another. Therefore, the path that begins with the instruction of '*Prajñānam Brahma*' (The Consciousness is Brahman)', leads to the realization of *Ayamātma Brahma*' (The Ātman is Brahman)' and the seeker discovers that he alone is the whole cosmos and is established in '*Aham Brahmāsmi (I am the Brahman)*'. At this stage, a being can be nothing but the well-wisher of all lives for he realizes the essence of everything moving and stationary as the 'Self'

21 Adi Shankaracharya, Swami Nikilananda (Tr & Com), '*Atmabodha*', Sri Ramakrishna Mission, Madras, 1947, pp. 195-196. (V.37)

5.3. Vyatireka-Anvaya: The Method of Negating and Accepting the World

In the classic work Aparokṣānubhūti, Ādi Śaṅkarācārya states that,

kāraṇam vyatirekaṇa pumānādou vilokayet।
anvayena punastaddhi kārye nityam prapaśyati॥[22]
(The seeker must first perform the spiritual practice of refutation (vyatireka) and then realize the Self in the effect through continued practice)

Vyatireka is a spiritual practice and training where in order to realize the Self, everything that one considers sentient and insentient, good and bad, mine and yours is negated, e.g. the body is not the Self, the animal is not the Self, the tree is not the Self. All entities are denied for the sake of negating the variety of forms and names that generate aversions and attachments. When the veil of dualism is lifted and this variedness is eliminated by method of refutation, the seeker realizes that Whatever he thought of as diverse is in reality the 'Unitary Whole.' Therefore, now when he looks at the world, he sees the animal as the Brahman, the tree as the Brahman and the whole of cosmos as the Brahman. He thus concludes that 'All is the Brahman'.[23] This acceptance of everything as the Brahman is Said to be 'Anvaya' The journey that starts from Neti-neti (not this, not this),[24] culminates with the wisdom of 'All is the Self'. By following the path or Vyatireka & Anvaya Thus, one realizes that-

- ***Brahman is the cause (kāraṇabrahman)***
- ***Brahman is the effect (kāryabrahman)***
- ***Brahman is the that which transcends the cause and the effect (kāryakaraṇatītaśuddhātman)***

---

22 Deshmukha Shrikrishna (Tr & Com), p.173. (V.138)

23 Swami Nikhilananda, '*The Upanishads: Taittirya and Chandogyopnisad*', Harper and Brothers, New York, 1959, pp.206. (V.3.14.1)

24 Swami Madhavananda, '*Brihdarnayakopnisad with Commentaries of Shankaracharya*', Advaita Ashrama, Himalayas, 1950, pp.336. (V.2.3.6)

In this respect, Ādi Śaṅkarācārya says,

adṛśyam bhāvarūpañca sarvametat cidātmākam ।
sāvadhānatayā nityṁ svātmānaṁ bhāvayedbhudaḥ ॥[25]
(the seeker should carefully think about the perceptible and non-perceptible aspects and conclude that 'All is the pure, conscious Self')

In the pot-clay analogy, the clay exists both as an effect (pot) and as the essential cause. When one initially sees the varied pots, he identifies the pots as 'small pot', 'big pot' and 'beautiful or ugly pot'. His identification is based upon names and forms in which the clay exists. The person sees the pots but is unable to see the clay that the pots are made up of. If one tells him that 'All this is a lump of clay', he will counter by saying 'This is not a lump of clay, it is a small pot or a big pot'. This refutation is technically known as 'Apavāda'. However, if he pays attention, he will realize that all pots are nothing but clay (Anvaya). Thus, it can be understood that humans, animals, birds, insects, mountains, oceans and every little atom that exists in the universe as an effect are non-different from the cause. In this regard, Ādi Śaṅkarācārya states,

kārya hi kārṇaṁ paśyetpaścatkāryaṁ visarjyate ।
kāraṇatvaṁ swato naś yedavaś iṣtam bhāvetmuniḥ ॥[26]
(One must see the cause in all the effects and then all effects must be dissolved in the cause. Therefore, what will remain is the cause alone which is the very 'Self')

Brahman is not only the cause of the cosmos, but It also becomes the entire cosmos of names and forms. It penetrates all living and non-living beings. As a result, dualism of all kinds ceases to exist for the enlightened one. However, multiplicity established in unity continues. Ādi Śaṅkarācārya further says,

---

25 Deshmukha Shrikrishna (Tr & Com), V.141, p.178. (V.141)

26 *Ibid.*, p.175. (V.139)

27 *Ibid.*, p.178 (V.142)

***ḍruśyam hyadṛśyatām nitvā brahmākāreṇa cintyate*।**
***vidvānnityasukhe tiṣṭheddhiyā cidrasapūrṇayā*॥[27]**
(For the perceptible world to dissolve in the Brahman, a seeker must consider that 'Everything is the Brahman'. By doing so he will be established in the supreme joy, eternal bliss and pure consciousness)

In addition to the same, the Māṇḍūkyakārikā also affirms that,

***jñātedvaitamnavidyate*[28]**
(An enlightened one sees no duality)

5.4. Śaṅkara's Fifteen Fold Yoga for Cosmic Harmony

The fifteen-fold yoga of Ādi Śaṅkarācārya appears in one of His Prakraṇagraṇthas called 'Aparokṣānubhūti'. The central theme of this glorious work is the realization of the non-duality of the effect and the Cause (Jīva and Brahman). Verses 100-129 of the text deal with the fifteen stages that one goes through while walking on the path of realization. In this glorious text, Ādi Śaṅkarācārya expounds upon fifteen yogic steps for the attainment of non-dual wisdom.[29] He states that the Ultimate Wisdom (Self) is unattainable without the continuous practice of meditation upon the Brahman.[30] Hence, one can understand that He stresses upon the practical application of knowledge in order to attain the highest state of being. The fifteen steps to realization as expounded by Ādi Śaṅkarācārya are,[31]

---

28 Mandukyakarika (V.1.18)

29 Swami Vimuktananda, '*Aprokshanubhuti of Adi Shankaracharya*', Advaita Ashrama, Himalyas, 1938, p.54, (V.100, *tripañcāṁ gānyatho vakṣye pūrvoktsyava siddhye*। *taiṣca sarveḥ sadākaryaṁ nididhyāsanameva tu*)

30 *Ibid.*, pp.54-55, (V.101,*nityābhyāsādṛte prāptirnabhavetasacidātmanaḥ*। *tasmādabrahma nididhyascjijñāsuḥ śreyase cirama*॥)

31 *Ibid.*,pp.55-56, (V.102-103, *yamo hi niyamast hāgo mounaṁ deśaṣca kālatāḥ*। *āsanaṁ mūlabandhaṣca dehasāmyaṁ ca dṛksthitiḥ*॥ *prāṇasaṁyamanaṁ caiva pratyāhārsca dhāranā*। *ātmadhyānaṁ samādhiṣca proktānyaḍgani vai kramāta*॥)

1.Yamaḥ[32]**:** In contrast to what Maharṣi Patañjali describes 'Yama' as (**Ahiṁsā, Satya, Asteya, Aprigraha and Brahmacārya**); Ādi Śaṅkarācārya suggests 'Yama' as practicing the control of senses repeatedly by the means of wisdom in the awareness of 'All is the Brahman'. It is to be understood that once a being understands everything as the Self, whom will he kill? Whom will he lie to? What will he try to pinch? What and whom will he possess and what sexual misconduct will he display? Therefore, the one who practices the control of senses by knowing 'All as the Brahman' will automatically work for the welfare of environment and the whole of cosmos. When one approaches all lives as the Brahman, he does not hurt, harm or kill any life in actions, words and thoughts. This is automatic and leads to universal compassion, non-duality and cosmic reverence. It is a state where one has no emotions of hate, harm and jealousy towards any creature of the world (**Ahiṁsā**). As a result, when humans pollute rivers or engage in deforestation, they forget that the woods and rivers are home to millions of sentient beings who sustain the human race, maintain ecological balance, and contribute to the earth's general well-being. At a higher level, they are the Supreme Brahman. Humans no longer see the earth as a living entity that breathes and feels. Thus, they destroy their own Annamayakośa when they destroy the earth's Annamayakośa. Moreover, each being has intrinsic worth in the material world. Indian culture has never seen the Pañcamahābūtas, flying birds, beautiful animals, mountains and lush green forests as entities to be destroyed rather they are seen as the very Self. Every spec of the universe has been raised to the level of the Brahman. In this regard, the Śrīmad Bhagvadgītā states,

---

32 Swami Vimuktananda, '*Aprokshanubhuti of Adi Shankaracharya*', p.56, (V.104, *sarvaṁ brahmeti vijñnādindriyagrāmasaṁ*। *yamoyamiti saṁproktobhyasanīyo muhurmuhuḥ*।)

raso'hamapsu kaunteya prabhāsmi śaśisūryayoḥ ।
praṇavaḥ sarvavedeṣu śabdaḥ khe pauruṣaṁ nṛiṣu ॥[33]
puṇyo gandhaḥ pṛithivyāṁ ca tejaścāsmi vibhāvasau ॥[34]
jīvanaṁ sarvabhūteṣu tapaścāsmi tapasviṣu ॥

(I am the taste in the water I am the light present in the sun and the moon. I am the sacred AUM of the Vedas; I am the śabda of the Ākāśa, and the ability in humans. I am the serene fragrance of the Pṛthvi, and the brilliance in the fire. I am the life in all beings, and the Tapas of an ascetic.)

When a person views everything as the Brahman, he or she is instantly established in truth **(Satya).** This all-encompassing truth invariably leads to everyone's happiness and well-being. He will accept all creations as they are, without attempting to alter or destroy them for the sake of temporary gains. Each creation will be the Supreme Self to him, and the Supreme Self alone will be the highest of Truth. A truthful attitude towards the entire cosmos will automatically lead to overall harmony and peace. Further, such a being will never indulge in stealing something that is of value to another being (**Asteya**). This arises out of self-satisfaction and non-attachment. When the whole of cosmos is seen as the Brahman, the very thought of stealing will lose its meaning.

Today, our greed has propelled us to the point where we have no remorse or shame in stealing someone's property, land, and money, and have even gone to the extent of stealing Mother Nature's bounties. We have deprived other sentient beings of their right to live and have killed them for their skin, their fur, for entertainment or merely to build fancy state-of-the-art malls on the land which belonged to them. The one who sees 'All as the Brahman' will appreciate each life form. He will not pinch away a peacock's life merely for the sake of its feathers and meat but will appreciate its melodious voice, dance and beauty. He will never steal away the right of a river to be pure and

---

[33] Adi Shankaracharya, '*Srimadbhagvadagītābhashya*', Manav Prabodhan Pranyasa, Bikaner, Rajasthan, 2016, p.119. (V.7.8)

[34] *Ibid.*, p. 119. (V.7.9)

enriching but will make every effort to maintain it's purity that enriches thousands of lives dependent upon it. Therefore, a being who realizes and understands that each life form is the Brahman will never deprive the universe of its serenity and bounty.

The abandonment of the urge to accumulate objects, feelings, and thoughts is referred to as non-possessiveness (**Aparigraha**). It can be followed only when one no more remains a slave in the hands of greed. Possessiveness arises out of fear, greed, insecurity and attachment. A person who eats more than he requires leads himself to health issues. He who sleeps a lot makes himself/herself prone to dullness, weight issues, lethargy and a hoard of other problems. Those who accumulate a lot of money suffer from the fear of losing it. Likewise, in our greed for technological advancements, we have looted the treasures of Mother Earth and have destined ourselves to global warming, oxygen depletion, deforestation, species extinction and more. When our desire to possess exceeds our need to survive there arises a state of disharmony on an individual, social, environmental, and cosmic level. However, when one sees everything as the Brahman, there is nothing and no one left to be possessed, looted or exploited.

Celibacy **(Brahmacārya)** is organically anchored in a being who controls his senses with the understanding that everything is the Brahman. Sexual urge is the most powerful and can lead to physical, mental, emotional and spiritual destruction if not controlled and directed appropriately. However, when all beings of the world are approached as the Brahman, there will be none who would become an object of sexual desire. Today, people have forgotten the virtue of Brahmcārya and have created chaos. A being established in the Brahman will never see women, children and animals as objects of sexual gratification.

It should be emphasized that the above mentioned have been explicitly discussed in this book just for the sake of understanding since people associate the above mentioned with thc word 'Yama as expounded by traditional Yogic texts.' On the other hand, the 'Yama' of Ādi Śaṅkarācārya, is the seat of all values, aesthetics, holiness, and greatest good, as Brahman becomes the essence of all existences. Therefore, Ādi Śaṅkarācārya's 'Yama' is not restricted to the afore mentioned. Practicing the control of senses 'Yama' with the wisdom that 'All is the Brahman' becomes the very base of an ethical life in the Vyāvhārika Jagat that goes beyond **Ahiṁsā, Satya, Asteya, Aprigraha and Brahmacārya**. It becomes the bedrock of existing in the non-dual wisdom and approaching the cosmos as the very Self. It can be concluded lucidly that Ādi Śaṅkarācārya's 'Yama' is all-encompassing and leads to cosmic and environmental welfare.

2. Niyamaḥ[35]: After one has attained 'Yama' where he views everything as the very Self, he moves on to 'Niyama'. At this stage, there is a continuous flow of the thought that 'The Self Alone Exists'. Here, the seeker disregards all dualities and sees the non-dual essence behind all distinctions. Although in the first stage a person views the dog as a Brahman, the tree as a Brahman, and everything in the universe as the Brahman, in the second stage he has a constant stream of thought that 'Brahman alone exists.' While Maharṣi Patañjali defines 'Niyama' as the practice of Śauca, Santoṣa, Tapaḥ, Svādhyāya and Īśvaraparidhāna, Ādi Śaṅkarācārya defines it as the steady flow of a single thought attained through constant practice. When all names and forms melt away, one automatically is established in cleanliness (**Śauca**), contentment (**Santoṣa**), penance (**Tapaḥ**), self-inquiry (**Svādhyāya**), and surrender (**Īśvaraparidhāna**).

3. Tyāgaḥ[36]: Tyāga for Ādi Śaṅkarācārya means giving

---

[35] Swami Vimuktananda, p.56-58, (V.105-106, *sajātīyapravāhaşca vijātyatiraskṛtiḥ। niyamo hi parānando niyamātkriyate budhaiḥ। tyagaḥ prapañcarūpasya cidātmat vāvaloknāt। tyāgo hi mahatāṁ pūjyaḥ sadhyo mokṣamayo yataḥ॥*)

[36] *Ibid*, p.57-58, (V.106)

up of material distinctions. For as long as a being exists in the material body, he will view distinctions. However, he must not consider these variations of names and forms as real and must be established in the reality of non-dualism that is the essence of all existences. Such a person not only relinquishes distinctions but also renounces Rāga-Dveṣa that are associated with these objects. When a person gives up dualities, he is endowed with equanimity, vision of truth, and is established in Tyāgaḥ (renunciation). Ādi Śaṅkarācārya does not advocate renunciation as a state of ceasing to act and accepting passivity. He rather propounds upon disinterested actions that are not performed in the mode of passion, ego and desire.

4. Mauna: Traditionally 'Silence' is understood as restriction of speech, deliberate cessation of words, communicating through gestures or writing. This is a primary stage of silence for a novice seeker. However, for Ādi Śaṅkarācārya silence has a different meaning altogether. The verse[37] that talks about silence can be interpreted in two ways-

- When one realizes the Self, 'Speech' just like names and forms retires and Brahman alone exists (*ṣāntam śivamadvaitam*).[38] At this stage words, speech, expression all merge into the Brahman and the highest of silence exists.
- When one realizes everything as the 'Brahman' (*sarvam khaluidam brahma*)[39] every object of the world from an animal, plant, tree to a tiny insect becomes indescribable. No words, speech or expressions can describe the cosmos.

---

[37] Deshmukh Srikrihna, pp.139-144 (V. 107,108,109, *yato vāco nivartante aprāpa manasā saha। vāco yasmānnivartante tadvaktuṁ kena śakyate। prapañco yadi vaktavyaḥ sópi śabdavivarjitaḥ।। iti vā tadbhavenmounaṁ satāṁ sahajasañjnitam। girā mounaṁ tu bālānaṁ prayuktaṁ brahmavādibhih।।*

[38] Joshi, Bimali, Trivedi, '*112 Upanishads, Vol-1, Mandukyopnishad*', Parimal Publications, Delhi, 2013, p.63. (V.7)

[39] *Ibid.*, pp.143-144. (V.3.14.1)

At this stage a being becomes silent for this stage can merely be experienced but cannot be explained in the finest of words. At this stage, one realizes all beings in the Self and the Self in all beings. Therefore, a wise Yogi is established in complete silence.

5. Ekānta[40]: In the classic sense 'Solitude' refers to an uninhabited place or a state of aloneness and loneliness. The entire entities of the cosmos exist in the realms of Vastupariccheda (limited by form), Deśapariccheda (limited by place), and Kālapariccheda (limited by time). However, Brahman pervades all entities of the universe. The whole of internal, external and cosmic environment is nothing but the Brahman. Therefore, Brahman exists in the highest solitude and in 'It' solitude exists. To know this highest solitude is to be established in Ekānta. Despite being surrounded by the varied entities of the world, a being is installed in the awareness that 'Brahman alone exists'.

6. Kāla[41]: Generally 'Time' is understood as that which the clock reads. It also refers to the measurement, calculation and comparison of events, irreversible existence and episodes in terms of past, present and future, quantifying the material changes of the cosmos and cosmic entities. For Ādi Śaṅkarācārya Brahman is Mahākāla (The Great time). Brahman exists without any divisions of seconds, minutes, hours, days, months, years, events, age, past, present and future. All these divisions are created by humans merely for the sake of operation and ease in the material world. However, at the highest state, all these retire into the Brahman. Just as one rises above the distinctions of names-forms, likes-dislikes, good-bad, and man-animal, he also rises above the dimensions of time for he is established in the Brahman (The Great Division-less Time).

---

40 Deshmukh Srikrihna, pp.144-145.(V.110, *ādāvante ca madhye ca jano yasmina vidyate| yenedaṁ satataṁ vyāptaṁ sa deśo vijanaḥ smṛtaḥ||*)

41 Swami Vimuktananda, p.60.(V.111, *kalanāta sarvabhūtānāṁa brahmādīnāṁ nimeśataḥ| kālaśabdena nirdiṣto hyakaṅdānandakodvayaḥ|*)

7. Āsanam[42]: In the traditional Aśṭāṇgayoga, Āsanam refers to a physical posture that one masters in order to meditate and can retain the same for long durations. Many Yoga Saṁpradāyas and traditions aim at teaching and learning various āsanas for the sake of attaining a healthy body. The benefits of Yoga are known to all. However, for Ādi Śaṅkarācārya realization of the Self is paramount. He is more concerned about postures that put no physical strain and allow one to concentrate on the Self. It is to be noted that Ādi Śaṅkarācārya's aim is the realisation of Brahman and for the same, a steady posture is peripheral. Therefore, one must sit in a posture that is comfortable and can be easily retained for long periods. It must not lead to numbness of feet, backache or strain in any part of the body. Ādi Śaṅkarācārya gives the freedom to elect a posture that is most suitable for a person depending upon his age, weight, and capability. However, one must not lie down or sit in a casual, slouching posture.

Here, an effort is being made to reinterpret 'Āsanam' in view of Advaita Vedānta. Since Āsanam means 'posture or position', it can also be understood as respecting one's own and other's position in the scheme of cosmos. As long as we do not interfere in the workings of Nature and allow all sentient beings to retain their position in the scheme of cosmos, each one will get an opportunity to step up the ladder and realize the Brahman. Further, Āsana can also be interpreted as our internal and external position. Unless equanimity, calmness and stability do not take their seat within and without us, we will continue to exist in ignorance. Therefore, being established in the Brahman is real Siddhāsana (attainment of the highest posture).

---

[42] Deshmukh Srikrihna, pp.146148 (V.112, *sukhenaiva bhavedyasmiṅjastraṁ brahmacintanam। āsanaṁ tadvijānīyānetaratasukhanāśanam॥*)

8. Mulābaṇdha[43]: In the classical Yoga system 'Mulābaṇdha' refers to root lock. It indicates a practice where one constraints, contracts and locks the perineal area. 'Mūlabaṅdha' is one of the three Baṅdhas along with Udyānabaṅdha and Jālandharbaṇdha that combine to make the Mahābaṇdha. These three are used together in order to control the Pañcaprāṇa. However, for Ādi Śaṅkarācārya 'Brahman' is the Mūla of all existences. It is the essence, root and base of all entities of the cosmos. Thus, being fixed in the 'Essence' is said to be 'Mulābaṇdha'. It is being established in the Brahman, which is the cause of all causes, and realizing 'Sat (pure existence)', 'Cit (all-pervasive consciousness)' and 'Ānanda (eternal delight). Therefore, when one realizes unity with all existences and sees them as the Brahman, he will experience complete non-dualism. This state is beyond description. The same is referred to as 'Mulābaṇdha' or being rooted in the Highest Truth 'Brahman'

9. Dehasāṁyam[44]: Equipoise of the body is generally described as a state of absolute stillness and lack of mobility. For Ādi Śaṅkarācārya, however, sitting in a position like a dried-out tree while the mind wanders is not a state of 'Dehasāmyam'. Instead, the same is accomplished when equanimity prevails within, without, and across the entire environment. It is this steadiness through which one is established in the Brahman. This is not merely attainable at an individual level but is also attainable at an environmental and cosmic level. When one approaches every creature as the Brahman and assists everything to operate in line with its Dharma, the entire cosmos is rooted in serenity and harmony reigns.

---

43 Deshmukh Srikrihna, pp.149 150, (V.114, *yanmūaṁ sarvabhūthanam yanmūlaṁ cittabandanam*। *mūlabhandhaḥ sadā sevyo yogyôsau rājayogināma*॥)

44 Tatya Tookaram, '*The Compendium of the Raja Yoga Philosophy with Treatises of Shrimat Sankaraacharya*', Bombay Theosophical Publication, Mumbai, 1888,p.25,(V.115, *aṅgānāma samatām avidyātasame brahmaṇi livate no cenaivas samānatva mrjutvaṁ śuṣkavṛkṣvata*॥)

10. Dṛṣṭi[45]: In the traditional Yoga 'Dṛṣṭi' refers to the fixed, firm and steady vision, which is attained by external techniques such as concentrating on the tip of the nose or the flame of a lamp (Trātaka). The practice works wonders in developing focus and concentration. However, outwardly focus and concentration are insufficient for Ādi Śaṅkarācārya unless they lead to developing an internal unifying vision that allows a person to see past the veil of Māyā and realize non-dualism as fundamental. Śaṅkara emphasizes the need for cultivating a noble vision that enables one to recognize 'Brahman' as the source of the cosmos via conscious effort. At this stage, the perceiver, perception and perceived (Draṣṭā, Dṛṣṭi and Dṛṣyam) melt into the Brahman. Therefore, one awakens to a world of diversity, with a vision of unity. This noble view leads to cosmic harmony, wellness and welfare.

11. Prāṇasāṁyam[46]: In the traditional Yoga, Prāṇāyāma refers to the technique of regulating the life forces through Recaka-Pūraka-Kuṁbhaka (exhaling-inhaling-retaining). However, for Ādi Śaṅkarācārya negation of duality of the world is 'Recaka'. Embracing the awareness that 'I' am the Brahman is 'Pūraka', and steadily being established in the 'Self' as the Ultimate Principle is 'Kuṁbhaka'. Ādi Śaṅkarācārya propounds that this alone is real 'Prāṇāyāma', which leads to realization of the 'Non-dual Principle', that is the cosmic breath. However, He says that "ignorant are those who merely torture the nose by pressing the nostrils". Here, Ādi Śaṅkarācārya has no intention of ridiculing the Yoga practitioners; rather, He wants to make it clear that one cannot realize oneself as the all-pervasive Brahman via

---

45 Tatya Tookaram, p.26, (V.116, *dṛṣtiṁ jñānamayiṁ kṛtvā paśyedihmayaṁ jagat। sa dṛṣti parmodāna nāsāgrāvalokinī*।)

46 *Ibid*, pp.26-27, (V. 118, 119, *citādisarvabhāveṣu brahmatvenaiva bhāvanāta। nirodhaḥ sarvavṛtīnāṁ prānāyāmaḥ sa ucchyate। niṣedhanaṁ prapañcasya recakākhyḥa samīraṇaḥ। brahmaivāsmīti ya vṛtiḥ pūrako vāyuṛritaḥ। tatasatadvṛtinaiṣcalyaṁ kuṁbhakaḥ prānasaṁyaṁḥ। ayam capi prabuddhānāmjñānāṁ ghrāṇapīnam*।।)

exclusive robotic practices. Only when one negates duality, names, forms and variations (Recaka), embraces the Self as whole, all-pervading reality (Pūraka) and exists in the unbroken wisdom that all is the Self (Kuṁbhaka) will he attain the highest state of being. Such a person alone will have the vision of non-dualism, self-sameness and Ekātman with all existences.

12. Pratyāhāra[47]: 'Pratyāhāra' is a term used in classical Yoga to describe the withdrawal of senses from the objects of pleasure. However, for Ādi Śaṅkarācārya the absorption of the mind in the highest consciousness and realizing all entities of the world as the very 'Brahman' is said to be 'Pratyāhāra'. By realization that the animal, the human, the plants and the whole of cosmos is the Brahman, the mind becomes calm and composed. Therefore, Śaṅkara declares unequivocally that "Pratyāhāra is seeing the non-dual Self in all objects of the world". Accordingly, all objects of the world that can be denoted, represented, and indicated are the 'Brahman.'[48] Consequently, it may be concluded that Idaṅta (objects denoted by he, she, it, this, that in regards to the world) and Ahaṅtā (I, me, mine in regards to an individual) are the Brahman. While apparently, they are a manifestation of ignorance, yet they are nothing but the Brahman. Hence, real Pratyāhāra is negating dualism and embracing non-duality and forever being established in '*Sarvam Khalu Idam Brahma* (all is the Brahman)'.

13. Dhāraṇā[49]: In the traditional Yoga 'Dhāraṇā' is understood as fixing one's mind on an object, sound or maṅtra of meditation. However, for Ādi Śaṅkarācārya, Dhāraṇā refers to being established and perceiving

---

47 Deshmukh Srikrihna, pp.154-155 (V.121, *viṣyeṣvātmtāṁ dṛṣtva manasaṣcitimajjanam* । *pratyāhāraḥ sa vijñeyob hyasanīyo mumukṣubhiḥ*।।)

48 *Ibid.,*

49 *Ibid,* pp.156-157 (V.122, *yatra yatra mano yāthi brahmaṇastatra darṣanāta* । *manasó dhāraṇaṁ caiva dhāraṇā sā parāmatā*।।).

everything within and without as the Brahman. At such a stage, one sees nothing but the Brahman, hears nothing but the Brahman, and understands nothing but the Brahman. This is Supreme Dhāraṇā.

14. Ātmadhyānam[50]: In the classic Yoga 'Dhyāna' refers to uninterrupted concentration. However, for Ādi Śaṅkarācārya, Dhyāna means being soaked in the awareness of 'Aham Brahmāsmi (I am the Supreme Spirit)'. At this stage, there remains no trace of worldly dualism. The poles of opposites (likes-dislikes, pains-pleasure, mine-yours, etc.) merge into the Brahman. 'Ego' which is the basis of the material world is dissolved into the Brahman and a person becomes Ānandasvarūpa'. This is the state of Paramānanda (Highest Joy) which is attainable by concentrating on Ātman which is the foundation of the entire cosmos.

15. Samādhiḥ[51]: Samādhiḥ is the stage of absolute non-duality. At this stage, the Antahkarṇa melts away into the Ātman. All distinctions of forms and names (human, animal, tree, nature) take refuge in the Brahman and Brahman alone exists. The Vṛttijñāna (qualified knowledge attained by knower-known-knowledge) and Avidyā ceases to exist at this stage. The stage cannot be explained in words but can merely be experienced. With constant practice, one attains a state where one can enter into Samādhi at will (Icchāsamādhi).

From the above, it can be understood that Ādi Śaṅkarācārya's fifteen-fold Yoga that starts with approaching every entity of the cosmos as the Brahman and ends with melting away of all names and forms in the 'Very Brahman' can prove to be a viable solution to the current environmental chaos. These steps cannot only help a person attain a

---

50 Deshmukh Srikrihna, pp.156-157, (V.123, *brahmaivāsmīti sa dvṛtya nirālaṁbatayāsthitiḥ। dhyānaśabdena vikhyātā paramānandā yinī॥*)

51 *Ibid,* pp.157-160,(V.124, *nirvikāratayā vṛttyā brahmākāratayā punaḥ। vṛptivismaraṇaṁ samyakasamādhirjñānasaṁjñakaḥ॥*)

balanced, peaceful and harmonious environment within but can also help him in attaining the same at a social, national and cosmic level.

CONCLUSION

Ādi Śaṅkarācārya provides an exceptionally well-thought-of, well-defined, logical, and methodical step-by-step technique that can assist a person in breaking free from the shackles of dualism, animosity, envy, and suffering in order to realise the Highest Truth 'Brahman'. On this path of gradual learning, change and realization 'Sādhanacatuṣṭya' becomes the foundation of self-control, ethics, intellectual query, spiritual patience and purity. It is by imbibing these four-fold qualities that one progresses on to the path of realization. After being entrenched in Sādhanacatuṣṭya, one progresses to and goes through the discipline of Śravaṇa, Manana, Nididhayāsna and Niṣṭhā in order to realize the Self as the Supreme Principle. Further, a person also goes through the practice of negating the duality of the world (neti-neti) and finally accepting everything as the Brahman under Vyatireka-Anvaya. Conclusively, the fifteen-fold Yoga of Ādi Śaṅkarācārya allows the seeker to approach all worldly entities as the living Brahman. Eventually, all these beings melt into the Brahman and Brahman alone exists. By this practice, the seeker is established in the Ultimate Self. With this wisdom, he knows everything that one aspires to know. This is the highest and noblest of vision. At this stage, one rises above all dualities. There exist no pains, sorrows, aversions and one is rooted in Dharma. Such a person exists as a Jīvanmukta who works for the welfare of all living creatures.

Ādi Śaṅkarācārya, therefore, leaves behind the gift of valuable methodologies in the form of Sādhanā. These methods act as a step-by-step guide in order to assist the deluded being to a stage of enlightenment. These practices, without a doubt, go hand in glove with ethics, morality, and respect for all lives. These methods not only help a seeker in establishing ethical foundations before embarking on the spiritual path, but they also assist him in purifying the inner environment. Only a pristine inner environment gives us the ability to perceive the entire universe as 'The Brahman'. This internal, external, and cosmic purity of environment brings us to a point where everything is embedded in the Self and there remains perfect wisdom, bliss, consciousness and being.

Oṁ Saṃsārṇavatārakāya Namaḥ

(I bow before Śaṅkara who handholds all beings in crossing over the ocean of Saṃsāra)

6.

Ādi Śaṅkarācārya's Works in View of Environmental Harmony

Ādi Śaṅkarācārya is indisputably one of the most celebrated philosophers in the history of the world. It is His immaculate elucidation of the basic texts of Vedānta, which become the foundation for the 'Classical Advaita'. He highlighted the universality and organismic wholesomeness of the Vedas. He further amalgamated Karma, Bhakti and Jñāna and assigned to each its necessitous position in the unitary process of realizing the Ultimate Reality. All of these were rooted in the sublime philosophy of 'Non-dualism', which He expounded upon as the heart of the Upaniṣdas, Bramhasūtras and the Bhagavadagītā which are collectively known as the 'Prasthānatrayī'. These three were elucidated upon logically and lucidly in a language distinguished as 'Praśnagaṃbhīraḥ'. A voluminous body of Advaita expositions, identified as 'Prakaraṇagranthas', are also accredited to Ādi Śaṅkarācārya. These become an important part of a seeker's quest. A large number of Stotras are further ascribed to Śaṅkara. He is also said to have composed copious Bhāṣyas on Yogasūtravivaraṇa, Adhyātmapatala (Āpastaṁbadharmasūtra), Viṣṇusahasranāma (Mahābhārata, Anuśasanaparva), Lalitātriśati (Brahmaṇḍapurāṇa), Jayamaṇgalā (Sāṃkhya), and Sthirasiddhi (Nyāya).

This chapter uses twenty-three of Ādi Śaṅkarācārya's most notable works in order to emphasize the aesthetical beauty and Divinity of environment. Depending on one's circumstances and point of view, these works can be understood. The best part about these works is that one cannot only see a sense of reverence but can also see a sense of appreciation for aesthetics in order to establish environmental harmony. These works further inject the heart with Bhakti, love and compassion that leads to Jñāna gradually. It must be noted that Bhakti and love are two different terms with the same meaning. He who has love for the Supreme is bound to see the whole of Nature as the very manifestation of the Divine (Advaitamata).

With this backdrop, let's have a look at some of Ādi Śaṅkarācārya's devotional works in the light of environmental harmony.

1. Ānandalahrī: The text forms a part of Ādi Śaṅkarācārya's much-acclaimed authoritative Tāṇtrika masterpiece 'Saundaryalehrī'. The first forty-one stanzas are referred to as 'Ānandalahrī (Wave of Bliss)', while the next fifty-nine stanzas are known as Saundaryalehrī (Wave of Beauty).

Ānandalahrī contains Stotras or hymns in praise of Devī Tripurāsuṇdarī. It deals with the worship of the Supreme Being in its (feminine) aspect of eternal creative power (Ādiparāśakti) known as 'Śrīvidyā'. There are thirty-five known commentaries on the same. The stanzas are arranged in the most logical, imaginative and creative manner. They exhibit exceptional spiritual fervor, devotional vehemence, fine touches of poetical ornamentation and an insight into the mysteries of the Āgamas and the Taṇtras. They contain various Maṇtras (mystic formula) along with Yaṇtras (diagrams) dedicated to the worship of Mother Goddess for the sake of attaininnng assorted Siddhis (powers). In the glorious work, Ādi Śaṅkarācārya profusely praises the Mother Goddess and in the spirit of Bhakti compares the marvels of the material world with Her incomprehensible grandeur. He then proclaims Her to be,

'The daughter of the Great Himālayas. The One who lives in Kailāśa.[1] She has a grandiose walk like that of an elephant.[2] She shines like the newborn sun and is elegant like the female deer.[3] Her hands are like the supple blossoming flowers of the Himālayas.[4] She is Pārvatī, the plant of everlasting bliss,[5] the cause of Dharma, the root of fortune and the seed of devotion.'[6]

As a result, the material world has immense value attached to it, making it fit enough to be used as a metaphor to laud the Ultimate. Further, that which is used to praise the Lord is itself held in reverence. Therefore, when Goddess is referred to as the daughter of Himālayas, the one who stays in Kailāśa, a non-dual relationship is established between the Creator (Goddess) and the created (Himālayas, Kailāśa). Due to the creation of a pious and revered relationship between the two, the created itself becomes worthy of worship. Just as the dance and the dancer, the wave and the ocean cannot be separated likewise the 'Creator' and the 'created' are non-distinct. As a result, when we worship the created, we actually worship the Creator.

---

1 *'Anandalahari', (V.15, nivāsaḥ kailāse vidhiśatamakhādyāḥ stutikarāḥ kuṭumbaṃ trailokyaṃ kṛtakarapuṭaḥ siddhinikaraḥ maheśaḥ prāṇeśastadavanidharādhīśatanaye na te saubhāgyasya kvacidapi manāgasti tulanā)*

2 *Ibid., (V.4, virājanmandāradrumakusumahārastanataṭī nadadvīṇānādaśr avaṇavilasatkuṇḍalaguṇā natāṅgī mātaṅgī ruciragatibhaṅgī bhagavatī satī śambhorambhoruhacamulacakṣurvijayate॥)*

3 *Ibid., (V.5, navīnārkabhrājanmaṇikanakabhūṣaṇaparikaraiḥ vṛtāṅgī sāraṅgīruciranayanāṅgīkṛtaśivā। taḍitpītā pītāmbaralalitamañjīrasubhagā mamāparṇā pūrṇā niravadhisukhairastu sumukhī॥)*

4 *Ibid., (V.6 himādreḥ saṃbhūtā sulalitakaraiḥ pallavayutā supuṣpā muktābhirbhramarakalitā cālakabharaiḥ। kṛtasthāṇusthānā kucaphalanatā sūktisarasā rujāṃ hantrī gantrī vilasati cidānandalatikā॥)*

5 *Ibid., (V.7, saparṇāmākīrṇāṃ katipayaguṇaiḥ sādaramiha śrayantyanye vallīṃ mama tu matirevaṃ vilasati। aparṇaikā sevyā jagati sakalairyatparivṛtaḥ purāṇópi sthāṇuḥ phalati kila kaivalyapadavīm॥).*

6 *Ibid, (V.8, vidhātrī dharmāṇāṃ tvamasi sakalāmnāyajananī tvamarthānāṃ mūlaṃ dhanadanamanīyāṃghrikamale। tvamādiḥ kāmānāṃ janani kṛtakandarpavijaye satāṃ mukterbījaṃ tvamasi paramabrahmamahiṣī॥)*

2. Kaṇakadhārāstotram: The word Kaṇakadhārā is a combination of Saṃskrit words Kaṇaka (gold) and Dhārā (stream). As a result, it means a constant flow of gold or prosperity. The Kaṇakadhārāstotram is a twenty-one stanza hymn dedicated to the Goddess of wealth and prosperity 'Mahālakṣamī'.

In this glorious hymn, Ādi Śaṅkarācārya not only requests the Goddess to bestow material wealth and well-being upon all lives but also states that the Divine resides in the bounties of Nature. In verse fifteen, He bows to Mahālakṣamī who is the source of monetary wellness and dwells in the beauty of a lotus flower, is the earth and also the Mother of earth.[7] As a result, viewing wealth in terms of financial well-being is a very limited perspective. Beautiful flora, peaceful woods, clear air, clean water bodies, joyful animals, chirping birds, and the very soil are all examples of natural wealth. Nature's bountries are the actual wealth and possessions that should be celebrated.

3. Dakṣiṇāmūrtistotram: This outstanding work is dedicated to Lord Śiva as the Guru. 'Dakṣiṇāmūrti' is the name given to Lord Śiva's all-knowing form as the Guru. In the much celebrated ten stanza work Ādi Śaṅkarācārya bows to Dakṣiṇāmūrti who dwells in all beings as the 'Self' and is the essence of all movable and immovable beings of the world.[8] There would be no inequity, exploitation, violence, or injustice when one realizes that all stationary creatures (trees, plants, mountains, rocks, stones) and moving lives (insects, reptiles, birds, animals, people) are manifestations of one's beloved Lord. A deer will not be hunted for

7 *'Kanakdharastotrami', (V.15, namóstu kāntyai kamalekṣaṇāyai namóstu bhūtyai bhuvanaprasūtyai। namóstu devādibhirarcitāyai namóstu nandātmajavallabhāyai॥)*

8 *'Dakshinamurthyashtakam', (V.8-9, bhūrambhāṃsyanalónilómbaramaharnātho himāṃśuḥ pumān ityābhāticarācarātmakamidaṃ yasyaiva mūrtyacmakam। nānyatkiicana vidyate vimṛśatāṃ yasmātparasmādvibhoḥ tasmai śrīgurumūrtaye nama idaṃ śrīdakṣiṇāmūrtaye।)*

enjoyment, nor will an eagle be murdered for wall dècor. A hen will not be slaughtered ruthlessly for the sake of taste, nor will trees be uprooted for monetary gain.

4. Dhanyāṣṭakam: In this eight stanza work, Ādi Śaṅkarācārya concludes by stating that the one who has realized the Brahman, considers the whole world as a garden, all trees become wish-fulfilling for him, each water body becomes the Ganges and is worthy of worship and the whole of universe is realised as the divine city of Kāśī.[9] As a result, the enlightened one is rooted in non-dualism and reveres all of the creation. Such a being has no preference for any creature, place, or event. To him, all beings are the manifestation of the non-dual supreme spirit 'Brahman', and so he bows before the entire cosmos as the very 'Self'.

5. Maṇīṣāpañcakam: While the Saṃskrit word 'Maṇiṣā' means 'certainty', the word 'Pañcakam' means five. Therefore, Maṇīṣāpañcakam means the five stanzas of utmost certainty of non-dualism. In this five verse glorious work, Ādi Śaṅkarācārya states that the non-dual essence of all existences resides within men, animals and devas.[10] It is essential to comprehend that not only all beings are equal in essence but also all forms are mere appearances and all likes and dislikes are rooted in Avidyā. As a result, all entities are worthy of adoration and play a vital part in the cosmic operation as well as in our spiritual evolution. One cannot say that humans are more significant than ants because importance cannot be judged based on one's size or nature. While man has his role to play, ants also play a major role in

---

9 *Dhanyashtakam', (V.10, sampūrṇaṃ jagadeva nandanavanaṃ sarvépi kalpadrumā gāṅgaṃ vari samastavārinivahaḥ puṇyāḥ samastāḥ kriyāḥ vācaḥ prākṛtasaṃskṛtāḥ śrutiśirovārāṇasī medinī sarvāvasthitirasya vastuviṣayā dṛṣme parabrahmaṇi।।)*

10 *Manishapanchakam',(V.4, yātiryaṅnaradevatābhirahamityantaḥ sphutā gṛhyate yadbhāsā hṛdayākcadehaviṣayā bhānti svatócetanāḥ। tāṃ bhāsyaiḥ pihitārkamaṇḍalanibhāṃ sphūrtiṃ sadā bhāvaya-nyogī nirvṛtamānaso hi gururityeṣā manīṣā mama।।)*

the universe by aerating the soil and allowing the water and oxygen to reach the roots of plants.[11]

6. Vivekacuḍāmaṇi: This text stands out as one of the most remarkable works of Ādi Śaṅkarācārya. In this text, He employs humble and eloquent language. The work aims at developing a vision of intellectual discrimination for the seeker which helps him in distinguishing between the temporary and the permanent. By cultivating this vision the seeker discovers that beneath all transitory names and forms of man, animal, and tree resides the everlasting 'Brahman'.

'Vivekacūḍāmaṇi', which may be translated as 'Crest Jewel of Intellectual Discrimination,' is a compendium of 580 verses that guides the seeker towards the realization of the Highest Truth. The work appears as a dialogue between a Guru and his Śiṣya. In this work, the qualified Guru puts an end to the various doubts that a Śiṣya holds. The Guru paves a path for the disciple to follow in order to realize his non-dual nature. The text emphasizes that no ritual can lead to Self-realization.[12] Here Ādi Śaṅkarācārya means that no ritual performed robotically without devotion and realization of non-duality can lead to liberation (*liberation is the realisation of the Self as the Ultimate Principle*) and that once a being realizes the non-dual essence, no rituals are required because a Jīvanmukta's life is naturally oriented toward the welfare of all. Only when one realizes the Self in all beings and all beings in the Self, he truly will be liberated. Bhakti remains a mere robotic ritual for as long as one is caught in a web of hate and like. Unless one develops the vision and sight to see the reflection of one's beloved Lord in each creation, 'Bhakti' remains far from reaching its pinnacle.

---

11 *Hölldobler, Bert, Edward Wilson, 'The Ants', Harvard University Press, USA, 1990, pp.77.*

12 *'Vivekachudamani', (V.6, vadantu śāstrāṇi yajantu devān var devān pamhantu kurvantu karmāṇ bhajantu devatāḥ। ātmaikyabodhena vināpi muktirn sidhyati brahmaśatāntarépi॥)*

7.Bhaja Govindaṃ: This distinguished work was composed in the city of Vārāṇasī and is also known as 'Moha Mudgara' which can be translated as 'The Destroyer of illusion'. Since the work has twelve magnificent verses, it also came to be known as the 'Dvādaśamaṇjarikāstotra'. Later, Ādi Śaṅkara's fourteen disciples who were accompanying Him contributed one stanza each. These fourteen verses together came to be known as 'Caturdaúamaṇjarikāstotra'.

In this popular work, Śaṅkara suggests the deluded being to chant the name of the Lord in order to break free from the clutches of Avidyā. When He employs the word 'Muḍhamate', He is not referring to a person of low intelligence; rather, He is referring to the one who has been duped by Avidyā and believes that duality is real and absolute.[13] Such a being is filled with love for God yet vehemently fosters hate for dogs. He is blinded by his ignorance to the truth that the God he venerates and the dog he despises are both manifestations of the same Reality. Therefore, a person caught up in Rāga and Dveṣa can be liberated by chanting the Lord's name and immersing himself in Bhakti. When his Bhakti reaches its climax, he will realise that the dog he once hated is the same God that he has always loved.

8. Ātmapañcakam: Ādi Śaṅkarācārya dedicates this popular five stanza work to Lord Śiva. Drenched in the sweet nectar of Bhakti verse four and five of the same states that-

matto nānyatkiñcidatrāpsti viśvaṃ satyaṃ bāhyaṃ vastu māyopakluptam।
ādarśāntarbhāsamānasyatulyaṇ mayyadvaite bhāti tasmācchivóham।।

(This world is non-dual from me; it is similar to everything that is reflected in a mirror of the Self. The entire cosmos is within me; therefore, I am the non-dual Śiva.)

Thus, to an enlightened one, all sentient beings appear as the very body of the 'Supreme Spirit'.

---

13 *'Bhajagovindam', (V.1, bhaja govindaṃ bhaja govindaṃ govindaṃ bhaja mūhamate।)*

9. Sādhanapañcakam: This classic five-stanza hymn offers eight instructions in each verse, making a total of forty glorious teachings of non-dualism that Ādi Śaṅkarācārya expounds upon. He suggests a being to be established in the devotion of God and foster virtues.[14] In the opening verse, He states that as worship to Lord, one must commit oneself to the study of the Vedas and performing acts in the mode of service to God.[15] The five recommended actions or Nityakarmas are-***Brahmayajña:*** offerings made to the study of Vedas, sages and the Guru. ***Devayajña:*** offerings made to the Īśvara, Pañcadevopāsna, and Pañcamahābhūtopāsna. ***Pitṛyajña:*** offerings made to the deceased ancestors and taking care of parents who are alive. ***Bhūtayajña:*** offerings made to animals, insects, birds and the plant kingdom. Installing a bowl of water for birds and animals. Watering plants and feeding cows, dogs, crows, and ants daily. ***Manuṣyayajña:*** offerings made to less fortunate human beings.

10. Viṣṇusahasranāmabhāṣyam: In the much celebrated 'Śrī Viṣṇusahasranāmabhāṣyam' Ādi Śaṅkarācārya comments upon the thousand names of Lord Viṣṇu. As '*Viṣvasmai*'[16], He manifests as the entire cosmos.[17] As '*Viṣṇu*', He pervades

---

14 *'Sadhanapanchakam' (V.2-4, saṅgaḥ satsu vidhīyatāṃ bhagavato bhaktirdṛḍhā'ghīyatāṃ śāntyādiḥ paricīyatāṃ dṛḍhataraṃ karmāśu santyajyatām । santyajyatām sadvidvānupasṛpyatāṃ pratidinaṃ tatpādukā sevyatāṃ brahmaikākṣaramarthyatāṃ śrutiśirovākyaṃ samākarṇyatām ।। vākyārthaśca vicāryatāṃ śrutiśiraḥ pakśaḥsa māśrīyatāṃ dustarkātsuviramyatāṃ śrutimatastarkónusandhīyatām । brahmāsmīti vibhāvyatāmaharahargarvaḥ parityajyatāṃ dehéhammatirujjhyatāṃ budhajanairvādaḥ parityajyatām ।। śudvyādhiśca cikitsyatāṃ pratidinaṃ bhiśauṣdhaṁ bhujyatāṃ svādvannaṃ na tu yācyatāṃ vidhivaśāt prāptena vidhivaśāt prāptena santuṣyatām । śītoṣṇādi viṣahyatāṃ na tu vṛthā vākyaṃ samuccāryatā maudāsīnyamabhīpsyatāṃ janaknpānaiṣthuryamutsṛjyatām ।।)*

15 *Ibid (V.1, vedo nityamadhīyatāṃ taduditaṃ karma svanuṣṭhīyatāṃ teneśasya vidhīyatāmapacitiḥ kāmye matistyajyatām । pāpaughaḥ paridhūyatāṃ bhavasukhe doṣónusandhīyatā mātmecchā vyavasīyatāṃ nijagṛhāttūrṇaṃ vinirgamyatām ।।)*

16 Shastry Ananthakrishnan, *'Vishnusahastranama with Commentary of Shankaracharya', 1927, Name-1, p.23.*

17 *'Vishnupurana', (V.1.2.69, sa eva bhūtātmā viśvarūpa yato avyayaḥ).*

everything.[18] As '*Bhūtakṛta*', He is the creator and destroyer of all the creatures.[19] As '*Bhūtabhṛta*', He is the nourisher and sustainer of all beings.[20] As '*Bhāvah*', He is the movable and immovable entities of the world.[21] As '*Bhūtātmā*', He indwells all living beings.[22] As '*Narsiṁhavapuḥ*', He appears as half man and half lion.[23] As '*Savaḥ*', He is everything.[24] As '*Śiva*', He is the auspicious one.[25] As '*Bhūtādye*', He is the five elements.[26] As '*Āditya*', He is the sun.[27] As '*Vriśākapaye*', He manifests as the boar to uphold Dharma.[28] As '*Govinda*', He is the earth, the cow, the speech and the Vedas.[29] As '*Bhujaṅgagotamaḥ*', He is the divine serpent.[30] As '*Siṁha*', He is the lion.[31] As '*Vahniḥ, Anila and Dharṇīdharaḥ*', He is the fire, the air and the earth.[32] As '*Śaśbindu*', He is the glowing dot of the moon.[33] As '*Vāyuḥ, Rituḥ and Kāla*', He is the wind, the seasons and the time.[34] As '*Nakṣatranemi*', He is the nave of all heavenly planets.[35] As '*Bhūtameśvara*', He is the Lord of all living creatures.[36] As '*Kapīndra*', He is the lord of monkeys.[37] As '*Vṛkśa*', He is the tree.[38] As '*Gohitaḥ*',

18 Shastry Ananthakrishnan, Name-2, p.32
19 *Ibid.*, Name-5, p.33.
20 *Ibid.*, Name-6.
21 *Ibid.*, Name-7.
22 *Ibid.*, Name-8, p.34.
23 *Ibid*, Name-21, p.36.
24 *Ibid.*, Name-25, p.37.
25 *Ibid.*, 26, p.37
26 *Ibid.*, Name-29.
27 *Ibid.*, Name-39, p.38.
28 *Ibid.*, Name-101, p.47.
29 *Ibid.*, Name-187, p.58.
30 *Ibid.*, Name-193, p.59.
31 *Ibid.*, Name-200, p.60.
32 *Ibid.*, Name-233, 234, 235 pp.75-76.
33 *Ibid.*, Name-285, p.71.
34 *Ibid.*, Name-414, 416, 418, p.87.
35 *Ibid.*, Name-440, p.90.
36 *Ibid.*, Name-489, p.97.
37 *Ibid.*, Name-501, p.98.
38 *Ibid*, Name-555, p.104.

He is the friend and protector of cows.[39] As '*Kunda*' He is thc flower.[40] Therefore, He alone is one (Ekaḥ) and the many (Anekaḥ)[41] If a person contemplates upon each name of Lord, he will come to conclude that the 'Supreme' is the One behind the many and the many that originates from the One. He is the cause and the caused. Therefore, one will realize that every spec of the cosmos is the 'Divine'.

11. Viṣṇuṣaṭpadī: Viṣṇuṣaṭpadī is a six verse hymn in praise of Lord Viṣṇu in which Ādi Śaṅkarācārya bows to the Lord and tells Him to fill His heart with compassion for all living beings.[42] He compares the feet[43] and face[44] of the Lord to the lotus flower, pollen and honey. Ādi Śaṅkarācārya further praises the sun and the moon as the very eyes of the Lord[45] and reveres His incarnation as 'The Fish'.[46] He also praises Him as the 'Maṇdarācala Mountain' that became the foundation while churning of the ocean.[47] The manner in which Ādi Śaṅkarācārya praises the Lord while comparing Him to the lotus, mountain, sun, moon and reveres Him as the fish demonstrates His adoration for God and for all the forms in which He appears. The fact that Ādi Śaṅkarācārya requests Lord to fill His heart with compassion for all beings illustrates His veneration for all lives.

12. Maṇikarṇikāṣṭakam: In this splendid text Ādi Śaṅkarācārya hails the Ghātas of the Ganges and states that it is here that one can attain enlightenment.[48] He goes on

---

39 Shastry Ananthakrishnan, Name -591, p.108.

40 *Ibid,* Name -809, p.133.

41 *Ibid,* Name-725, 726, p.124.

42 Adi Shankaracharya, '*Vishnushatpadi*', Kamakoti Kanchi Peeth Publication, Kanchipuram, 2017. (V.1)

43 *Ibid.,* V.2

44 *Ibid.,* V.6

45 *Ibid,* V.4

46 *Ibid,* V.5

47 *Ibid.,* V.6

48 '*Manikarnikashtakam*', (V.1, *atha māhātmyam।anekajanmasāhasrata-podhyānaśivārcanaiḥ। advaitānandasaṅgena labdhavedāntisatpadaḥ।।*)

to extol the city of Kāṣī and refers to it as "better than the heaven above."[49] This clearly shows His reverence for the material world, which is non-distinct from its cause.

13. Gaṇgāṣtakama: In the Gaṇgāṣtakama, Ādi Śaṅkarācārya praises Mother Gaṇgā who descends from the trees of sandalwood and from the mountains of Meru, who touches the earth and fortifies it, who washes away all sins and nourishes all beings.[50] While penning down the joy of all beings, He states "bees (who are the source of honey) rush to taste your water, the elephants and little calves play and bathe in your glory, women are drenched with your holy water, devotees worship you with flowers and sages bow to you. Dear Mother! Protect us all."[51] He further highlights that the Gaṇgā nourishes all beings without any discrimination. In verse six, Ādi Śaṅkarācārya demonstrates the interconnectedness of life when He refers to the Gaṇgā as being born from the far off mountains. The verse highlights that near-far, this-that, mine-yours are untrue notions and in reality, we all are connected in the cosmic wheel. Similar thoughts can be seen in His glorious work Gaṇgāstotram.

14. Yamunāṣtakam: In this magnificent hymn Ādi Śaṅkarācārya establishes the unity of all existences by referring to Yamunā as the daughter of the Kalinda mountain who with Her playful waves washes away all sins and brings joy to all beings. He mentions that it is on the

---

49 *'Manikarnikashtakam', (V.3, ānandakānanamidaṃ sukhadaṃ puraiva tatrāpi cakrasarasi maṇikarṇikātha। svaḥsindhusaṅgatiratho paramāspadañca viśveśituḥ kimiha tanna vimuktaye yat॥)*

50 *Gangastakam', (V.3, brahmāṇaṃ khaṃayantī haraśirasi jaṭāvallimullāsayantī kharllokātāpatantī kanakagiriguhāgaṇḍśailāt skhalantī। kṣoṇī pṛṣmhe luṭhantī duritacayacamūnimṛbharaṃ bhartsayantī pāthodhiṃ purayantī suranagarasarit pāvanī naḥ punātu॥)*

51 *Ibid., (V.4, majjanamātaṃgakuṃbhacyutamadamadirā modamattālijālaṃ snānaḥ siddhāṃganānāṃ kucayugavigalat kuṃkumāsaṃgapiṇgam। sāyaṃprātarmunīnāṃ kuśakusumacayaiḥ channatīrasthanīraṃ pāya nno gāṃgamaṃbhaḥ karikalabhakarākrāntaraṃ hastaraṃgam॥)*

banks of Yamunā that the Chatka bird (Jacobin cuckoo) and the white swans reside.[52] He further praises the quiet and pure wind on the Her banks and the indescribable beauty of Her waves.[53] Therefore, one may deduce that diverse living species like to congregate in an atmosphere that is clean, calm, serene and peaceful. Sadly, today's water bodies are either unclean or dead, making it impossible to experience tranquility, fresh air or witness exotic birds and animals. Ādi Śaṅkarācārya then goes on to praise the shining sand on the banks of Yamunā which looks magnificent when the moonbeam falls on it on an autumn night. He describes how the Yamunā banks are adorned with blossoming Kadaṁba flowers (butter flower tree).[54]

The beautiful writings of Ādi Śaṅkarācārya prove His subtle and deep connection with Nature. Only when one has lived in close proximity with Nature and has formed an intimate relationship with its varied beings can he write such wise words brimming with love, beauty, and compassion.

15. Śrī Mūkaṃikā Stotram: Ādi Śaṅkarācārya praises Śrī Mūkaṃikā in this stotram stating that She alone manifests as the whole of cosmos. He prays to the Devi and associates the cause with effect by saying that,

"Śrī Mūkaṃikā manifests as the mountains, the center of the lotus flower, the color of the Baṇḍūka flower, the blue light of the moon and the pane that holds a parrot. She is the rising sun and Her eyes are the crescent of the moon. She is the one who protects and sustains everything by wielding the conch, mace, and Cakra. She remains with Lord Śiva in Tripurā. She is the afternoon sun, the bewildering Māyā, the holder of the spear, skull and the book. She is pure wisdom and the music of the dawn. Her hands

---

52 *Yamunastakam', (*V.3, *navinamādhuṅdhūriṇbhaktijāta cātaka।)*

53 *Ibid, (*V. 5, *taraḍgsḍgsakatākincitāntarā sādasitā śaranni śākrāṁ śumkjumkjrīsabhājitā। bhvārcanaya caruṇāmbynādhunā viśāradā dhunotu we manomalaṁ kalindanadivī sadā।)*

54 *Ibid., (*V.8, *tatotthaphullamalikākadaṁbareṇusūjjvalā)*

shine like the bamboo plant. She dwells in the woods and is adorned with gems. Her ears are the sun and the moon and Her face is like the white cloud. She is the consort of Maheśvara, is worshiped by Nārāyaṇa and is praised by the Vedas, Purāṇas and all other Divine texts. She appears as the Vindhyā Mountain and is the lightning in the skies. She is the One who is the entire world and soul of the cosmos. She alone preserves and redeems all Jīvas. She exists in the Mūlādhāra, Svādhiṣthāna, Maṇipura, Anāhata, Viṣuddha, Ajnā and Sahastra and is the unity of all. She is the Śrī Cakra and the potency of all Mantras."[55]

From the above it is not difficult to deriul cosmic & environmental worth, Values & renevenel. One can lucidly see That it is the 'One' who appears as many.

16. Hymn to Harī-Harā: While passing through the state of Mahārāṣtra and Āndhrapradeśa, Śaṅkara reached the Divine Jyotir Liṅga of Śrīśailam where He offered His prayers to Lord Śiva who rests there as Mallikārjuna and then reached the town of Gokarṇa[56] in Karnātaka. At this place, Śaṅkara worshiped Śiva as Mahābaleśvara. He then moved to Harśaṅkara temple situated at the Gandhamardhan hills in Orissa where He worshiped the combined form of Śiva and Viṣṇu that depict non-duality of the Supreme Spirit. In the glory of Harī-Harā, He dedicated an eleven verse hymn to the Supreme in accordance with Śāṅkaradigvijay[57],

---

55 (i) Ramchander P.R, 2015,'*Śāī Mūkaṃikā Strotam'*, Online, Strotra Ratna, http://stotrarathna.blogspot.com/2015/12/sri-stotram-translated-by-p.html., (Accessed April 10, 2021)

(ii) Vidyaranya Mdhava, Swami Tapasyananda(Tr) pp.139-140.

56 *'Gokarna'* lies in the state of Karnataka and the word is a derivative of Saṃskrita words 'Go (cow)' + 'Karna (ear)'. Thus, the word 'Gokarna' means 'the ear of a cow'. However, a deeper contemplation on the word will bring us to a conclusion that it refers to the ear shaped adjoining of two rivers namely- Gangavali and Aghanashani. It is believed that Lord Shiva had appeared frm the ear shaped land that exists between the adjoining rivers. According to the Srimad Bhagvad Purana, the place 'Gokarna' was home to two brothers- Gokarna and Dhundhakari.

57 Vidyaranya Mdhava, Swami Tapasyananda (Tr), pp.136-139.

"I bow to the Supreme Spirit Śiva whose head is decorated with the shining moon, who holds His Naṇḍī dear and who sits with Mother Pārvatī. He alone manifests as the entire cosmos and whose abode is the glorious Mount Kailāśa. He is decorated with the Mandāra flowers and wears Vāsukī around His neck. He is the One who drank the Halāhala to protect all. He is the Supreme Spirit whose five faces depict the five great elements. He alone upholds the Gaṅgā in His matted locks and protects the Devas by killing the demon of ignorance-Gajāsura. May the Great God who destroyed Kāmdeva lead us from darkness unto light. May the cosmic dancer Natarāja who is Himself Mokṣa and Dharma bestow us with wisdom and grace. I worship the brilliance of Mahādeva who is all-knowing, who is the slayer of Māra, the one who resides in Kāṣī and who is wisdom Himself.

I bow to the Supreme Spirit Viṣṇu who manifests as the 'Fish' in the cosmic waters. He is the divine 'Trtoise' who supported the Samudra Maṇthana in the form of the Maṇdāra Mountain. He alone appears as the 'Cosmic' Boar and 'Narsiṃha', the destroyer of demon king Hirṇyākṣyapa and the protector Prahlāda. He incarnates as the 'Brahmcārī Vamana' for the protection of the world from the demon Bāli. He also was born as the fierce 'Parśurāma', the 'Great Rāma' with His consort Sītā in order to end Rāvana and as the voice of eternal Dharma 'Balrāma'. He is the one who holds dear the king of birds Garuḍa and seems fearsome to those who are evil. As 'Kṛṣṇa', He is adorned with peacock feathers and appears enchanting. He alone is the One who manifests as 'Buddha', the one who defeated Māra, is wise, kind and is appreciated by those who oppose the Yajña. As 'Kālkī' He will end all evils to restore 'Dharma' with His unmatched splendor.

I bow to 'Śiva-Viṣṇu' who are the non-dual Supreme Spirit!"

From the above it can be comprehenced that for the restoration of 'Dharma,' the Supreme Spirit can appear not only as a human but also as an animal, reptile or tree depending upon The time and see of the hour.

17. Praśnottara Ratna Mālikā: This is one of the most overwhelming works of Ādi Śaṅkarācārya. In merely sixty-seven verses, He puts an end to all the uncertainties and inquisitiveness of a seeker. The glorious work addresses various questions including those related to spirituality, religion, ethics, morals, as well as the ones concerning compassion, humans, animals, and all other species. This work can surely be a foundation for non-dual awareness. One may readily discover references that can be applied to today's societal vices and can aid the fight against environmental vulnerability, animal abuse, and other issues. Let's have a look,

"Indeed, it is 'Life' that is dear to all beings.[58] The most cherished virtue of all is compassion towards all living beings.[59] Love and compassion are indeed the virtues that please the celestial Devas.[60] Blind is he who commits evil despite knowing it.[61] A virtuous character is indeed a revered ornament.[62] Cow is the mother of all beings.[63] The most heinous is 'Hiṃsā' itself.[64] The dearest to Lord is he who never causes pain to others." [65]

18. Nṛsiṁha Tāpanīya Upaniṣda Bhāṣyam: In this work Ādi Śaṅkarācārya bows in reverence to Lord Nrsiṁha who appears as half man and half lion. This aspect can alternatively be seen as the mutual coexistence of all entities for the operation of Dharma. It also implies that God is not restricted to appearing as a human, but may also take the shape of an

58 Adi Shankaracharya, Sharma Vandana and J.Thirumal (Tr and Commentary), '*Prashnottara Ratna Malika*', Origionals Publication, Delhi, 2019, p.84. (V.12.3, *'asavaḥ'*)

59 *Ibid.,* p.114. (V.16.1, *karuṇā dineṣu; sajjane maitrī*)

60 *Ibid.,* p.130. (V.19, *dayā pradānāya*)

61 *Ibid.,* p.137. (V.21, *yogākrya rataḥ*)

62 Ibid., p.147. (V.22.2, *śilam*)

63 Bhagvadpada Shankara, Prama Kruna Devi (Tr), '*Prashnottara Ratna Malika*', Jagganath Vallabh Vedic Research Centre, Orissa, 2016, pp.69-70. (V.40.1, *ḍhenuḥ*)

64 *Ibid.,* pp.74-75. (V.42.1, hiṁsa)

65 *Ibid.,* (p.75. (V.42.2, *yónyaṁ na udvejyate anudviṅgḥ*)

animal, human-animal, tree, or any other living creature for the sake of re-establishment and preservation of Dharma, depending on the place, time, and circumstance. As a result, reverence for all lives should be the foundation of one's existence. Here, Ādi Śaṅkarācārya begins by referring to Lord Ṇrsiṁha as Śiva, He further calls Him Paśupati (the Lord of animals including humans) and then refers to Him as Viṣṇu.[66] He with His power makes all men, Bhūtas and animals play and act.[67] In verse three, Ādi Śaṅkarācārya says that "There is nothing in the cosmos that is not Him, He alone exists as the sun, moon and fire"[68] Further, it is stated that all Devas, all beings and all Bhūtas shine because of His luster.[69] In the beginning, He alone existed and then He became all this (the world). Everything comes from Him exists in Him, and merges into Him.[70] Ādi Śaṅkarācārya also states that Lord Ṇrsiṁha is present in the entire cosmos but lives on the mountain.[71] Here, 'Mountain' is used as a metaphor for the 'Highest Reality'. He further referrers to the Lord as the Ākāśa, the source from which all living beings emerge, in which they live and into which they disintegrate.[72] As a result, it is reasonable to conclude that divinity is all-pervasive, and all beings (humans, animals, birds, trees, mountains, rivers, and even objects) are rooted in the light of Divinity.

19. Upadeśasahasri: In this celebrated text, Ādi Śaṅkarācārya uses two characters; Guru and Śiṣya to communicate one thousand splendid teachings that are spread over nineteen valuable chapters and are divided into prose and poetry. The work not just features the teachings

---

66 '*Narsimha Purva Tapaniya Upanishad Bhashyam*', (V.1)

67 *Ibid.*, Second Upanishad, (V.2)

68 *Ibid.*, (V.3)

69 *Ibid.*, V.4)

70 *Ibid.*, (V.5)

71 *Ibid.*, (V.6)

72 *Ibid.*, (Third Upanishad)

of non-dualism but also goes on to emphasize the preliminary codes of ethics and morals that are to be observed for the realization of the highest non-dual state. Thus, one can easily witness a sense of unmatched compassion in this glorious work. The text undoubtedly stands in favor of environmental care and compassion if seen from a holistic perspective. The text highlights that,

'All these creatures, be it a tiger or any other are the 'Ultimate One'. By comprehension of non-difference one continues to be in a state of transmigration and accepts all names and forms as the non-dual Highest Truth. Anyone who perceives existence in terms of hierarchies or classes, and regards himself as separate from these beings, remains unaware of his/her identity with the Supreme Self. [73] ***'I have assumed various bodies as humans, animals and insects.'*** [74] ***The Supreme Ruler not just created all these names and forms but also thought 'Let me enter into these creatures and live through them'. Thus, 'The Supreme Self' is not only all these names and forms but is also concealed in them."*** [75] ***I bow down to the all-pervading, all-knowing consciousness that resides in the heart of all creatures and all objects of the world.*** [76] ***The Supreme Brahman is the same in all creatures.*** [77] ***When all elements (Pañcabhūtas) either external or the ones present in the body are seen as the 'Self', there remains no distinction and only 'Self' exists.*** [78]

From the above-said verses, one can see the lucid spirit of compassion which is part-less and wholesome. Throughout the text, one can see various verses that stand in favor of

---

73 Swami Jagadananda(Tr), '*Updeshasahesri: Prose and Poetry of Shankaracharya*', Sri Rama Krishna Matha, Madras, 1949, pp.18-119. (V.29)

74 *Ibid.*, pp.8-9. (V.1.1.16)

75 *Ibid.*, pp.15-16. (V.23)

76 *Ibid.*, p.79. (V2.1.1)

77 *Ibid.*, p.105. (V 2.8.6)

78 *Ibid.*, pp.107-108. (V.2.9.2)

environmental harmony. The text raises all entities to the highest spirit 'Brahman' at a transcendental sphere.

20. Aprokṣānubhūtī: This work is one of the most acclaimed treatises of Ādi Śaṅkarācārya. It not only deals with the core philosophy of non-dualism but also deals with the application of the same in one's day-to-day life for the realization of the Highest Principle. Further, in this work, Ādi Śaṅkarācārya uniquely presents the Aśtāṅgayoga practices in the light of Advaita Vedānta in fifteen glorious steps. The work focuses on the identity between the individual Self and the Cosmic Self. Here, the term 'Individual' should not be seen as limited to only the human species rather it refers to all entities of the cosmos that are in essence 'The Brahman'.

21. Bhagavadagītābhāṣyam: The much sought-after Bhagvadgītābhāṣya is impregnated with references of non-duality and compassion. The pinnacle of the same is evident in chapter twelve-

"The one who sees me in all creatures without any hate or animosity, the one who sees me in those who have caused harm, the one who sees me in all lives as the non-dual Self, the one who fosters friendliness and compassion towards all beings, the one who no creature fears, the one who remains tranquil in joys and sorrows, the one who is free from likes and dislikes, and the one who forgives everyone is my beloved devotee. The one who is unaffected by the poles of opposite, who accepts profits and losses as my will, who remains single-pointed, who has immovable faith, who surrenders to me completely is dear to me and to him I am dear. He who is free from fear and from whom none fears, who is joyous and happy by the progress of others, is adored by me. Who has no preferences, who is pure within and without, who is dutiful and skilled, who refrains from any sort of discrimination, who surrenders all his Karmas to me and in me, he is my cherished devotee. He who is never elated by joy nor is he depressed due to

sufferings, he who remains calm and composed, he who has given up all desires, the one who is beyond auspicious and inauspicious is my cherished devotee."[79]

22. Brahmasūtrabhāṣya: As mentioned earlier that Ādi Śaṅkarācārya doesn't specifically talk of environment in the Brahmasūtrabhāṣya if one understands the term environment in the limited sense. However, one must understand this in a broader sense. Since He sees no distinction in the Self, He avoids specifications. Just because He doesn't use the word 'Woman' in the Bhāṣya, one can't boil down to the conclusion that the work is neither meant nor can be applied to women. Thus, when Ādi Śaṅkarācārya uses the word 'Jīva', it is to be understood that the same applies to every entity of the cosmos in a general sense. Also, through implication based upon His statement mentioned below one can conclude that wherever Brahman appears with attributes it is worthy of worship and whoever sees variedness destines himself to the cobweb of birth and death,

"It may be deduced from 'Śrutatvāccha' that the all-knowing Brahman is the first cause of the world. The Upaniṣdas speak of Brahman as Saguṇa and Nirguṇa. Wherever Brahman appears with attributes, it is to be worshiped.[80] ***He goes from death to death for there exists no manifoldness"***[81]

Prof. Srinivas Rao remarkably expands his vision and propounds in his article '*Advaita as the Foundation of Morality*',

---

[79] *Adi Shankaracharya, 'Shrimadbhagvadgita Bhashya', Manav Prabodh Pranyasa, Bikaner, 2019,pp.191-192. (V.12.13-12.17, adveṣṭā sarvabhūtānām maitraḥ karuṇaeva ca । nirmamo nirahaṅkāraḥ samaduḥkhasukhaḥ kṣamī ॥ santuṣṭaḥ satatam yogi yatātmā dṛḍhaniścayaḥ। mayya arpitamanobuddhir yo madbhaktaḥ sa me priyaḥ॥ yasmān nodvijate lokolokān nodvijate ca yaḥ। harṣāmarṣa bhayodvegairmukto yaḥ sa ca me priyaḥ।) anapekṣaḥ śucir dakṣa udāsīno gatavyathaḥ। sarvārambha parityāgī yo madbhaktaḥ sa me priyaḥ। yo na hṛṣyati na dveṣṭi na śocati na kāṅkṣati। śubhāśubha parityāgī bhaktimān yaḥ sa me priyaḥ।)*

[80] Swami Vishveshwarananda, '*Brahmasutrabhashya*', Advaita Ashrama, Kolkata, 2014, pp.36-37. (S.1.1.11, *śrutatvāccа॥*).

[81] *Ibid.*, p.28. (S.1.1.4) (also see *Kaṭha Upaniṣad* 2.4.11).

"Unequal and unfair treatment extends much beyond the strict confines of human society. It is a well-known fact that animals do not receive any kind of fair treatment at the hands of humans. It is only a few years ago that the west started recognizing animals as conscious beings and began accepting that they also exhibit intelligence and emotions just like humans. This however was a recognized fact in India long ago and can be seen through Śaṅkara's statement in His famous Adhyāsabhaṣya on the Brahmasūtra that transactions involving objects (pramāṇa-prameya-vyavahāra) are common to both men and animals. This is why animals run away from those who approach them with a stick while they eagerly approach those who are compassionate towards them. The treatment that we meet out towards animals is due to being rooted in difference (Avidyā/ duality) which we all seem to value and celebrate. However, these differences have deadly consequences."[82]

23. Upaniṣdabhāṣya: Ādi Śaṅkarācārya's Upaniṣdabhāṣya's are well decorated with verses of compassion towards Nature and its sentient beings. Verses such as 'your own Self is within all'[83], 'all is the Brahman'[84], 'the wise look at all beings in the Self and the Self in all beings'[85], 'I am One and I become many'[86], 'It is from the Brahman that all beings are born'[87] point towards non-dualism, cosmic reverence which in no way excludes environmental wellness. Further, in chapter-6 of the Taittiriyaopaniṣdabhāṣya, 'Brahman' is said to be the source of all.[88] In chapter-12 (Udgīta of Dogs), a white dog has been announced as the symbol of 'Prāṇa'.[89] The Chāndogyaopaniṣdabhāṣya recommends one to meditate on

---

82 Swami Gyanananda Sarasvati, pp.353-354.

83 Swami Mdhavananda, p.466-467. (V.3.4.1)

84 *Ibid.*, p.466-467. (V.3.4.1)

85 Joshi, Bimali, Trivedi, pp.2-3. (V.6)

86 Jha Ganganatha, pp.304-305. (V.6.2.3)

87 Swami Nikhilananda, p.67. (V.3.1.1)

88 *Ibid.*, p.51. (V.2.6.1)

89 *Ibid.*, pp146-47. (V.1.2.5)

the rain as the Brahman,[90] water as the Brahman,[91] seasons as the Brahman,[92] animals as the Brahman,[93] and the sun as the Brahman.[94] In the Aittariyaopaniṣdabhāṣya, it is propounded that 'the five elements, horses, cattle, elephants, men, creatures that fly, move and do not move have consciousness which is the Brahman'.[95] Therefore, one can see a sense of all-encompassing reverence, value and compassion in the Upaniṣdabhāṣyas of Ādi Śaṅkarācārya.

CONCLUSION

The reasons and sources presented above support the conclusion that Ādi Śaṅkarācārya had a profound understanding of 'Mother Nature'. His writings throw light on the intimate relationship that He shared with rivers, cities, mountains, animals, trees and all beings of the cosmos.

If one carefully comprehends His works, one will come to conclude that He not only shared a deep bond with various sentient entities but He also observed and studied them minutely. The conclusion of His observation and relationship with environment is highlighted in His writings when He uses sentient beings as a metaphor (i.e. rivers, flowers, animals, sun, moon and more) to express the indescribable glory of the Highest Reality 'Īśvara'. It becomes very clear from His writings that He considers a lotus petal to be the most appropriate expression of 'Lord's' soft and supple skin and so He must have realized aesthetic perfection in it. Likewise, when He compares the walk of the Goddess with an elephant, He must have seen, evaluated, pondered, and come to the conclusion that only the magnificent walk of an elephant can adequately express the grandeur of Devi's walk.

---

90 Swami Nikhilananda, p.155 (V.2.2.3).

91 *Ibid.*, p. 156. (V.2.2.4)

92 *Ibid.*, p.157. (V.2.2.5)

93 *Ibid.*, p. 158. (V.2.2.6,)

94 *Ibid.*, p. 218. (V.3.19.4)

95 Swami Gambhirananda, p.71. (V.3.1.3)

Only someone who embraces, appreciates, observes, and has a profound relationship with Nature can write hymns as eloquently as Ādi Śaṅkarācārya does. His works are rooted in reverence for all beings. On a mundane level, they vividly emphasize the aesthetic value and inherent worth of these sentient creatures, and on a transcendental level, they realize them as the Supreme Spirit.

Oṁ Sarvalokahitotsukhāya Namaḥ

(I bow before Śaṅkara who causes the welfare of all creatures.)

7.
Ādi Śaṅkarācārya's Establishments in View of Environmental Harmony

Ādi Śaṅkarācārya not only propagated a philosophy that could be employed to any sphere of life in order to realize harmony but He also made practical endeavors that could become the source of attaining a world installed in the purity of inner and outer environment. In His own profound words, He states,

yeṣām vṛttiḥ samāvṛddhā paripakvā ca sa punaḥ।
te vai sad brahmatām prāptā netare śabdavādinaḥ॥[1]
(Those alone who realize the 'Self' evolve fully into the Brahman while others who merely use words (talk for the sake of proving points) never attain this stage.)

The preceding verse emphasises that Ādi Śaṅkarācārya gave utmost importance to practical efforts and experiences and discarded mere philosophical sermons, proving empty points, and intellectual speculations. Undoubtedly, Ādi Śaṅkarācārya's philosophical contribution has established the foundation of India's identity; nevertheless, it is important that His practical contribution should be recognised and viewed in the context of environmental congruence, awareness, and consciousness. Therefore, this chapter makes a positive endeavor to elaborate on Ādi Śaṅkarācārya's

---

1 Swami Vimuktananda, '*Aprokshanubhuti of Shri Shankaracharya*', Advaita Ashram,Himalayas,1938. pp.71-72

practical efforts that can assist in coping with environmental deterioration on an internal, external, and cosmic level.

7.1. The Chaturāmnāya Pīthams (Four Maṭhas) and their Environmental Significance

In the four directions, Ādi Śaṅkarācārya established the four Maṭhas that are the four spiritual centers of the country. In Indian tradition, 'Spirituality or Divinity' is all-pervasive, indwelling, and that in which the entire cosmos is rooted. It is material and transcendental, temporary and permanent, limited and unlimited. To consider these spiritual centres as places for mere cultural events, religious activities, and discourses is reducing the very understanding and purpose for which these centres were set up. In the Maṭhāmnāyasetu, which is also referred to as the Mahānuśāsanam, Ādi Śaṅkarācārya states,

kevalaṁ dharmudiśye vibhavo brahmacetasāma ।
vihitaścopkārya prajñpatranyaṁ vrajeta ॥[2]

(Only for the sake of Dharma, its glory and Supreme Consciousness the majesty is conferred upon them (present Śaṅkarācārya) who must act like a lotus leaf in the water with benevolence towards all lives.)

It should be emphasized that the aim of establishing the four Maṭhas was to,

- Establish centres in four directions that could assist in realizing the 'Self,' and were ecologically, geographically, spiritually most ideal locations for the comprehensive growth of an individual, community, and nation.
- To conserve and maintain the region's natural-environmental aura, which comprised the air, water, soil, trees, rivers, mountains, animals, birds, and ecology. The goal was to preserve a sense of balance, serenity, and harmony both externally and internally.

2 Mishra Parmeshvarnatha Nath (Com) '*Adi Shankaracharya's Mathanushasanam Setu or Mahanushasanam*', Shankaracharya Memorial Trust, Dwarka, 2001, V.54, p.38. (V.54)

- For the spiritual growth and well-being of all living creatures. The goal was to educate the human race about life, responsibilities, duties, and gradually alter their attitude toward themselves, their families, the environment (both internal and external), and the universe while eventually guiding them to the ultimate realization.
- To promote environmental reverence through 'Nature Worship' of mountains, rivers, sea, air, fire, animals, trees, the performance of Yajña, and more.
- For the sake of cultural exchange throughout India. It is to be noted that when people from South will travel to North and vice-versa it will lead to cultural exchange and respect for each other.
- To disseminate authentic and unaltered Vedic wisdom for the attainment of universal peace and harmony.
- To bind all living creatures together in a single thread and to enable the human race with the ability to recognize the eternal in the ephemeral.
- To protect Bhāratavarṣa's frontiers against external invasions by ensuring that there remained continuous activity on the borders owing to spiritual and religious events, ceremonies, discourses, and meetings.
- For the sake of economic upsurge and financial prosperity. It is to be comprehended that when people travel, there will be an economic boost for all macro and micro businesses.
- To leave a historical mark through these centres of living traditions and to teach future generations about compassion, non-dualism, and universal brotherhood.
- Through these centres, guide the society on the path of Dharma. These centres could assist humans during emergencies related to ethics, crimes, environmental deterioration, educational invasions and more by highlighting the non-dual essence of all lives.

Therefore, the Maṭhas were not established for the welfare and well-being of the human race alone. Contrary to the West where philosophy, ethics, and religion not just exist as separate but are also human-centric, Indian traditions view 'Humans' as an extremely small part of the whole. In this way, we have always seen the cosmos having multiple centres and each life as wholesome in itself. Each life has its own Svabhāva, Dharma and as a result, it has its worth in the larger scheme. It is therefore important to realize that the establishment of Maṭhas was not a random activity but was well thought and flawlessly executed. It is for this reason that not just the four Vedas are associated with each Maṭha but even a 'River' is connected with each centre exclusively (Mahānadī, Tuṇgabhadrā, Gomtī, Alakhanandā). Moreover, each centre is established alongside natural icons, i.e. snow clad mountains (Himālayas, Jyotirmaṭha), Mahodadhi (Bay of Bengal, Purīmaṭha), forests, waterfalls (Narsiṃha Vana, Śriṅgerīmaṭha), and sea (Siṅdhūmahāsāgara, Okhmaṇdala Peninsula, Dwārkāmaṭha). It will be desirous to throw light on the environmental significance of these four Maṭhas.

1. Dwārkā Kālikā Maṭha: It lies in the Western part of India on the Okhamaṇdala Penninsula at the mouth of the Gulf of Kutch. At the Western end, it faces the Arabian Sea (Sindhusāgara).[3] The ancient city of Dwārkā situated along the coast of Gujarat was also referred to as Mokṣapurī.[4] The possible reason why Dwārkāṣetra was elected by Ādi Śaṅkarācārya for the establishment of the 'Pascimāmnāya Maṭha' is due to the value that it holds historically, culturally, geographically, and environmentally. It is one of the seven sacred cities that find mention in the Garuḍapurāṇa.[5] The

3 Wikipedia contributors,2002 '*Arabian Sea*', Online, Wikipedia, https://en.wikipedia.org/wiki/Arabian_Sea. (Accessed on 13 April 2021)

4 Wikipedia contributors, 2004 '*Dwarka*',Online, Wikipedia, https://en.wikipedia.org/wiki/Dwarka. (Accessed on 13 April 2021)

5 Garudapurana, Ch.14, V.114
(अयोध्या मथुरा माया काशी कांची अवन्तिका। पुरी द्वारावती चैव सप्तैते मोक्षदायका:।।)

name is believed to be given by Lord Kṛṣna and connotes to 'Gateway to wisdom/ liberation.'

The first Śaṅkarācārya appointed by Ādi Śaṅkarācārya for this Maṭha was Hastāmalakācārya.[6] The Maṭha is allied with the Sāmaveda[7] along with the Mahāvākya '*tat tvam asi* (You are That)'.[8] The Maṭha is related to the Tirtha and Āṣrama Sampradāyas.[9] Further, Mother Gomatī is associated with the Maṭha[10] in terms of river. Mother Gomatī holds immense importance for the people of Sanātana Dharma. It is one of the important tributaries of Gaṇgā. It is believed that Mother Gomatī is home to 'Gomatī Chakra' an exquisite circular sea snail belonging to the Turbinidae family of snails.[11] The Gomatī Chakra is a natural form of Yaṅtra that points towards Supreme Consciousness. It is on the divine Ghāts of River Gomatī that Lord Kṛṣna had served Sage Durvāsa, who was an ardent devotee of Lord Śiva. The river also finds mention in the Nāḍsūkta of the Ṛgveda.[12] The great epic Māhābhārata makes a reference to the river as a place of pilgrimage.[13] Further, the Skaṇdapurāṇa has a complete chapter dedicated to the glory of Mother Gomatī.[14]

The Maṭha also stands close to Bet Dwārkā[15], an island dedicated to Lord Śiva, where Viṣṇu in the form of 'Matsya (fish)' killed the demon Śaṅkhāsura.[16] Further, the Maṭha was located near the 'Raivataka Mountain' which finds

---

6 Swami Gyananada Saraswati , p.210

7 Mishra Parmeshvarnatha Nath (Com), p.4. (V.3)

8 *Ibid.*, (V.4)

9 Swami Gyananada Saraswati, p.210.

10 Mishra Parmeshvarnatha Nath (Com), p.4. (V.4)

11 Barbosa Duarte, "*A Description of the Coasts of East Africa and Malabar*", Johnson Reprint Corporation,London, 19701.

12 Rigveda (10.75.6)

13 Mahabharata (3.85.5, 6.10.17)

14 Skandapurana, '*Chapter 62 - The Glory of GomatÓ KuG a*'

15 Wikipedia contributors, 2004 '*Dwarka*',Online.

16 *Ibid.*

mention in the epic Māhābhārata[17] and the Harivaṃśapurāṇa.[18]

This Maṭha has a dedicated Gauśālā for the protection of cows. It is also dedicated to the preservation of flora and fauna. Sadly, the entire area surrounding the Maṭha is now affected by population explosion, urban growth, coastal erosion, wildlife destruction, etc. that is leading to environmental haphazard.

The Maṭha has a glorious past. However, not many people are aware of its history, culture, and philosophy which are also linked to its geographical placement and environmental importance. An effort to introduce the common man to his glorious past can become a viable solution in dealing with the environmental chaos that is negatively affecting the entire region.

2. Govardhan Purī Maṭha: It rests in the East of India.[19] The first Śaṇkarācārya appointed by Ādi Śaṅkarācārya for this Maṭha was Padmapādācārya[20]. The Ṛg Veda[21] is associated with this Maṭha along with the Mahāvākya '*prajñānam brahma* (The Consciousness is Brahman)'.[22] The Maṭha takes in its sphere the states of Jharkhand, Bihar, Chattisgarh, Orissa, Andhra Pradesh, Bangladesh, West Bengal, Mizoram, Sikkim, Nepal, Tripura, Bhutan, Meghalay, Manipur and Uttar Pradesh including Gaya and Banaras. The River 'Mahānadī'[23] is connected with this Maṭha along with Araṇya and Vana Sampradāyas. The Maṭha is not merely a place of learning, teaching, religion and culture but has

17 Mahabharata, Adiparva, Ch.217, V.8

18 Nagar Shanti Lal, '*Harivamshapurana,* Vol.2', Eastern Book Linkers, Delhi, 2012, p.551

19 Mishra Parmeshvarnatha Nath (Com) p.7. (V.10)

20 *Ibid.,* (V.11)

21 *Ibid.,* (V.13)

22 *Ibid.,* (V.12)

23 *Ibid.*

immense importance in terms of being a place of environmental purity both internally and externally.

The Purī Maṭha follows traditions and rituals that are meant for cosmic environmental harmony. One such ritual is the daily worship of the sea. This daily fire offering to the sea is known as 'Samudrāratī'[24] which is performed by the disciples of the present Śaṅkarācārya. A Mahāratī dedicated to the sea also takes place annually on the Pauṣa Pūrṇimā by the Śaṅkarācārya Himself. Pauṣa Pūrnimā marks the end of winters and the beginning of summers. Pūrnimā or full moon day holds an important place in the Vedic culture as it divides the month into two Pakṣas (parts)-Śuklapakṣa and Kṛṣṇpakṣa. Pūrṇimā is a time when the sun, moon and earth are in a perfect line and the angle between the sun and moon is zero degree (the opposite side of the earth from the sun and the bright side of the Moon is facing the earth). During Pūrnimā the moon is completely illuminated and it leads to high tides in the water bodies.

The colossal water body that is worshiped is called 'Sāgarasvargadvāra or the gateway to heaven',[25] this is so because it is water that sustains all beings of the earth and if this water is revered, respected and regarded it will become a gateway to a world that is heavenly. In such a world all beings of different names and forms will be nourished and sustained by this water. When this water will nourish Mother Earth, the trees, the insects, the birds, the animals and the humans, it will not only lead to a healthy, happy and harmonious environment externally but will also become a source of peace, calm and harmony within. It is also to be understood that the vastness of the sea symbolizes the infinite cosmos and the Divine which we hold in reverence and bow down to.

---

24 Wikipedia contributors, 2012, '*Pancha Teertha-Puri*', Online,https://en.wikipedia.org/wiki/Pancha Tirtha of Puri. (Accessed on 13 April 2021)

25 *Ibid.*

The Maṭha continues to works for the welfare of all sentient beings. It is working tirelessly for the protection and preservation of Gaumātā.[26] It is also involved in the protection of various rivers, plants, trees, animals and the Rāmasetu. The present Śaṅkarācārya of the Maṭha Svāmī Niṣcalānanda Sarasvatī states,

"One can realize Parmātmā who is devoid of any distinctions by revering the distinctions of nature."[27] Gau-mātā's gentle nature should be an inspiration for compassion, forgiveness, non-violence and non-enmity towards all living beings."[28]

3. Jyotir Maṭha: The Maṭha lies in the Northern[29] part of India. It cradles in the lap of the magnificent Himālayās and is the Uttarāmnāyamaṭha. The sacred Alakhanaṅdā nourishes the entire region of the Maṭha.[30] The first Śaṅkarācārya appointed by Ādi Śaṅkarācārya for this Maṭha was Toṭakācārya.[31] It is associated with the Atharvaveda[32] along with the Mahāvākya '*ayamātmā brahma* (The ātman is Brahman)'.[33] The Maṭha is related to the Girī, Parvata and Sāgara Sampradāyas.[34]

The Maṭha works for the joint welfare of humans, animals, Vanaspatī and adds to the quality of environment by following the pūjāpaddhathī as established by Ādi Śaṅkarācārya. It also prides itself with a 2400-year-old Mulberry tree, which is

---

26 Govardhan Matha, 2020, *'Cow Protection'*, Online , Govardhan Peeth, https://govardhanpeeth.org/en/activities-en. (Accessed on 13 April 2021)

27 *Ibid.*

28 *Ibid.*

29 Mishra Parmeshvarnatha Nath (Com), p.10. (V.18)

30 *Ibid.*, (V.21)

31 *Ibid.*, (V.20)

32 *Ibid.*, (Com), (V.22)

33 *Ibid.*,(p.10 (V.18 ; V.21)

34 *Ibid.*, (Com), p.10. (V.19)

known as 'Kalpavṛkṣa'[35] and remains green throughout. It is here that Ādi Śaṅkarācārya meditated on Lord Śiva and then established the Jyotirmaṭha. The Liṅgam has now been covered and the temple is known as '*Jyoteśvara Mahādeva Maṅdira*'.[36] The Kalpavṛkṣa covers the whole of the temple with a radius of 21.5 meters.[37] Today, the Indian Armed Forces are responsible to protect and preserve this tree, which has a historical, cultural, philosophical, spiritual and religious worth.[38] If we philosophically try to interpret the significance of the tree, we will conclude that,

'When one elects the path of wisdom, he becomes a replica of the Kalpavṛkṣa that lives for the well-being of all. Without discrimination of animal, or human and without any desire, it blesses everyone with shade, fruit, medicine, calmness, peace and rejuvenating energy. This selfless service makes it evergreen. If humans imbibe these valuable lessons from the Kalpavṛkṣa, they too will be established in immortality.'

The Kalpavṛkṣa for thousands of years silently continues to add value and aesthetic beauty to the environment. It is a source of relief and peace to all beings who take refuge in it. The tree that everyone bows down to continues to be one with nature and nature remains one with it.

The Maṭha also stands near the Tapovana. The word Tapovana means 'a forest of austerities, spiritual practices or penance grove.'[39] Tapovan has exotic plants, trees and deep woods and holds value at a mundane, spiritual, transcendental and aesthetical level.

---

35 Limaye Anita, 2006 '*Visit the 2,400 year old Kalpavriksh*', Online, The Economic Times, https://economictimes.indiatimes.com/visit-the-2400-year-old-kalpavriksh/articleshow/1600283.cms. (Accessed on 13 April 2021)

36 *Ibid.*

37 *Ibid.*

38 *Ibid.*

39 Shivamahapurana, 2.2.5

4. Śriṅgerī Maṭha: The Maṭha lies in the Southern slice of India.[40] The name 'Śriṅgerī'is derived from Riṣyaśriṇgagirī, a hill that is near the Maṭha and which finds mention in the great epic Rāmāyaṇa (Bālakāṇda).[41] The first Śaṅkarācārya appointed by Ādi Śaṅkarācārya for the Maṭha was Sureśvarācārya. It is associated with River Tuṇgabhadrā[42] along with the Mahāvākya '*aham brahmāsmi*'[43] and the Yajurveda.[44] The Maṭha is related to the Sarasvatī, Bhāratī and Purī Sampradāyas.[45] It is surrounded by the thick Narsiṃha forest while the Narsiṃha hill stands elegantly decorating its bountiful surroundings. It also has a nearby fall known as the 'Sirimāne'

Following the hagiographic records, when Ādi Śaṅkarācārya arrived at the holy Śriṅgerīṣtra on the banks of River Tuṇgabhadrā, He witnessed a supremely sacred site where a cobra snake opened his complete hood like an umbrella in order to protect a laboring frog from the hot sun and was helping her in giving birth to tadpoles.[46] On seeing the view that was flowing with compassion, love, kindness and Ekātman, Ādi Śaṅkarācārya decided to establish the Śriṅgerī Maṭha at this very place. The incident is a symbol of compassion across apparent variations. It exhibits mutual respect, mutual care, mutual wellness, co-existence, peace and harmony despite material distinctions. Even today, one

---

[40] Mishra Parmeshvarnatha Nath (Com) p.12. (V.28)

[41] The legend of Rishyashringa, https://sringeri.net/history/sage-rishyashringa (Accessed on 13 April 2021)

[42] Mishra Parmeshvarnatha Nath (Com), p.12. (V.30)

[43] *Ibid.*, (V.31)

[44] *Ibid.*, (V.32)

[45] *Ibid.*, (V.29)

[46] (i) Shringeri Matha, 2004, '*History of Mathas*',Online, Shringeri, https://www.sringeri.net/history. (Accessed on 13 April 2021)

(ii) Wikipedia contributors, 2005, '*Sringeri Sharada Peetham*', Online,Wikipedia,https://en.wikipedia.org/wiki/Sringeri Sharada Peetham. (Accessed on 13 April 2021)

can witness a stone structure of the snake and frog at the Maṭha that captures the compassionate and serene moment witnessed by Ādi Śaṅkarācārya.

The Maṭha continues to work tirelessly towards the protection of cows,[47] fishes and other sentient beings. It also protects an endangered species of fishes called 'Mahsīra' and further restricts anyone from fishing in and around the area that comes under the Maṭha's jurisdiction.[48] The Maṭha also uses a solar panel to cook food and preserve environment.

7.2. The Daśanāmīsaṃpradāya and Their Environmental Significance

Ādi Śaṅkarācārya classified the Saṃnyāsī Saṅgha into ten Saṃpradāyas namely: Vana, Araṇya, Sarasvatī, Bhāratī, Purī, Tīrtha, Āśrama, Girī, Parvata and Sāgara. The classification was made in order to bring about unity and give strength to the country. It also aimed at giving specific duties to each Saṃpradāya and preserving the country internally and externally by protecting its forests, mountains, seas, education system, and pilgrimage.

The ten Saṃpradāyas are normally understood as 'Spiritual' in the light of the modern understanding of the word that limits spirituality to an internal state of humans, which is to be attained through some mysterious practices. In this regard, it is important to take note of the following,

- If a profound philosophy like Advaita Vedānta restricts itself to such definitions or establishes itself in uncalled for divisions like man-animal, human-nature, it will lose its grounds completely.

---

47 Shringeri Matha,2004,'*Shri Bharti Teertha Mahasvami on Cow Protection*',Online,Shringeri,https://www.sringeri.net/activities/other-activities/goshala-cowshed. (Accessed on 13 April 2021)

48 Wikitravel,2007, '*Sringeri*', (See: '*Matha-Ban on Fishing*'), Online. Wikitravel.org, https://wikitravel.org/en/Shringeri. (Accessed on 13 April 2021)

- When people choose not to see the practical environmental significance of Ādi Śaṅkarācārya's endeavors, it is because of partial understanding of His philosophy and life that is in reality installed in cosmic welfare in the most practical manner.
- It must be understood that the cosmos and 'Environment or Nature' are not distinct from each other. As mentioned before, internal, external and cosmic environment are not separate, they merely appear to be distinct due to ignorance. Likewise, humans, animals, plants or birds are not divisible in their essence; they only appear to be varied forms due to the veil of Avidyā.

It is to be comprehended that just as the material world is important to realize the Ultimate, likewise these ten material divisions were necessary to realize the 'Highest Division-less Reality'. The ten Saṃpradāyas were certainly meant for environmental consciousness, preservation and reverence because national and spiritual enhancement cannot be viewed in compartments.

It is desirable to intricately see the ten Saṃpradāyas that Ādi Śaṅkarācārya established in the light of practical environmental consciousness and protection. Before one concludes that the ten Saṃpradāyas have no environmental significance, it is important to ponder over the following questions,

a) Why would a being as enlightened as 'Ādi Śaṅkarācārya' make these ten divisions if metaphysics (as understood in the modern context) alone was His concern? There must be some deeper Vyāvahārika (mundane) significance attached to these divisions that would ultimately lead to 'Supreme Realization'.

- Why would Ādi Śaṅkarācārya choose the above mentioned ten names like Vana, Girī and Sāgara while He could have chosen other names?

- Why did Ādi Śaṅkarācārya choose Paryāyavācī words like Vana and Araṇya or Girī and Parvata?

Based on a talk delivered by the present Śaṅkarācārya of the Govardhan Maṭha 'Svāmī Niṣcalānanda Sarasvatī',[49] it may be concluded that the ten names of the Saṃnyāsī Saṇgha are not merely spiritual but are also of worldly importance that can bring about environmental, educational, religious and spiritual advancement. Let us see how the Daśanāmī divisions promote harmonious co-existence,

1. Vana and Araṇya[50]: In the Mahāmnāyasetu, Ādi Śaṅkarācārya states,

surmaye nirjane sthāne vane vāsam karoti yaḥ।
āśābandhavinarmukto vananāma sa ucchyate॥
āraṇye saṁsthito nityamānande nande vane।
tyatva sarvamidaṁ viṣvamārṇyaṁ parikītryate॥[51]

(He who indwells in the harmonious wilderness of the forests, liberated from binding desires is called 'Vana (Vanasaṁnyāsī)'. He who stays in the delight of the deep forest with eternal joy moves from the enumerated to the 'One, Non-dual Whole' and is said to be 'Araṇya (Araṇyasaṁnyāsī)'.

The Vana and Araṇya come under the Govardhan Maṭha and their Mahāvākya is '*prajñānam brahma* (The Consciousness is Brahman)' which means that the whole cosmos of names and forms exist in the non-dual Divine consciousness and thus every life from a little bugs to the magnificent mountains are the Supreme. This Mahāvākya appears in the Aitarīya Upaniṣad (3.3) of the Ṛgveda and is a Lakṣṇavākya.[52] Commonly Vana and Araṇya are used interchangeably and are considered to be synonyms.

---

49 Swami Nischalananda Saraswati, 2017, '*Dashnami Sampradaya Ka Mahatva*', Online,Youtube,https://www.youtube.com/watch?v=hkfcUkMoyYE. (Accessed on 14 April 2021)

50 Mishra Parmeshvarnatha Nath (Com), p.7. (V.10)

51 *Ibid.*, 15, pp.7-8. (V.14)

52 *Lakshanavakya* is the sentence that defines the nature of Brahman. It is also known as Svarupa Bodha Vakya.

However, Dr. Shaikh Ahmad in his book '*Environmental Science and Ecology*' mentions,

'Vana is that which provides timber to the villagers, and is home to animals, it is rich in Vanaspatī, Ouśadhi and it adjoins the village. However, Araṇya is distant, dark and exists in the wilderness of the Vana'.[53]

Further, it may be noted that in the Mahābhārata the Araṇya Parva is a part of the Vana Parva, which also throws light on the fact that Vana is a bigger forest while Araṇya is a deeper wood. As a result, it may be concluded that 'Vana' is the exterior while 'Araṇya' is the heart of the forest. Hence, a smaller but denser forest is known as 'Araṇya' while a larger forest that has the denser forest as a part of it is called 'Vana'. Vana and Araṇya not only depend upon each other for existence but are also non-dual in essence. The distinction of Vana and Araṇya is merely for intellectual deliberations just as Pārmārthika and Vyāvhārika. According to Svāmī Niṣcalānanda Sarasvatī,

"Vana and Araṇya Saṃnyāsīs were initiated by Ādi Śaṅkarācārya to protect the Vana (forests), Araṇya (deep woods), and the Vanavāsīs (all sentient beings residing in the forest) who are the very identity of these forests. It was the duty of the Vana and Araṇya Saṃnyāsīs to stop Vidharmīs from entering these forests and destroying them and making their way into the villages in order to ruin peace and harmony. However, due to slack on the part of the 'Śaṅkarācāryas' who failed to implement the subtle ideas of Ādi Śaṅkarācārya and who further failed in order to explain the duties and responsibilities to the Saṃnyāsīs, our forests and those sentient beings who live in these forests have suffered a great deal".[54]

---

53 Sheikh Ahmad, '*Environmental Science and Ecology*', Sankalpa Publication, Bilaspur, 2019, pp.219-221.

54 Swami Nischalananda Saraswati, https://www.youtube.com/watch?v=hkfcUkMoyYE. (Accessed on 14 April 2021)

Following the above-said, it may be understood that,

- Ādi Śaṅkarācārya established the Vana and Araṇya Saṃpradāyas with the aim that the Saṃnyāsīs will protect the forests and all sentient beings that exist in the forest for the sake of maintaining universal harmony, and mutual co-existence.
- Ādi Śaṅkarācārya established the Vana and Araṇya Saṃpradāyas so that the Saṃnyāsīs propagate the physical importance and spiritual significance of the forests in due course. The fact that all great works, texts and Bhāṣyas have been written in the natural surroundings of forests, rivers and mountains ascertains that such natural surroundings assist a being in touching higher spiritual and creative realms of one's existence. Thus, forests are not only a source of keeping the earth and it's sentient beings healthy but are also an extremely important milestone for the realization of the 'Self' as the 'Ultimate Principle.' They are essential at an individual, social and cosmic level. Just as one thorn is needed to get rid of another thorn, likewise material bondages can be transcended only through the material. Hence, to understand spiritual significance one needs to first understand the material significance.
- Ādi Śaṅkarācārya established the Vana and Araṇya Saṃpradāyas so that the Saṃnyāsīs could act as a force in order to refrain the Vidharmīs from entering these forests and ruining their peace. The Saṃnyāsīs also acted as a wall in order to stop Vidharmīs from entering villages through the forests and create any sort of disturbance. Had the Saṃnyāsīs understood the spirit of Ādi Śaṅkarācārya's vision the new age Vidharmīs in the name of urban development and infrastructure would not have been able to damage the forests, wildlife, ecological balance and the very essence of the Saṃpradāyas who were supposed to live in Vana and Araṇya.

It is to be taken note of that the straying of carnivorous animals into the cities is due to the cutting down of Vana and Araṇya which were supposed to be the homes of these beings. Because humans indulged in deforestation, the animals and species like leopards, tigers and bears were forced to invade the cities for food and survival which further led to man-animal conflict.

As in the case of 'Chinese whisper' where the message is maligned by the time it reaches the last person, the message of Ādi Śaṅkarācārya has been either misinterpreted, inferred as per will or has been purposefully maligned. Negligence on the part of the succeeding Śaṅkarācārya along with a complete failure on part of the various governments that did not support the efforts of Ādi Śaṅkarācārya has led to the destruction of flora-fauna.

2. Giri, Parvata, Sāgara: In the Mahānuśāsanam Ādi Śaṅkarācārya states,

vāso girivane nityam gītadhyayantatparaḥ।
gaṁbhīrācalbuddhiṣca girināmā sa uccyate॥[55]
(He who forever lives in the hill forest and with eagerness studies the Gīta, he who has a mature and immovable intellect (like that of a hill) is said to be a 'Giri (Girisaṃnyāsī)')

vasan parvatamleśu proṇa jñāna vibharti yaḥ।
sārāsāraṁ vijānāti parvataḥ parikītryate॥[56]
(He who stays at the foot or base of the mountain and spreads his wisdom in the truest sense (practically) is 'Parvata (Parvatsaṃnyāsī)')

tattvasāgaragaṁbhīra jñānaratnaparigreḥ।
maryādāṁ vain a laṅghayta sāgaraḥ parikītryate॥[57]
(He who limits himself to residing by the shore (water bodies) while making sure that he collects the jewels of wisdom from the ocean of life that is rooted in the Supreme in the most dedicated manner is said to be 'Sagara (Sagarasaṃnyāsī)')

---

55 Mishra Parmeshvarnatha Nath (Com), p.11. (V.23)

56 *Ibid.* (V.24)

57 *Ibid.*, (V.25)

Girī, Parvata, Sāgara belong to the Jyotir Maṭha and their Mahāvākya is '*ayam ātma brahma* (The ātman is Brahman)'. This Mahāvākya comes from the Māṇḍūkya Upaniṣad (1.2) of the Atharvaveda and is a Anusandhānavākya.[58] Once the Śiṣya has realized the 'Self' as the Ultimate Principle, the Guru advises the Śiṣya to be established in the wisdom of non-duality with continued determination. Thus, the Śiṣya is not only established in Advaita like a sturdy mountain but also allows the river of compassion to flow and expands its identity into the ocean of wisdom by seeing the whole cosmos as Divine (*sarvam khalu idam brahma*).

Śaṅkarācārya Svāmī Niṣcalānanda Sarasvatī ji expounds upon the idea of Ādi Śaṅkarācārya by pointing out the apparent differences and similarities of Girī and Parvata,

"Referring to the Matsyapurāṇa, I will tell you that a greater Girī (hill) is known as Parvata (mountain) while a smaller Parvata (mountain) can be referred to as Girī (hill). Thus, Ādi Śaṅkarācārya aimed at protecting and maintaining the purity of our mountains, hills, all lives that exist on and within these hills and mountains. The mountains also protect us from Vidharmīs. Today, the hills and mountains are not secure because the Saṃnyāsīs called Girī and Parvata are not made to realize their lofty goals by the current Śaṅkarācāryas."[59]

From the above one can conclude that Girī and Parvata are interwoven like the ocean and the wave. When the little Girī expands its identity, it is called 'Parvata' while every Parvata has a 'Girī' in it. Ādi Śaṅkarācārya established the Girī and Parvata Saṃnyāsīs Saṁpradāyas to not only shield the country from foreign invasions and attacks but to also maintain and protect the natural beauty, splendor and balance of the mountain ranges and further preserve the

---

58 *Anusandhanavakya* is the sentence of enquiry.

59 Swami Nischalananda Saraswati, https://www.youtube.com/watch?v=hkfcUkMoyYE. (Accessed on 14 April 2021)

natural habitat of all animals, plants, humans and birds who livcd in these ranges.

The protection of the mountains and sentient beings was also related to the preservation of culture and religion because in the Vedas and Purāṇas several rivers, mountain ranges, plants that grow on these mountains, animals and birds that live in these ranges have been mentioned. Besides this, no one could have understood the physical value of more than Ādi Śaṅkarācārya who Himself wrote the Bhāṣyas in the serenity of the Himālayās amidst varied beings.

Only recently, environmentalists and scientists have woken up to the importance of mountain ranges and the sanctity of all beings that live in these areas. However, the Vedas have been stressing upon it since time immemorial. Thus states Charles Allen, a well-known historian,

"The entire Himālayan mountain range is important for the well-being of the earth but I am amazed at the Mount Kailāśa which is geometrically and mathematically accurate and lies in the centre of the earth. It is known as the spine or the 'Axis Mundi' of the earth. The Viṣṇupurāṇa refers to it as the home of the Great God Śiva that has four faces and each face of the mountain is made of crystal, ruby, gold and lapis lazuli. This spine of the earth lies in the heart of six glorious mountain ranges and symbolizes a lotus"[60]

Hence, it can be understood that mountains are extremely important for the health of the earth, for the Himālayan region, for all beings of the cosmos and especially Mount Kailāśa which is said to be the centre of the earth not just by ancient texts but also by contemporary researchers and scientists.

---

60 Allen, Charles, '*A Mountain in Tibet: The Search for Mount Kailasa and the Sources of the Great Rivers of India*', Future Publications, London, 1991. pp. 21–22.

Mountains and hills also have immense spiritual significance as they are not only a symbol of unshakable balance, determination and vow but have the potency to elevate a person to higher spiritual states and are thus considered most appropriate for creative arts, learning, writing, spiritual practices and mysticism. Ecologically they are not only home to various animal and plant life but act as an instrument that balances the earth's temperature and health. Further, all water bodies are born in the mountains and finally merge into the ocean.

As mentioned previously by Śaṅkarācārya Svāmī Niṣcalānanda Sarasvatī that it has been an error on the part of the existing Śaṅkarācāryas and the Girī-Parvata Saṃnyāsis who have confined their roles and ignored the execution of their duties and responsibilities. The Sāgarasaṃnyāsis were meant to protect the seas, oceans, rivers and all beings who lived within and along these water bodies. If Sāgarasaṃnyāsis had operated in accordance with the instructions laid down by Ādi Śaṅkarācārya the water bodies would not have been contaminated with plastic and the water beings would not have died due to choking. It was also the duty of these Saṃnyāsis to protect Vidharmīs from entering through the sea route during 26/11 Mumbai attack. Those who attacked the Taj, Oberoi and Trident hotels entered the city via the sea and created havoc and violence within the city.[61]

Ādi Śaṅkarācārya's bifurcation of Saṃnyāsis if understood in the right context and with a broader vision could have led to securing and enriching of the nation, its culture, and its environmental bounties. It is also the ignorance and negligence on the part of the government, which has not abided by the ancient laws and chose to be governed by laws that disregarded the Vedas and voices of enlightened beings

61 Debashish Panigrahi,2009, '*26/11 Attackers Took Sea Route, Assert Cops*',Online,HindustanTimes,https://www.hindustantimes.com/india/26-11-attackers-took-sea-route-assert cops/storyA3JwFGqqlang2TxuJbeEgN.html. (Accessed on 14 April 2021)

like Ādi Śaṅkarācārya. The past governments elected to forego these teachings to establish themselves as secular, modern and to gain popularity amongst those who followed Abrahamic faith systems. Further, poor environmental, wildlife and animal cruelty laws have led to the ruining of the mountain ranges, melting of glaciers, and extinction of rare species of animals, birds, plants, unimaginable cruelty towards sentient beings and at a larger scale they have added to climate change and global warming. Moreover, at an individual level, an attitude of 'Dualism' has also added to the running of our natural bounties.

3. Sarasvatī, Bhāratī, Purī: In the Maṭhāmnāyasetu, Ādi Śaṅkarācārya states,

svarajñānarato nityaṃ svarvādi kaviṣvraḥ।
saṁsārasāgarāsārahaṇtasau hi sarasvatī॥[62]

(He who is decorated with the whole of wisdom and speaks as though he is the Lord of sound (Svara) and with this wisdom approaches the ocean of Saṁsāra is said to be Sarasvatī (Sarasvatīsaṃnyāsī)')

vidyābhareṇa saṁpūrṇaḥ sarvabhāraṁ parityajan।
dukhbhāraṁ na jānāti bhārati parikītaryate॥[63]

(The one who carries all responsibilities in the light of wisdom and sacrifice yet remains without an iota of suffering is said to be 'Bhāratī (Bharatisaṃnyāsī)')

jñānatattvena saṁpūrṇaḥ purṇatattvapade sthitaḥ।
parabrahmarato nityaṃ purīnāmā sa ucchyate॥[64]

(He who realises the essence of wisdom by being constantly established in the Parabrahman is said to be 'Purī (Purīsaṃnyāsī))

Sarasvatī, Bhāratī, Purī belong to the Śriṇgerī Maṭha[65] and their Mahāvākya is '*aham brahmāsmi* (I am the

---

62 Mishra Parmeshvarnatha Nath (Com) p.13. (V.33)

63 *Ibid.*, p.14.

64 *Ibid.*, (V.35)

65 Swami Gyananada Saraswati, 'p. 210.

Brahman)'[66] which means that all existences from a small leaf to a sage are the Self. This Mahāvākya appears in the Bṛhadāraṇyaka Upaniṣad (1.4.10) of the Yajurveda and is an Anubhavavākya[67] where by the Śiṣya meditates in order to overcome the notion of the temporary Self that he associates himself with as the body, mind and intellect. With the dint of his experience, he realizes that he is not distinct from all other creatures of the cosmos and the self-shining, all-knowing, omnipresent 'Self' that exists in him is the same Self that exists in all. While the word 'Purī' means place or country. The words 'Sarasvatī' and 'Bhāratī' are not only the names of the Goddess of wisdom but are also names of rivers.

Let's first understand 'Purī'. There are eight holy cities of Ayodhyā, Mathurā, Māyā, Kāśī, Kāṇcī, Avantikā, Dwārkā, and Purī, which are said to be the external cities. However, there are eight cities within our bodies called Purīaṣtaka which include: 1.five sensory organs, 2.five organs of action, 3.five Prāṇas, 4.Antahkarṇa, 5.Tanmātras, 6.Avidyā, 7.Kāma and 8.Karma. The inner cities of our being have nine gates called 'Navadvārapurī', which are: 1. Two eyes, 2.Two ears, 3.Two nostrils, 4.One mouth, 5.One anus and 6.One sexual organ. In order to make sure that we visit the external eight cities and realize ourselves as the Ultimate Truth, we must first make sure that our internal cities and all that enters and exits from our nine gates should be such that brings about a sense of peace, calm and harmony in and around us. Only when we are purified from within will we approach all that is external with a sense of reverence instead of a sense of greed and exploitation.

The Purīsaṃnyāsīsaṃpradāya was established to not only maintain harmony and peace within the eight external cities but they were also expected to handhold people and develop

---

66 Swami Gyananada Saraswati, 'p. 211.

67 *Anubhavavakya* is the sentence of experience.

a vision through which people could see the reflection of these eight cities within themselves and finally realize their spiritual essence. Purī Saṃnyāsīs were not only meant to lighten up the external eight cities during festivals and occasions instead they were also supposed to dispel the darkness of the inner eight cities by giving spiritual, religious and ethical education and sermons. By doing so they not only changed the way a person saw himself but also changed the way he saw all living beings of the cosmos. The lighting of lamp while visiting these cities was a symbol of the light of wisdom within. In this regard, Śaṅkarācārya Svāmī Niṣcalānanda Sarasvatī states,

"The Purīsaṃnyāsī's duties and responsibilities was to maintain the sanctity of the external and internal Purīs (cities) so that no unholy thought, unholy cultures, unholy people and unholy acts could contaminate these cities in which we live and in us they live. This was the true message of Jagadguru Ādi Śaṅkarācārya"[68]

Sadly, with time people have forgotten the internal cities that exist in every being and even the external cities have become mere symbols.

Human's polluted internal states, unholy acts of raping women, children and animals, unholy desires of non-vegetarianism, alcoholism, drugs, urban development, unholy thoughts of possessing, greed, trying to overpower natural elements, trying to be superior to all other forms of lives have led to ruining the holy cities, polluting the natural elements, and increased violence. This maligning of internal and external states has posed a threat not only for the human race but also for other sentient beings. This so happened because the Purīsaṃnyāsīs have turned a blind eye towards their duties and responsibilities by understanding the message of Ādi Śaṅkarācārya in the most narrow fashion. Had they understood the subtle ideas of Ādi Śaṅkarācārya,

---

[68] Swami Nischalananda Saraswati, https://www.youtube.com/watch?v=hkfcUkMoyYE. (Accessed on 14 April 2021)

the internal Purīs and external Purīs would have remained pure, serene and could have led the society to a higher state of being.

Let us now look at Sarasvatī and Bhāratī. While Sarasvatī is a larger water body, Bhāratī was a tributary of the same. The latter merged into the former and expanded its identity. Similarly, the Sarasvatī and Bhāratī Saṃnyāsīs are initiated into taking up the responsibility of higher and primary education system. Just as Bhāratī merges into Sarasvatī and there is an expansion of identity, likewise primary education leads to higher education that becomes the base of an educated nation, which is led to wisdom and realization of the Ultimate Principle. Undoubtedly, education and wisdom are distinct. However, right education based upon spirituality and science leads to the path of wisdom.

The aim of Ādi Śaṅkarācārya in establishing Sarasvatī and Bhāratī Saṃnyāsī Saṃpradāya was to make sure that the education system remains uncontaminated. No foreign element invades the education system and propagates Vidharma. All humans get an opportunity to explore themselves with the right education. People develop skills and abilities and thus economy booms. Along with material development, the whole country must develop spiritually and further develop the vision of non-duality. Environment and nature can be revered only when children from a tender age are enabled with the vision to see unity in diversity. A wise nation not only chooses sustainable development but also focuses on preserving, protecting and enhancing the bounties of Mother Nature. Such a nation makes efforts to understand 'Material Matter' but refrains from exploiting it. It may want to understand the chemistry of the Pañcamahābhūtas but it does so with reverence and without bothering their very balance. Such a country would choose to nourish itself with milk and milk products but would also bow down to the cow as 'Mother' and would nourish it twice as much.

A country that has a spiritual base and scientific oriented education system will indulge in travel, tourism, development and all sorts of businesses with a holistic view. It will take into account not just the welfare and well-being of the human race but will be concerned about its forests, wildlife, birds, mountains and rivers. A country of this kind will rather elect the preservation of its land, air, sea, animals and plants than developing malls and cinema halls that are temporary and serve a limited purpose. This judgment of electing the most appropriate is rooted in not just education but in education that is spiritual, scientific and aims at the realization of the Self. Śaṅkarācārya Svāmī Niṣcalānanda Sarasvatī in this regard states,

"Bhiṣmapitāmaḥ tells Yūhiśthira! The one who uses and invests all of their education, intelligence and skill for the sake of wealth and fulfilling desires is a sinner. Therefore, most of the educated people today are sinners for they hardly think of anything other than fulfilling their own personal desires. These people practice all that is Adharmic. Accept one to two percent of educational institutions rest all are centres for preaching Adharma and Anti-nationalism. Hence, if the Sarasvatī and Bhāratī Saṃnyāsīs had truly understood their role, duties, and responsibilities and had implemented them under the Śaṅkarācāryas, then our education system would not have been corrupted as was desired by Ādi Śaṅkarācārya"[69]

4. Āśrama and Tīrtha: Āśrama and Tīrtha belong to the Dwārkā Maṭha[70] and their Mahāvākya is '*tat tvam asi* (Thou Art That)'.[71] This Mahāvākya comes from the Chāṇdogya upaniṣad (6.8.7) of the Sāmaveda and is a Updeśavākya.[72] Through this Vākya the Guru instructs the Śiṣya that 'There

---

[69] Swami Nischalananda Saraswati, https://www.youtube.com/watch?v=hkfcUkMoyYE. (Accessed on 14 April 2021)

[70] Swami Gyananada Saraswati, p.210

[71] *Ibid.*, p. 211.

[72] *Updeshavakya* is the sentence of instruction by the Guru.

is none other to be sought but his own Self'. Hence, by knowing the 'Self', one can know everything else.

'Āśrama' refers to taking a step in the direction of purifying the Self via: *Brahmacārya, Gṛhastha, Vānaprastha,* and *Saṃnyasa.* Here a person's life is divided into four stages and accordingly one performs his duties towards gaining education, performing responsibilities towards the Guru, the family, the environment, all sentient beings, nation, cosmos and finally he retires and leads a life of renunciation in action.

S.S.Chandra describes Āśrama as *'A Step in the Journey of Life'.*[73] 'Āśrama' also refers to a hermitage or monastery that is situated in the natural surroundings of mountains, forests, seashores and is conducive for spiritual enhancement[74] where people stay and lead a life of Dharma, Ahiṃsa, Jñāna that is aimed at the attainment of realization of the Self.

'Tīrtha' on the other hand refers to a holy place of pilgrimage. The word 'Tīrtha' refers to *'a ford, a crossing, a transition'*. Thus, one can understand that 'Tīrtha' is a transition from material to spiritual through nature and therefore 'Tīrthas' exist amidst hills, near water bodies, in the mid of forests and so on. Natural environment acts as a crossing point between the seen and the unseen worlds. Through the experiences narrated by various Yogīs, Ṛṣis and Saṃnyāsīs it can be concluded that Nature can assist and easily lead a person to higher states of consciousness. Jacobson Kunt, a well-known scholar of Indian philosophy and history states,

"Tīrtha is anything that has a salvific value to a Hindu, and includes pilgrimage sites such as mountains, forests, seashores,

73 Chandra S.S & Sharma Rajendra, '*Philosophy of Education*'. Atlantic Publishers & Dist. Delhi, 1996, pp. 173.

74 Gopal, Madan, K. S. Gautam (ed.), '*India Through The Ages*'. Publication Division, Ministry of Information and Broadcasting, Government of India, Delhi, 1990, p.70.

rivers, ponds, as well as virtues, actions, studies or a certain state of mind."[75]

Therefore, one starts by entering into various Āśramas, purifying himself by the performance of duties. He then travels to Tīrthas that exist amidst Nature. All of this acts as a crossing point that allows a person to transcend his physicality and touch higher realms of consciousness.

The Āśrama and Tīrtha Saṃnyāsīs were not merely supposed to take care of the Āśramas and Tīrthas but were also supposed to explain to the layman, their physical and spiritual significance. It became the responsibility of the Āśramasaṃnyāsīs to explain to the general man about the duties related to each Āśrama and further maintain the natural environment of the monasteries. It also became the Dharma of the Tīrthasaṃnyāsīs to preserve the cultural, religious, spiritual and ecological environment of the pilgrimages. The spiritual army of Āśrama and Tīrtha Saṃnyāsīs were also meant to stop any Adharmic forces that could ruin environmental harmony, cultural splendor, religious peace and spiritual unity.

Unfortunately, due to lack of understanding of Ādi Śaṅkarācārya's message and due to continues ignorance of the Saṃnyāsīs and Śaṅkarācāryas the Āśramas and Tīrthas have been transformed into money pinching institutions and places. Contrary to the vision of Ādi Śaṅkarācārya, one can observe mindless practices that prevail in the name of religion in order to fool innocent devotees at various pilgrimages. The forests, mountains, seas and rivers which acted as a crossroad between the physical and transcendental world have become garbage dumping arenas. People have forgotten the concepts of Sarvabhūtāhita and Bhūtariṇa. Today cows, dogs, monkeys, birds and other life forms go hungry and thirsty in these places of pilgrimages. With

---

75 Knut A. Jacobsen, '*Pilgrimage in the Hindu Tradition: Salvific Space*', Routledge, London, 2013, pp.157-158.

foreign influences, people have abandoned the 'Āśrama Dharma' and have forgotten their duties, responsibilities and concerns towards their family, society, religion, environment, country and cosmos. Had the Śaṅkarācāryas and the Saṃnyāsīs of the Āśrama and Tīrtha been dedicated in executing their responsibilities, such a day would not have been witnessed. Rightly says Śaṇkarācārya Svāmī Niṣcalānanda Sarasvatī,

"May the Tīrthas do not fitter away from their holiness in pursuits of material development and may the Āśrama system prosper, such auspicious roles were assigned and determined for the Saṃnyāsīs named- Āśrama and Tīrtha by Ādi Śaṅkarācārya"[76]

7.3. Nāgās-The Protectors Rooted in Dharma

The word 'Nāgā' is derived from the Sanskrit word 'Nāg', which means 'Mountain' and those who dwell in these mountains are referred to as the 'Nāgās. The word 'Nāgā' also refers to those who remain naked and ornament themselves with arms, matted locks and ashes. Typically, the Nāgāsādhus behold an appearance that can be extremely fearful.

The establishment of the Nāgāsādhusaṅgha is accredited to Jagadguru Ādi Śaṅkarācārya who understood that along with spiritual strengthening, physical strength was equally important in order to protect the glories of Bhāratvarṣa.

The Nāgāsādhus are perhaps the most mysterious, enchanting and the most misunderstood. They suddenly appear during the Kuṁbha celebrations and disappear thereafter. No one knows from where they appear and where do they disappear. Traditionally, the Nāgāsādhus have dwelled in the mountains in order to protect the borders.

---

76 Swami Nischalananda Saraswati, https://www.youtube.com/watch?v=hkfcUkMoyYE. (Accessed on 14 April 2021)

Despite being apt in martial arts and the art of using weapons, they are essentially spiritual and rooted in Dharma. As and when one starts understanding them, one realizes that they are extremely calm and never bother or harm anyone. They resort to weapons only in order to save the weak or for greater good and not for any personal gain. The chief aim of the Nāgāsādhusaṅgha was to protect Bhāratvarṣa from any external harmful elements and invasions and for this reason, Ādi Śaṅkarācārya established Akhādās where the Nāgāsādhus were strengthened mentally, emotionally, physically while being rooted in the basic tenets of Sarvabhūtahita (welfare of all) by fighting the Vidharmīs.

It is indeed sad that we remain ignorant towards the sacrifices of the Nāgāsādhus. Each time evil invaders have tried to snatch away the bounties of Bhāratmātā, Gaumātā and have tried to exploit us spiritually, culturally or otherwise by looting our temples, women and other glories, the Nāgāsādhus have stood before us like a shield with the compassion of a mother. Be it Mohammad Gauri, Taimur Lang or Mohammad Shah Abdali, the Nāgāsādhusaṅgha have fought them to ruins and have allowed us to live with freedom.

The Nāgāsādhus retire into the caves of the mountain and give up all worldly pleasures, they go through tremendous Tapasyā merely for the sake of maintaining harmony and protecting the environment of the country.

Their role in protecting the borders, mountains and the environment of the entire country must be recognized and applauded. In the same breath, it is important to bow in reverence before Ādi Śaṅkarācārya and His vision that has given us the wealth of the Nāgāsādhusaṅgha and the priceless Akhādās.

7.4. The Unifying Pañcadevopāsanā and the Pañcamahābhūtas

Ādi Śaṅkarācārya propagated the worship of 'Five Devas' namely Gaṇeśa, Śiva, Nārāyaṇa, Sūrya and Śakti. The aim was to tie up the whole country into a single thread and here 'The Whole Country' also takes into account the environment and all its creatures which the modern man seems to forget time and again.

The Pañcadevas are regarded as a manifestation of 'The One Ultimate Brahman'. Each Deva has a unique quality as Saguṇa Brahman and symbolizes the five great elements respectively. The five Deities also represent the five functions of the Divine as Sriṣti (creation), Stithi (preservation), Saṇhāra (destruction for the sake of reconstruction), Tirobhāva (veiling) and Anugraha (grace). While creation is associated with the earth, preservation is connected to water, destruction is connected to fire, veiling is associated with the air and grace is connected to Ākāśa.

'The One Ultimate' as the Pañcamahābhūtas gives rise to the entire cosmos and into 'It' the whole universe dissolves. The coming together of the five elements in a certain proportion creates various objects of the world and they merge back into the five great elements.

The concept of Pañcadevopāsanā not only brought about social, cultural and religious unity amongst people but also brought about unity in diversity at a cosmic, spiritual and environmental level. It not only made a devotee realize that Gaṇeśa, Śiva, Nārayaṇa, Sūrya and Śakti are varied names of the 'One Non-dual Reality' but it also made people realize that these five exist in each human, animal, bird, insect, tree, river, mountain and pervades the whole of cosmos. As says the Bhagwadgīta,

vidyāvinayasaṁpanne brāhmaṇe gavi hastini।
śuni caiva śvapāke ca paṇḍitāḥ samadarśinaḥ॥[77]

(The wise one is he who sees the non-dual self with an equal eye in a Brahmṇa, in a cow, in a dog and even in a person of low class.)

For a common devotee these five are the Pañcadevas that exist in the whole of cosmos and thus everything is the Divine to him. To a Ṛṣi these five are the Pañcamahābhūtas that combine in a certain proportion and give rise to the world of variation which is rooted in the Saguṇa Brahman. For a Jīvanmukta or a Paramjñāni the Pañcamahābhūtas, Pañcadevas and the Jagat are nothing but the 'Brahman'.

It is also important to note here that each Deva is associated with an animal, tree, plant, reptile, weapon, river, element, function, Guṇa and more, for e.g. Śiva is associated with bulls, snakes, scorpions, and dogs in terms of reptiles, insects and animals. Rudrākṣa, Bilva, Dhattura, Bhāṅga, Bera are associated with the Great Lord Śiva in terms of trees, plants and flowers that are medically rich. The Gaṇgā is associated with Him as a river. Mount Kailāsa is said to be His sacred abode. Ākāṣha is His element and Moon is associated with Him that He adorns as an ornament. Therefore, worshiping any of the above is worshiping Lord Śiva.

Pañcadevopāsanā brought about reverence for all lives. This reverence can be seen as the spirit of India even today. An Indian is often seen worshiping a tree, a river, a cow, a dog, and the earth. In fact, people around the world consider India as the country of 'Nature Worshipers'. The Rudrākṣa seeds and Bilva are considered to be Sākśāta Śiva. Banana trees are worshiped as Sākśāta Viṣṇu. An elephant is seen as Sākśāta Gaṇeśa. Even today the Sun is prayed by giving Argha and cow is prayed as the Universal Mother. It is not that an Indian is superstitious when he prays to various forms instead even the most uneducated Indian is aware that behind varied names and forms exists the non-dual Ultimate Reality. In this regard, Ādi Śaṅkarācārya in His work Pañcikarṇa Pranavārtha states,

77 Adi Shankaracharya, '*Shrimadbhagvadgitabhashya*', p.95. (V.5.18,)

"pañcamahābhūtebhyokhilam jagat"[78]
(from the five elements the world comes into being)

Further, each Deva has been associated with an element: Gaṇśa (Pṛthvi), Śiva (Ākāśa), Nārayaṇa (Jala), Sūrya(Agni) and Śakti (Vāyu).[79] Hence, the perceiver may refer to the Brahman as Pañcadevas, Pañcamahābhūtas, Jagat or as the Ultimate Truth depending upon his mental, spiritual and intellectual acumen.

It is to be comprehended lucidly that the 'One Ultimate' appears as the soul of the cosmos, as the material, as the inner, and the outer environment. 'It' alone becomes the flower, the fire, the fish, the water, the bird, the food and all that exists, all that has ceased to exist, all that will never exist and all that will ever exist in the womb of time. However, for a layman it becomes very tough to comprehend that which is beyond names and forms. Therefore, when he is told that it is his beloved deity that becomes the whole of cosmos, he sees the cosmos with reverence. He then has no desire to exploit it. This vision makes him see the water bodies, the hills, the sky, the fire, the air, and all living beings as his beloved Deity. Thus, internal, external and cosmic environment become the manifestation of the One Ultimate. Further, the Chāndogya Upaniṣad declares that,

tenobhau kuruto yaścaitadevaṃ veda yaśca na veda
nānā tu vidyā cāvidyā ca yadeva vidyayā karoti ।
śraddhayopaniṣadā tadeva vīryavattaraṃ bhavatīti
khalvetasyaivākṣaras yopavyākhyānaṃ bhavati ॥[80]
(The one who knows and the one who is ignorant both operate with the grace of AUM. However, knowledge and ignorance produce varied results.)

---

78 Adi Shankaracharya, Pt. Sharma Mahadev, '*Pañcikarna Pranavārtha*', Kanoon Press, Kanpur, 1941, p.4.

79 *Ibid.*, p.12.

80 Swami Lokeshwarananda,'*Chāndogyopniṣadāśānkarabhāṣya*', Ramakrishna Mission Institute of Culture,Kolkata,2017,pp.16-17. (V.1.1.10,)

The above said can be explained by the example of the 'gravitational force'. Thc gravitational force operates throughout the world. However, the ignorant never even comes to think or it, leave alone talking about it or having reverence for it. On the other hand, the same gravitational force is a subject of astonishment, miracle, research, reverence and wisdom for a Ṛṣi, scientist or Panḍita (wise one). Similarly, when one sees the cosmos in the realm of wisdom and as a manifestation of the Divine his relationship with all lives changes. However, when he sees everything in the realm of ignorance, he becomes the cause of the destruction of flora, fauna, the five elements and himself. The Chāndogya Upaniṣad also states,

***'One can perform the five-fold worship during rains by bowing to the water, the clouds, lightning, the thunder and the Ākaśa'*[81]**
***'We worship animals for the nourishment that they give us and help us sustain. Their milk becomes our body, blood and is spread all over us. Their bodies, feces and bones after death become the trees and the earth and we thus worship the trees.'*[82] *'Those who know these Five (elements) are led from death to immortality.'*[83]**

From the above said, it can be concluded that the whole cosmos is rooted in the Divine and the propagation of Pañcadevopāsna by Ādi Śaṅkarācārya was,

- *A step to realize* the 'One Whole' that manifests as Pañcadevas and creates the Divine world of names and forms by becoming the Pañcamahābhūtas.
- *A step to make* people realize cultural, social, ecological, spiritual and cosmic non-duality.
- *A step to preserve* the purity of individual and cosmic nature and environment.
- *A step to establish* equality of all beings that goes beyond names and forms.

---

81 Swami Lokeshwarananda, pp.127-128. (V.2.3.1)

82 *Ibid.*, pp.174-177. (V.2.19.1)

83 *Ibid*, pp.431-435. (V.5.10.1 ; 5.10.2,)

- *A step to establish* a culture that is founded in sublime philosophy of non-dualism which can carry on for future generations.

7.5. Chāradhāmayatrā-The Divine Circumambulation

Chāradhāma is an important set of four pilgrimage sites established by Ādi Śaṅkarācārya that lie in the four directions of the country. All know the importance of visiting the Chārdhāma once in a lifetime. The act of pilgrimage in performing clockwise circumambulation encompassing the four directions familiarises the pilgrims with the sacred geography of India. The four cardinal points where the Chārdhāma is established represent 'Maṇḍala (cosmos)'. Wikipedia defines the Maṇḍala as,

'a diagram, chart or geometric pattern that represents the cosmos metaphysically or symbolically; a time microcosm of the universe, meant to represent wholeness and a model for the organizational structure of life itself, a cosmic diagram that shows the relation to the infinite and the world that extends beyond and within minds and bodies.'[84]

The aim of Chāradhāmayātrā was not merely pilgrimage but was also traveling through divine landscapes, waterbodies, variety of plants, humans, animals and connecting with the culture, tradition, faith and belief of the whole country. This wholesome pilgrimage automatically leads to revering all lives and viewing selfsameness. It further purifies one's internal states. The sites that were chosen by Ādi Śaṅkarācārya for the establishment of these Dhāmas lie amidst natural surroundings. The Chārdhāmas are so deeply interwoven with religion, culture, environment and philosophy that it becomes extremely difficult to separate any of these. Taking up a Chāradhāmayātrā is moving towards the understanding of the divine movement of the cosmos,

[84] Wikipedia contributors, 2002 '*Mandala*', Online,Wikipedia, *https://en.wikipedia.org/wiki/Mandala.* (Accessed on 14 April 2021)

through a formative journey down the living divine rivers, mountains, Śāligrāmas, forests, cities, and temples. A devotee travels through great expanses of time, space, forces of nature and the complex network of various kinds of lives (animals, trees, birds, saints, humans and more). He eventually realizes kinship and oneness amongst all beings. He understands that the variation of names and forms have little meaning because in essence, every creature is shining with divinity. He awakens to a world that is 'One Family (*vasudhaiva kuṭuṃbakam*)'. Let's look at the four Dhāmas in the same view,

1. **Baḍrīdhāma:** 'Baḍrī' is a Saṃskrit word that means 'Berry'. It is believed that the area of Baḍrīnātha was rich in berries. In a few Indian scriptures, the 'Baḍrī' is referred to as Baḍrīnātha.[85] The Taptakuṅda from where Ādi Śaṅkarācārya recovered the statue of Mahāviṣṇu is a hot sulphur spring that lies below the temple and maintains a temperature of 55 degrees throughout the year. The natural hot spring is said to have medicinal properties.[86] The Śrīmadbhāgvatam without any limitations talks about the welfare of all entities while announcing the incarnation of Nara-Nārāyaṇa at Baḍrikāśrama in the following verse,

yatra nārāyaṇo devo naraś ca bhagavān ṛṣiḥ।
mṛdu tīvraṁ tapo dīrghaṁtepāte loka-bhāvanau॥[87]
(In the Badarikāśrama the Supreme Lord, in His incarnation as Nara and Nārāyaṇa, is going through Divine penance since time immemorial for the welfare of all living creatures).

The Dhāma is established amidst the magnificent Himālayas on the banks of River Alaknaṅdā. It is further surrounded by the Nara-Nārāyaṇa, Nīlakaṅtha and

85 Wikipedia contributors, 2004 '*Badrinath*', Online, Wikipedia,https://en.wikipedia.org/wiki/Badrinath. (Accessed on 14 April 2021)

86 *Ibid.*

87 Maharishi Vyasa, '*Shrimadbhagvatam Purana*', Online, srimad.in, https://srimad.in/bhagavatam/verse/3/4/22. (V.3.4.22) (Accessed on 14 April 2021)

Naṅdādevi peaks.[88] It must be noted that the idol of Mahāviṣṇu established by Ādi Śaṅkarācārya is made of Śāligrāma stone. The Śāligrāma stone is worshiped as 'Mahāviṣṇu' not only because it is not man-made but also because the geological formation of the landscape gives it a living essence of its own.[89] Thus, Śāligrāma is worshiped as living 'Mahāviṣṇu'. This highlights the fact that Divinity is all-encompassing and exists equally in things that we may discard off as non-living in view of modern science. Śāligrāmas appear in accordance with the incarnations of Mahāviṣṇu. Therefore, there are Matsyaśāligrāmas, Kurmaśāligrāmas, Rāmaśāligrāmas and others.[90]

According to a research called '*Badrivana Restoration Programme*' that was launched in 1993, it has been found that the area that was selected to develop the Dhāma had dense forests, vegetation and biodiversity around it.[91] The research further states that Ādi Śaṅkarācārya named the forest around the Baḍridhāma as 'Baḍrivana' due to the presence of Baḍriphala.[92] Unfortunately, the forest disappeared in the due course.[93] Further, it is to be noted that the tree seedlings are ritually distributed as 'Vrikṣaprasāda' by the chief priest of the shrine and hold immense value for the devotees. These seedlings are planted by the devotees around the area. This ceremonial practice highlights the value of adopting 'Cultural Approach' for reviving our forests. It also illustrates the coming together of science and religion for the protection and promotion of environment and biodiversity conservation.

---

88 Wikipedia contributors, 2004 '*Badrinath*', Online.

89 Walters Holly D, '*The Living Fossils*', The Fimmiliar Strange, 2018.

90 *Ibid.*

91 Dhyani, P.P, '*Badrivan: An Innovative Model in The Indian Central Himalaya for Restoration of Degraded Lands and Biodiversity Conservation*', Himavikas Publishing, 1998, pp. 387-405.

92 *Ibid.*, p. 406.

93 *Ibid.*, pp. 408-410.

2. Purī Dhāma: The Purīdhāma is situated in the east of India alongside the Bay of Bengal and at the coastal delta of Mahānadī.[94] It is accepted that before the appearance of the wood quartet idol of Lord Nila Mādhava, He was worshiped as Nīlāṅcala (Blue hill).[95] In texts like Vāmadevasaṁhita and Nīlādarimahodaya the disappearance of Lord Nila Mādhava and appearance of Lord Jagannātha is clearly mentioned. Purīdhāma situated on the coastal delta has been home to various animals, reptiles, trees and plant species. The Jagannātha Purī temple declares that,

In Skaṇdapurāna (Utkalakhaṇda) it is mentioned that this beautiful Śrī Kśetra is spread over 10 yojanas (128km or 80 miles) and surrounded by sand. Utkala is another name of Orissa. Utkala is divided into four parts- Saṇkhakṣetra (Purī town), Padmakṣetra (Koṇārk), Cakrakṣetra (Bhubaneśwara) and Gadākṣetra (Jajapura). Within this area of ten yojanas, Purī is known as Saṇkhakṣetra because its shape resembles a conch shell. This Purīkṣetra covers an area of five kośas, three of which are immersed under the ocean, and two on land. This land is covered with golden sand and is decorated with a blue mountain (Nīlāṇcala). The Lord Himself is residing here on the banks of the ocean on top of the blue mountain. Saṇkhakṣetra spreads from east to west. Its head is towards the west where Lokanātha Mahādeva resides.[96]

As mentioned before, at this Dhāma Smudrārti is carried out for the welfare and well-being of all lives. The Dhāma is home to Śveta Gaṇgā a self-sustained bathing tank that never dries up and nourishes all beings.[97]

---

94 Wikipedia contributors, 2004 '*Puri*', Online, Wikipedia,https://en.wikipedia.org/wiki/Puri. (Accessed on 14 April 2021)

95 *Ibid.*

96 Jaggannathpuri, 2020 '*History*', Online, Jaggannatha Puri Temple, https://www.jagannathpuri.in/. (Accessed on 14 April 2021)

97 *Ibid.*

3. Rāmeśvaram Dhāma: is established in the state of Tamilnadu.[98] The Dhāma rests at the very edge of the Indian Peninsula in the Gulf of Munnar.[99] The Dhāma is dedicated to Lord Śiva. It is here that Śrī Rāma built a Pārthiva Śivaliṇgam to pray to Lord Śiva. Between the Rāmeśvarama and the Mannar lies the Rāmasetū constructed by the Vānarasenā.[100] The location of the Dhāma not only has a spiritual significance but also has an ecological importance. The Dhāma is connected to Rāmāyaṇa and Ādi Śaṅkarācārya. Further, it is an important centre of culture, tradition and religion. Being situated at an environmentally rich site, surrounded by water bodies and being home to rare variety of water fishes and other species, this Dhāma holds a prime position. The entire place is an example of the interdependence and non-duality of all species. The Dhāma has twenty-two wells that have water with medicinal properties.[101] It is also home to the divine site of Jatāyutīrtham dedicated to 'The King of Birds-Jatāyu'who assisted Lord Rāma in His mission. At a physical level the Dhāma it promotes us to live in tune with environment; so that the essential continuity of both life and Nature is assured. However, at a metaphysical level, it raises all beings to the divine status.

4. Dwārkādhāma: For a detailed understanding of Dwārkādhām in view of environment kindly refer to 'Dwārkā Kālikā Maṭha' on page 230.

---

98 Wikipedia contributors, 2009 '*Char Dham*', Online, Wikipedia,https://en.wikipedia.org/wiki/Char_Dham (Accessed on 14 April 2021)

99 Wikipedia contributors, 2003 '*Rameshwaram*', Online, Wikipedia,https://en.wikipedia.org/wiki/Rameswaram (Accessed on 14 April 2021)

100 *Ibid.*

101 Tourmyindia, 2019, '*Rameshwarama*', Online, Tourmyindia,https://www.tourmyindia.com/states/tamilnadu/rameswaram.html, (Accessed on 14 April 2021)

CONCLUSION

From the above, it can be concluded that Ādi Śaṅkarācārya was a visionary and had multiple reasons to elect specific places for the establishment of the four Maṭhas and Chāradhāmayātra. He also had an all-encompassing vision when He established the ten Saṃpradāyas, Pañcadevopāsana and the Nāgāsādhusaṇgha. It is extremely unfair to box up these efforts and announce them as merely 'Spiritual' while compartmentalizing the term 'Spirituality' as something internal and specific to human beings. Even if one chooses to refer to the above said as 'Spiritual', it is important to use the word in an all-inclusive manner that pervades the entire cosmos. An appropriate, unbiased and unprejudiced understanding of Ādi Śaṅkarācārya will make us realize that all His establishments were meant for wholesome cosmic welfare and not well-being that is pigeonholed. His enterprises aim at purification of the internal, external and cosmic environment. His endeavors take into account the entire course without discriminating between any.

It is particularly unfortunate that today scholars understand Ādi Śaṅkarācārya based upon preconceived notions and see Him as a mere 'Metaphysicist'. It is imprudence on part of the teachers and professors who announce His philosophy as one that has little or no practical application in the world of material. It is for this reason that the new generation has become ignorant towards Ādi Śaṅkarācārya's practical contributions who was not merely a stupendous metaphysicist but was also a Yogi, poet, writer, thinker, philosopher, teacher, methodologist, environmentalist, psychiatrist, visionary and a being of the highest stature.

Ādi Śaṅkarācārya's enterprises mentioned in the chapter are a manifestation of His philosophy of non-duality. These enterprises aimed at making the common man realize 'Oneness of All Existences'. It is therefore imperative that the new age seekers, philosophers, and teachers broaden their vision in order to realize the compassion, which is the canvas of Ādi Śaṅkarācārya's endeavors.

Philosophers are not meant to compartmentalize thoughts or base their judgments upon any previous prejudices instead, they are supposed to develop a vision that helps the Society in Seeing meaning and worth even in the material. They are not supposed to pass verdicts rather they are supposed to encourage thinking, ideas, and point of views.

Once Ādi Śaṅkarācārya's endeavors are recognized and His philosophy is seen with a holistic vision, it is important to reinterpret the same in relation to the present times. If we aspire to be benefited by the unmatched wisdom of Ādi Śaṅkarācārya, we must make desirable efforts to reinterpret His philosophy and efforts in a new light while making sure that its soul remains unadulterated. With this thought, we must progress and make the most of His philosophy in the field of environment, social sciences, technology, politics and more.

It is important for philosophers to come out of their old boring shell and see Ādi Śaṅkarācārya's enterprises with a fresh, crisp and renewed perspective. If one develops a novel vision of looking at Ādi Śaṅkarācārya's efforts with the backdrop of His sublime philosophy, it will not be difficult to draw valuable meanings from His endeavors and thoughts in view of environmental harmony. With this innovative vision, one will be able to see that all the Maṭhas, and the Chāradhāmas were established amidst nature, near hills, water bodies and had supreme ecological importance. Further, the Daśanāmīsaṃpradāya, Nāgāsādhusaṇgha and the Pañcadevopāsana were founded with a vision to revere the natural bounties and to protect the country. Sorrowfully, due to a gloomy vision, these centres exist as mere places where rituals are carried out today.

One possible reason for establishing the Dhāmas in the lap of nature could be that these act as a confluence between the material and spiritual world. The subtle and euphoric effect of nature leads to the realization of self-sameness with all existences. Thus, Ādi Śaṅkarācārya's efforts have to be seen in a state of tranquillity, with a newfound perspective and with the desire to tackle the current environmental glitches.

Oṁ Trayīmārgaprakāśkāye Namaḥ

(I bow before Śaṅkara who illumines the three paths of Karma, Bhakti and Jñāna)

Conclusion

Ādi Śaṅkarācārya has been one of the greatest exponents of Vedic wisdom which is evident from His erudite commentary on the Prasthānatreyī. Therefore, the book begins with expounding upon Vedic perspectives on environment.

The Vedas are the highest of all Pramāṇas in the material world and they serve as the basis for all Indian philosophical systems. Without an iota of doubt, the Vedas speak compassionately about environmental harmony and global peace. They embrace a holistic and benevolent vision for all lives. Further, they are adorned with rituals, verses and philosophy that lead to the purification of internal, external and cosmic environment. The Vedas aim at comprehensive peace, and plentitude. The 'Divine' becomes the ground of the cosmos and its sentient beings which may be lucidly summed up as,

- Divine is both; the cause and the effect
- Divine alone indwells, pervades and manifests as everything and everyone.
- 'The Effect (World and all entities)' merges back into its 'Cause (The Divine)'

As a result, the whole cosmos is the breathing body of the Supreme and so 'Environment' is just another term for it. This Divinity should not be exploited, rather it is to be cherished.

The Vedas do not disagree with science and technology; rather, they are in harmony with material development so long as this development is meant for universal well-being and greater good. However, when materialism becomes the end all and be all, when there is a deliberate abandonment of the wellness of all other sentient beings, and when there is an unyielding desire to suppress Nature under the guise of technology and scientific discoveries, a crack between Vedic view and scientific attitude emanates.

The book goes on to concentrate upon Ādi Śaṅkarācārya's life, works, philosophy and His efforts in order see environment from an Advaitic perspective. A comprehensive review of Ādi Śaṅkarācārya's life can reveal His personality that was studded with the jewels of wisdom, scholarship, compassion, love and generosity. One can certainly take note of His taintless ideals and virtuous life. It was His internal environmental purity and reverence for the external world that led natural forces, humans and animals to assist Him in His journey in order to establish the doctrine of non-dualism. The joy of 'Mother Nature' and all the sentient beings at the birth of Ādi Śaṅkarācārya, the role played by the 'Gaṇdharva Crocodile' in assisting Him to take up the path of Saṃnyāsa, the gathering of 'River Narmadā' in His Kamaṇdala, the supporting of the 'Pañcamahābhūtas' at various stages of His life, the assisting of the 'Himālayan Region' while He wrote the Bhāṣyas and His disappearance into the 'Kedārnātha' on His beloved Naṇdī are examples of how the whole of Environment in varied names and forms assisted Him in His efforts to propoused the doctrine of Advaita Vedānta.

Mother Nature's veneration and compassion for Ādi Śaṅkarācārya, as well as His adoration, love, and reverence for Her, were natural. His life exemplifies how a Jīvanmukta devotes Himself to the benefit and service of all beings. Thus, He practically lived the teachings that He propagated and never gave up working for the well-being of others. He never led a life of ease, retirement, idleness and indulgence.

Ādi Śaṅkarācārya's life is itself a glaring testimony of His comprehensive compassion towards all beings. Therefore, His life is in symphony with environmental awareness and a profound bond shared with 'Mother Nature'. His writings also shed light on the special bond He had with rivers, mountains, animals, plants, and all other creatures of the cosmos. If one closely examines His works, one will see that He not only had a profound relationship with all creatures but also meticulously observed them. His respect for Nature may be seen in His legendary Stotrams, where He compares the beauty of the Ultimate Reality 'Īśvara' to the entities of the material world, such as rivers, flowers, animals, the sun, moon, and more. Only someone who fathoms, cherishes, and shares an intimate bond with 'Mother Nature' can write hymns as brilliantly, aesthetically and dramatically as Ādi Śaṅkarācārya did.

The book also sheds light on Ādi Śaṅkarācārya's impeccable vision for choosing precise places for the establishment of Maṭhas. He was far sighted when He formed the ten Saṃpradāyas, promoted Pañcadevopāsana and initiated the Chāradhāmayātra. It is erroneous to classify the aforementioned as just "spiritual," while confining the word "spirituality" to that which is internal and unique to humans. If the foregoing is referred to as "Spiritual" in a broad and all-encompassing sense, it is perfectly acceptable. It is further to be reckoned that all entities of the cosmos are essentially 'Spiritual/Divine/Ātman/Brahman'. How we understand these varied words, depends upon where we stand in life.

Ādi Śaṅkarācārya's efforts were a manifestation of His philosophy and His entire being. These efforts were directed at making the common man realize 'Oneness of a All lives'. If one develops a novel vision of looking at Ādi Śaṅkarācārya's efforts with the backdrop of His sublime philosophy, it will be effortless to draw valuable meanings from His endeavors and thoughts in view of environmental harmony. With a newfound perspective, one will be able to see that the Maṭhas, and Chāradhāmas were established amidst nature, near hills, water bodies and had undeniable ecological significance. Additionally, the Daśanāīṃsaṃpradāya and the Pañcadevopāsana were also established in order to revere the natural bounties of the 'Mother Earth'. The holiness and sanctity of these places lie in their environmental glory and the subtle effect of their natural surroundings that lead to the realization of self-sameness with all existences. Regrettably, these centres now remain as places where only rituals are performed, while their environmental value and essence have withered away.

It is a matter of great melancholy that researchers and scholars have merely concentrated upon Ādi Śaṅkarācārya's metaphysics and have elected to completely turn a blind eye towards His life and works that were flowing with wholesome-ness. To pronounce an enlightened being like Ādi Śaṅkarācārya as a 'Mere Metaphysicists' while ignoring His works, misinterpreting His thought, overlooking His virtuous life and disregarding His establishments, is simply boiling down to fallacious conclusions. Indian philosophy refuses to see ethics as distinct from life. This book has made desirable efforts to see Ādi Śaṅkarācārya's life, works, philosophy and His practical endeavours in continuity and not in seclusion of one another.

Ādi Śaṅkarācārya bestows to the world a well-defined and well-considered technique for liberating oneself from the vices of duality; hatred, jealousy, and suffering, and realizing the Greatest Truth, 'Brahman'. On this path, 'Sādhanacatuṣṭya' becomes the fountainhead of self-restraint, ethics, intellectual inquiry, spiritual endurance and chastity. It is through 'Sādhanacatuṣṭya' that one becomes qualified in order to move forward on to the path of realization. The process of 'Śravaṇa-Manana-Nididhyāsana-Niṣṭhā', further assists a being in realizing 'The One' that sans any gulfs. The seeker also goes through the well-structured method of Anvaya-Vyatireka where he accepts and refutes all names and forms in order to realize them as the 'Supreme Truth'. Ultimately, the fifteen-fold Yoga of Ādi Śaṅkarācārya lets the quester see all the worldly entities as the 'Breathing Brahman' and eventually these entities melt into the 'Ultimate Cause' and Brahman alone exists.

A being who sees everything as the 'Self' is a 'Jīvanmukta' who continues to work for the welfare of all living creatures. The saints from the Advaita Vedānta order are a testimony of how a 'Jīvanmukta' remains dedicated towards the well-being of all lives. Therefore, Ādi Śaṅkarācārya endows us with methodologies that aid us from darkness unto light. These approaches are undeniably founded in ethics, morality, and reverence for all living things.

As ethics in view of Advaita Vedānta have been highlighted in this book, they also become the foundation of comprehensive environmental harmony. The beauty of this philosophy lies in its unanimous, organic and non-dual approach towards all entities of the universe that are permeated, in-dwelled, and founded in the Supreme Being. Sadly, the environmental disharmony is a consequence of the alteration of a man's internal environmental conditions that lead to cosmic mayhems, devastations, upheavals and unrests.

The relationship between ethics and metaphysics has been emphasized the most in case of Advaita Vedānta and this book has made efforts to bring to fore the same. A philosophy that sees Mokṣa as the final end, cannot be anything but 'Ethical' and this alone becomes the very identity of India, where humans, animals, birds and the entire nature is worshiped as the Supreme. Advaita Vedānta thus stands in favour of environmental harmony and ethics.

The book also goes on to throw light upon the Pravṛtti and Nivṛtti Dharma, which encompasses not just human ethics but also ethics for all cosmic entities, that are explained on the basis of Ādi Śaṅkarācārya's metaphysics.

Ethics play a critical role right from the point a seeker starts his journey to the very realization of the Self as the 'Highest Principle'. Ādi Śaṅkarācārya's contribution towards ethics that are rooted in His metaphysics have been cold-bloodedly disregarded. Philosophers, intellectuals and theorists elected to focus only upon His debating proficiencies, logic and repudiation of other schools. Even those who claim to abide by the conventional Advaita Vedānta chose to become blindly ritualistic and failed to notice Ādi Śaṅkarācārya's concepts of 'Sarvabhūtahita and Loksaṃgraha'. The Maṭhas that were founded by Ādi Śaṅkarācārya in order to uphold the spirit of non-dualism, overlooked His philosophy and resorted to mindless ritualism that Ādi Śaṅkarācārya Himself had negated.

The absence of code of conduct in Advaita Vedantic literature is not because it is frivolous, but because the same is inexorably tied to its philosophy. Ethics and morals are addressed in a substantial corpus of Advaita Vedntic literature. However, before exploring these works, one must first grasp Advaita Vednta's primary premise. It must be also understood that Advaita Vedānta takes into account universal morality for granted. The same will lose its grounds if ethics and morals are not abided by in the process of realizing 'The Highest Good-Brahman'. The one who is established in the Brahman will automatically have his actions rooted in cosmic welfare, well-being, amity and concord. The philosophy emphasizes enlightenment manifests as acts of eternal wisdom rather than actions that are peripheral, transitory, robotic, and result from dread of commandments of 'must and must not.' Dualism is an effect of Avidyā and so, commands like 'you must be good' or 'you must not be evil' become pointless in view of Advaita Vedānta for a realized one but the same are valid for a seeker and the worldly man.

It is to be unconditionally appreciated that if Advaita Vedānta merely addressed humans and had ignored other 'Sentient Beings' of the world in which the Brahman appears, its very foundation would have been demolished. Furthermore, to boil down to the conclusion that the entire world is a 'Void or Illusion' is refuting the very theory of 'Sarvabrahmavāda'. If the entire world was like the sky flower, Ādi Śaṅkarācārya's philosophy, works and efforts would have no meaning and His endeavors would be standing in contrast with His philosophy. The universe, in all of its flux, is unquestionably transitory, but it cannot be rejected as unreal like the son of a barren woman.

The final goal of Advaita Vedānta is realization of the 'Non-dual Self'. However, this awareness is only possible through the material world, and hence this world has its own worth and value. As a part of the cosmos, the environment, animals, and birds become tools for experiencing the Self at a physical level, and at a higher level, all of these become the body of the Īśvara. Further, at a transcendental sphere, all these entities are realized as the 'Brahman'. Therefore, one cannot have an approach of apathy towards these pure sentient beings.

The concept of non-dualism is rendered meaningless if one chooses to be concerned only with the human race while remaining indifferent towards all other beings. The world's ontological standing is maintained by those who go on to disapprove of it. One cannot realize non-duality by being apathetic to the realm of duality. Therefore, iniquitous conduct because of which the entire ecological unit suffers, gluttony that becomes the source of misery for all sentient beings and the yearning to subdue Nature becomes the reason for damaging of our internal and external environment. All of this stems from the unawareness of our factual nature and in the obliviousness of me nature of all beings of the world, who are the 'Non-dual Brahman'.

Ādi Śaṅkarācārya's philosophy beautifies a being with selflessness, stability, wisdom and ethics and allows him to take control of his impulses. In order to appreciate Ādi

Śaṅkarācārya's ethics one has to clearly understand His Pārmārthika, Vyāvhārika and Pratibhāśika positions. Ādi Śaṅkarācārya acknowledges the world of names and forms as: 'Momentarily real', 'Undivided whole that appears diverse', 'More real than the dreams and less real than the Highest Reality-Brahman', and 'Indescribable'. At no point, Ādi Śaṅkarācārya has concluded the world to be a 'Void' like the horns of a rabbit.

Ādi Śaṅkarācārya establishes the importance of 'Jñāna' by announcing it as the only means to realization. He concentrates on the internal purification of one's states which automatically lead to external purification. The purification of our internal states will lead us to realize the 'Nature of Reality' as Sat (Truth), Cit (Consciousness), Ānanda (Bliss). It is to be taken into account that we are already pure (Nityaśuddha), all-knowing (Nityabuddha) and liberated (Nityamukta). This is possible only with a spiritually oriented holistic education that becomes a means to unfold our true nature.

The current educational system, which focuses on exterior beauty, has to alter dramatically. Unfortunately, education is reduced to being a source of information and its aim is mere monetary gains. The 'Vedantic Education System,' on the other hand, focuses on realizing the 'Self' by knowing which everything else can be known. This education system strives to realize the 'Non-dual Truth,' which is the essence of all existences. It inquires, explores, investigates, seeks solutions, finds answers, and weighs those findings using the Pramāṇas (Valid Sources of Knowledge) as a guide. All of this is done in order to attain excellence because every spec of the cosmos is flawless in essence and realization of this perfection is the final quest. This essential perfection can be realized only with the dint of 'education that is rooted in spirituality'. An education that is scientific yet spiritual and allows us to realize ourselves through the world of material because you need material to be liberated from material and so material world and entities have an extremely important role to play in realizing perfection. Therefore, the aim of education is to realize our 'Perfect Self'. Only when one endeavors to realize one's nature of perfection will he seek the 'Permanent' through the temporary rather than seeking the temporary as the permanent.

Today, merely for the sake of academic research, problems like 'Locus of Avidyā', 'Nature of Brahman', 'Reality of the World' and more are taken up repeatedly. Old concepts are rewritten in new and fancy words and are served like old wine in a new bottle. Sorrowfully, no one is eager to investigate Ādi Śaṅkarācārya's philosophy from a fresh perspective in terms of environment, social sciences, physics and more. The pragmatic applicability of Advaita Vedānta must be explored while making sure that the metaphysics of the same is not maligned. It can be said that the philosophy can be reinterpreted and can be put to use but due to utmost laziness and orthodoxy, it has purposefully been reduced to being a philosophy that has no practical application left.

The human race's inner ecology must undergo a full transition, and for this reason, a spiritually based education system is urgently required. There will be a progressive change outwardly and cosmically as a result of this inner transformation. For the same, the entire education system should be revamped. This alone can rid the society from the shackles of vices.

It is also important that texts such as the Bhavadgītābhāṣya and the hymns of Ādi Śaṅkarācārya are not looked upon as 'Texts of Religion'. It is to be lucidly comprehended that these texts are meant for the welfare and well-being of the entire cosmos and so they must be introduced in the education system. It has already been pointed out in this book that Ādi Śaṅkarācārya's texts are relevant to bring about a sense of reverence for all lives and thus strike a remarkable balance socially, mentally, spiritually and environmentally. It is further recommended that these texts should be researched upon and must accordingly be introduced in schools and colleges in order to bring about internal ecological change that will automatically change the entire world in which we live.

An introduction to Ādi Śaṅkarācārya's life, events and hymns at a young age through pictorial images and short stories is highly recommended. The same will serve as a foundation for an individual's character, which will be decorated with the jewels of self-sameness, compassion, and virtue. A person who develops the vision to perceive non-duality cannot behave in any other way than that which is beneficial for the whole of cosmos. Therefore, Ādi Śaṅkarācārya's philosophy, life, works, and establishments can surely serve as a practical guide for achieving environmental harmony.

Once Ādi Śaṅkarācārya's efforts are acclaimed and His philosophy is lucidly comprehended, it is crucial to reinterprct its core concepts concerning the existing times. A philosophy that is not reinterpreted, rejuvenated and refreshed following the demands of the society becomes static, redundant and uncalled-for. The splendor and chasteness of a river lies in its flowing and in its enlargement. The moment it halts; it becomes susceptible to amassing filth. Therefore, in order to be benefited from the unsurpassed wisdom of Ādi Śaṅkarācārya, we must make appropriate labors to reinterpret His philosophy and thought while making sure that we do not limit, manipulate or after His metaphysics. It is critical for philosophers to break free from their old, dull shells and look at Ādi Śaṅkarācārya's endeavors with a new, fresh, and reinvented viewpoint.

The present book emerges as one of the unique works as no known research work related to Advaita Vedānta and environment has come to fore in India or internationally.

With contemporary environmental concerns emerging as an international emergency, the philosophy of Advaita Vedānta as propounded by Ādi Śaṅkarācārya can certainly be a viable solution in confronting the same.

Oṁ Ajñānatimirādityāye Namaḥ

(I bow before Śaṅkara who like sun dispells the darkness of ignorance.)

BIBLIOGRAPHY

A

ACHARYA TIRTHA VEDANTA, '*Atharvaveda*', Manoj Publications, 2018.

AIYER. P.SIVASWAMY, '*Evolution of Indian Moral Ideals*', University of Calcutta, Kolkata, 1945.

ALLEN, CHARLES, '*A Mountain in Tibet: The Search for Mount Kailasa and the Sources of the Great Rivers of India* ', Futura Publications, London, 1991.

ARYA SHARDA, '*Sanctity of Environment in Ancient Hindu Scriptures*' Parimal Publications, Delhi, 2018.

ATHALYE D.V, '*Neo Hinduism Vivekananda's Concept of Vedantism*', Mumbai, 1922.

B

BALASUBRAMANIAM.R, '*Concept of Mukti in Advaita Vedanta*', Madras University, 1981.

BALASUBRAMANIAM.R, '*Concept of Vyyavharika in Advaita Vedanta*', Madras University, 1980.

BALASUBRAMANIAM. R (Ed), '*The Voice of Shankara, Vol.29, No.2*',

ADI SHANKARA ADVAITA RESEARCH CENTRE, Chennai, 2004.

BALASUBRAMANIAM. R (Ed), '*The Voice of Shankara, Vol.30, No.1*', Adi Shankara Advaita Research Centre, Chennai 2005. '*Jagadguru Adi Shakaracharya Ka Samaya Chintan*' Pratibh Prakashan, Delhi,1999.

BANERJEE SURES CHANDRA, '*Aspects of Ancient Indian Life Form Sanskrit Sources*' Punthi Pustak, Calcutta, 1972.

BHAGVADPADA SHANKARA, PRAMA KRUNA DEVI (Tr), '*Prashnottara Ratna Malika*', Jagganath Vallabh Vedic Research Centre, Orissa, 2016.

BHATT S.R (Ed), '*Reality, Knowledge and Value*' Sundeep Prakashan, Delhi, 2004.

BHATT S. R, '*Vedic Wisdom, Cultural Inheritance and Contemporary Life*' Bhartiya Vidya Prakashan, Delhi, 1999.

BHATT S.R, '*Indian Spirituality: Theory and Praxis*' Indian Council of Philosophical Research, Delhi, 2018.

BHATT JEET RAM, '*Shatpat Brahman*', Eastern Book Linkers, Delhi 2009.

BHATTACHARYA KALIDAS, '*A Modern Understanding of Advaita Vedanta*', L.D. Institute of Indology, Ahamdabad, 1975.

BHAVI S. S, 'Soma Hymns in the Rigveda', Oriental Institute, Badoda, 1957.

BLOOMFEILD MAURICE, '*Hymns of the Atharvaveda*', Pinnacle Press, USA, 2017.

BRADLEY. F.H, '*Appearance and Reality*', Oxford Press, London, 1966.

C

CHAKRAVARTI RANABIR, '*Materials Background of Darius I's Invasion of India, Vol.43*', Proceedings of the Indian History Congress, Delhi, 1982.

CHANDRA S.S & SHARMA RAJENDRA, '*Philosophy of Education*'. Atlantic Publishers & Dist. Delhi, 1996.

CHANDRA SURESH, '*Jagadguru Adi Shankaracharya: A Short Biography*', Sri Jagadguru Shankaracharya Mahasamsthanam Dakshinamnaya Sri Sharda Peetam, Shringeri, 2010.

CHAPPLE CHRISTOPHER, Elvin Mary Tucker (Ed), '*Hinduism and Ecology; The Interaction of Earth, Sky and Water*', Harvard University Press, Cambridge, 2000.

CHAPPLE CHRISTOPHER, '*Non-violence to Animals, Earth and Self in Asian Traditions*', State University of New York, Albany, 1993.

CHATTOPADHYAYA D.P, BHATT S.R, SINGH S.P, KUMAR S.P (Ed Board), '*Quest for Excellence*', Richa Prakashan, Delhi, 2000.

CHAUDHARY B.R, TRIVEDI PRIYA (Ed), '*Economy and Eco-dharma for a Sustainable Society*', Institute of Ecology and Environment, Delhi, 1996.

CHAUBEY. B.B, '*Treatment of Nature in Rigveda*', Vedic Sahitya Sadan, Punjab, 1970.

CRAWFORD CORMWELL.S, '*Evolution of Hindu Ethics*', University Press Hawaii, Hawaii, 1982.

D

DATTA AND CHATTERJEE, '*An Introduction to Indian Philosophy*', Rupa Publications, Delhi 2007.

DESHMUKHA SHRIKRISHNA (Tr & Com), '*Aproksanubhuti*', Motilal Banarsidas, Delhi, 2019.

DEVASENAPATI V.A, '*Komakottam, Nayanmars and Adi Shankara*', University of Madras, Chennai, 1993.

DHYANI, P.P, '*Badrivan: An Innovative Model in The Indian Central Himalaya for Restoration of Degraded Lands and Biodiversity Conservation*', Himavikas Publishing, 1998.

DIVEDI KAPILDEV, '*Vedon Mein Vijnan*', Vishvabharti Anusandhana Parishad, Bhadohi, 2014.

DRAVID R MANI (Ed) and Bhumneshwari S (Tr), '*Samnyasavichara*', Adyar Library and Research Centre, Chennai, 2016.

E

EGGLING JULIUS, '*Shatpath Brahman*', Create space Publishing, Amazon, USA, 2015.

G

GOEL ARUNA, '*Environment and Ancient Sanskrit Literature*' Deep and Deep Publications, Delhi, 2003.

GOENDKA HARIKRISHNA, '*Shrimadbhagvad Gita Shankara Bhashya*', Gita Press, Gorakhpur, 2016.

GOPAL, MADAN, K. S. GAUTAM (ed.), '*India Through The Ages*'. Publication Division, Ministry of Information and Broadcasting, Government of India, Delhi, 1990.

GRIFFITH RALPH T.H, '*The Rigveda*', Védico Antiguo Einglés, Spain, 1896.

H

HLLDOBLER, BERT, EDWARD WILSON, '*The Ants*', Harvard University Press, USA, 1990.

HOLDREGE BARBARA, '*Veda and Torah: Transcending the Textuality of Scripture*', Suny Press, New York, 1996.

HOPKINS E.W, '*Ethics of India*', Yale University Press, London, 1924.

HIRIYANNA. M, '*Outlines of Indian Philosophy*', Motilal Banarsidas Publications, Delhi, 1932.

I

IYER P.S.S, '*Evolution of Hindu Moral Ideas*', Calcutta University, Kolkata, 1935.

J

JAMES KING, '*The Holy Bible*', American Bible Society, New York 1999.

JAVADEKAR A.G, '*Reality of the World in Shankara Vedanta*', Journal of M.S.University of Badoda, Badoda, 1962.

JAVADEKAR A.G, '*Constructive Reinterpretation of Advaita Vedanta*', Philosophical Quarterly, Amalner, 1964.

JHA GANGANATHA, '*The Chandogyaupanishad with Shankara Bhashya*', Oriental Book Agency, Puna, 1942.

JONES WILLIAM, '*Botanical Observations on Select Indian Plants*', Vernor and Hood Museum Publication London, 1876.

JOSHI, BIMALI, TRIVEDI, '*112 Upanishads, Vol-1, Mandukyopnishad*', Parimal Publications, Delhi, 2013.

K

KAPOOR RAJIVE, '*Shivsankalpasutra*', Ideal Print Links Pvt Ltd, Mumbai, 2016.

KAREN ARMS, '*Environmental Sciences*', Holt, Rinehart and Winson, Inc., Florida,1996.

KAUSHAL RADHEY SHYAM, '*The Philosophy of Vedanta: A Modern Scientific Perspective*' Satguru Publications, Delhi, 1994.

KING SHUDRAKA, RYDER ARTHUR WILLIAM (Tr), '*Mrichchakatikam –Samskrit Play (The Little Clay Cart)*', Harvard University, Massachusetts, 1905.

KUMAR SURENDRA, '*Manusmriti*', Aarsh Sahitya Prachar Trust, Delhi, 2017.

KNUT A. JACOBSEN, '*Pilgrimage in the Hindu Tradition: Salvific Space*', Routledge, London, 2013.

L

LOSTY J.P AND OZA SUMEDHA, '*Ramayana*', Lustre Publications, Delhi, 2016.

M

MALKANI G.R, '*Metaphysics of Advaita Vedanta*', Indian Institute of Philosophy, Amalner, 1961.

MANDANMISHRA, SHASTRI KUPPUSAMI S (Ed), '*Brahmasiddhi*', Madras, 1937.

MAULANA ALI MUHAMMAD, '*The Holy Quran*', Ahmadiyyah AnjumanIsha'at Islam, Lahore, 1991.

MAYEDA SENGAKU, '*Updeshsahasri*', Motilal Banarsidas, Delhi, 2006.

MISHRA PARMESHVARNATHA NATH (Com) '*Adi Shankaracharya's Mathanushasanama Setu or Mathanushasanama*', Shankaracharya Memorial Trust, Dwarka,2001.

MITTAL KRISHNA KEWAL '*Materialism in Indian Thought*', Munshiram Manoharlal, Delhi, 1974.

MULLER MAX, 'SHATPAT BRAHMAN', Motilal Banarsidass, Delhi, 1982.

MURTHY KRISHNA S.R, '*Science and Hinduism*', Sharda Prakashan, 2015.

N

NANDA KUMARA PREMA, '*ādi Śaṅkara-Finite to the Infinite*' Chinmayaa International Foundation, Ernakulam, 2013.

NARAYANA RAJADEVA AND KUMAR JANARDAN, '*Ecology and Religion: Ecological Concepts in Hinduism, Buddhism, Jainism, Islam, Christianity and Sikkhism*', Deep and Deeo Publications, Delhi, 2008.

NARAYANASHARMA, MOHANTA DILIP KUMAR (Ed), '*Advaita Siddhanta Sara Samgrah*', Ramakrishna Mission Vivekananda University, West Bengal, 2012.

P

PADMAPADACHARYA, '*Panchapadika*' Calcutta Sanskrit Series, Kolkata,1932.

PANDE GOVINDA CHANDRA,'*Life and Thought of Śaṅkarācārya*' Motilal Banarsidass, Delhi, 2011.

PARPOLA ASHKO, '*The Roots of Hinduism: Early Aryan and Indus Civilizations*', Oxford University Press, New York, 2015.

PT.SHARMA MAHADEV, '*Pañcikarna Pranavārthaya*', Kanoon Press, Kanpur,1941.

R

RAJA RAM MOHAN ROY, '*Vedic Physics, Scientific Origin of Hinduism*', Golden Egg Publishing, Toronto, 1999,

RAJU P.T, '*Structural Depths of Indian Thought*', South Asian Publishers, Delhi,1985.

RAM TULSI, '*Hymns of Yajurveda*', Vijaykumar Govindram Hasanand, Delhi, 2011.

RAVI ILLA, '*Foundations of Indian Ethics*' Kaveri Books, Delhi, 2002.

S

SADANANDA ACHARYA, '*Vedantasara*', Chaukhamba Publication, Delhi, 2003.

SANGHVI NAṆDĪTA, '*Vedon Me Paryavarana*', Sonali Publications, Jaipur, 2004.

SHANKARACHARYA '*Brahmajnanawalimala*', Delphian Books, Australia, 2011.

SHANKARACARYA, PANSIKAR W.L (Ed), '*Gita Bhashya*', Nirnayasagar Press, Mumbai, 1934.

SHANKARACARYA, BAKRE M.S (Ed), '*Brahmasutrabhashya*', Nirnayasagar Press, Mumbai, 1934.

SHANKARACARYA, '*Shrimadhagvadagita Bhashya*', Manav Prabodhan Pranyasa, Bikaner, Rajasthan, 2016.

SHARMA ARVIND, '*On Hindu, Hindustān, Hinduism and Hindutva Vol.49*', Numen, Netherlands, 2002.

SHARMA CHANDRADHAR, '*The Advaita Tradition on Indian Philosophy*', Motilal Banarsidass, Delhi, 2016.

SHARMA GANGA SAHAY '*Rigveda*', Vishva Books Pvt.Ltd, Gaziabad, 2014.

SHARMA I.C, '*Ethical Philosophies of India*', Johnsen Publishing Company and Harper and Raw Company, USA, 1991.

SHARMA PUSHPENDRA, TRIPATHI C.N, AJNAVI S AND DUBEY S.K, '*Agnihotra-A Non-Conventional Solution to Air Pollution*', International Journal of Innovative Research in Science & Engineering, UP, 2014.

SHARMA VANDANA AND THIRUMAL J, '*Prashnottara Ratna Malika*', Origionls Publications, Delhi, 2020.

SHASTRI SATVIR, '*Rigveda*', Hindi SahityaSadan, Delhi 2011.

SHASTRI N.S ANANTHAKRISHNA, (Ed), '*Śaṅkara Digvijay*', Sringeri Math, 1956.

SHASTRY ANANTHAKRISHNAN, '*Vishnusahastranama with Commentary of Shankaracharya*', Theosophical Publishing House, Madras, 1927.

SHASTRI KOILESHVARA, '*An Introduction to Advaita Vedanta*', University of Calcutta, 1926.

SHEIKH AHMAD, '*Environmental Science and Ecology*', Sankalpa Publication, Bilaspur, 2019.

SRI SHANKARA, ACHARYA PRANIPATCHAITANYA (Tr), Dhiman Satinder (Ed) '*Vivekachudamani*', Chinmaya Mission Foundation, Tamil Nadu, 2012.

SINGH BALBIR, '*Hindu Ethics: An Exposition of the Concept of Good*', Arnold Heinemann, Delhi, 1984.

SINGH R.P, '*The Vedanta of Shankara, Vol.1*', Jaipur Bharat Printing House, Jaipur, 1949.

SINHA JADUNATH, '*A Manual of Ethics*', New Central Book Agency, India, 2009.

SRI SHANKARA, ACHARYA PRANIPATCHAITANYA (Tr), Dhiman Satinder (Ed) '*Vivekachudamani*', Chinmaya Mission Foundation, Tamil Nadu, 2012.

SRIDHAR N, '*Samanya Dhama and Spirituality*', Prabuddha Bharat, Kolkata, 2015.

SRI HARIKRISHNADAS GAOYENDKA, '*Srimadbhagvada Gita Shankar Bhashya*', Gitapress, Gorakhpur, 2019.

SURESHVARACHARYA, SHASTRI KRISHNA PANDITA, '*Nishkarmayasiddhi*', Achutyagranthamala Karyalaya, Varanasi, 2013.

SVAMI VIRESWARANANDA, '*Brahmasutra Bhashya*', Advaita Ashrama, Kolkata, 2014.

SWAMI CHINMAYANANDA, '*Śrī Ādi Śaṅkarācārya*', Chinmaya International Foundation, Ernakulam, 2014.

SWAMI GAMBHIRANANDA, '*The Eight Upanishads with Commentary of Shankaracharya, Vol. 2*', Advaita Ashrama, Kolkata, 1937.

SWAMI GAMBHIRANANDA, '*The Eight Upanishads with Commentary of Shankaracharya, Vol.4*', Advaita Ashramaa, Himalayas, 1957.

SWAMI GYANANADA SARASWATI, '*Ādi Śaṅkara*', Neeta Publications, Delhi, 2006.

SWAMI HARIBRAHMENDRANANDA TIRTHA, '*Sri Shankara Sarasvata Sarvasvam: Complete Works of Sri Shankara*', Arsha Vidya Prathishthanam, Kerala, 2019.

Swami Isvarananda Giri, '*UpanisahadAloka*', Samvit Sadhnayana, Mount Abu, 2018.

Swami Lokeshwarananda, '*Cāndogya Upaniṣad-Śaṅkara Bhāṣya*', Ramakrishna Mission Institute of Culture, Kolkata, 2017.

Swami Sri Jananananda Bharti, '*Outlines of Vedanta*', Sri Ganananda Bharti Grantha Prakashana Samithi, Chennai, 2015.

Swami Lokeshwarananda, '*Shvetashvatara Upanishad-Shankara Bhassya*', Ramakrishna Mission Institute of Culture, Kolkata, 2000.

Swami Prakash Satya, '*AumAgnihotra - An Ancient Process of Fumigation (A Study From the Chemical Standpoint)*', Jan Gyan Prakashan, India, 1974.

Swami Madhavananda (Tr), '*Vivekachudamani*', Advaita Ashrama, Kolkata, 2015.

Swami Mdhavananda, '*Brihdarnayakopnishad with Commentaries of Shankaracharya*', Advaita Ashrama, Himalayas, 1950.

Swami Nikhilananda, '*The Upanishad-Taittirya and Chandogy Based on Shankara's Commentary, Vol-IV*', Harper Brother Publishers, New York,1959.

Swami Nikilananda (Tr & Com), '*Atmabodha*', Sri Ramakrishna Mission, Madras, 1947.

Swami Shantananda Saraswati, '*Brihdarnayakopnishad Based on Shankara's Commentary*', Advaita Ashrama, Himalayas, 2019.

Swami Tejomayananda '*Shiv Manas Puja by Shri Shankaracharya*', Central Chinmaya Mission Trust, Mumbai, 2014.

Swami Vishveshwarananda, '*Brahmasutrabhashya*', Advaita Ashrama, Kolkata, 2014.

Swami Vividatmananda '*Vedanta in Present Day*', Adhyatma VidyaMandir, Ahamdabad, 1995.

SWAMI VIMUKTANANDA '*Aprokshanubhuti of Shri Shankaracharya*', Advaita Ashram, Himalayas, 1938.

SWAMI VIVEKANANDA, '*Jnanayoga, Vol-II*', Ramakrishna Vivekananda Centre, New York, 1982.

SWAMI VIVEKANANDA, '*The Complete Works of Swami Vivekananda Vol. I*', Vedanta Press, USA, 1947.

T

TATYA TOOKARAM, '*The Compendium of the Raja Yoga Philosophy with Treatises of ShrimatSankaraacharya*', Bombay Theosophical Publication, Mumbai, 1888.

THAKUR S BHART (Ed), "*The Future of Leadership: Addressing Global Issues Complex*", Palgrave, Mcmillan,USA, 2018.

TRIPATHI D.K, '*Revelation, Intuition and Reason in Shankara Vedanta*', Arti Prakashan, Faizabad, 1986.

V

VEDA VYAS, '*Mahabharata*', Bharat Press, Kolkata, 1884.

VIDYARANYA MADHAVA, Svami Tpasyananda (Tr), '*Shankar Digvijay*', Ramakrishna Math, Chennai, 2008.

VIDYARANYA, '*Jivanmuktiviveka*', Ananda Ashram Sanskit Series, Puna, 1916.

W

WILLIAMS GEORGE, '*Handbook of Hindu Mythology*', Oxford University Press, London, 2008.

WILLIAMS MONIER SIR, '*Hinduism*', Society for Promoting Christian Knowledge, Pott Young & Co, New York, 1877.

Online Sources

Adi Shankaracharya, Shastri. S.N (Tr), '*Atmapanchakama*', Shastra.com, 2018.

Adi Shankaracharya, P.R.Ramachandra (Tr), '*Anandalehari*', Shastra.com, 2018,

Adi Shankaracharya, Shastri.S.N (Tr), '*Bhaja Govindam*', Shastra.com, 2018.

Adi Shankaracharya, P.R.Ramachandra (Tr), '*Dhyanashtakam*', Shastra.com, 2018,

Adi Shankaracharya '*Gangastakam*', Sanskrit Documents, 2010

Adi Shankaracharya and P.R.Ramachandra (Tr), '*Manishapanchakam*', Shastra.com, 2018.

Shankaracharya '*Narsimha Porva Tapaniya Upanishad Bhashyam*', Vdocuments, 2019.

Adi Shankaracharya, Swami Chinmayananda (Tr), '*Sadhanapanchakam*', Chinmaya Mission International, www.chinfo.in, 2018.

Adi Shankaracharya, '*Ymunastakam*', Green Message, 2020,

Bhumisuktam, greenmessage, 2020.

Britannica Encyclopedia, '*Environment*', 2020.

Bhagvad Gita USA, 'Kashmir Shaivism, 2020'

Cambridge Dictionary '*Environment*', Cambridge University, 2020.

Dikpanchanga, '108 Names of Lord Krishna', 2020.

Encyclopedia Britannica, '*Environment*', 2020, E-Uttaranchal.com, '*Kalpavriksha*', 2020.

Govardhan Matha, '*Cow Protection*', 2019.

Govardhan Matha, '*Swami NishcalanandaSarasvat Quotes'*, 2019.

Gupta Kritika, '*Mumbai Male Dog Brutally Gang Raped by four, Dies After Fighting for His Life*', India Times, 2018.

Jagannathpuri.in, '*Jaggannatha Puri Temple History*', 2020.

K.Jayalakshmi, '*Cull of 40, 000 Dogs in Kerala*', International Business Times, 2015,

Limaye Anita, '*The Oldest Tree*', The Economic Times, 2006.

Maharishi Vyasa, '*Shrimad Bhagvatam Purana*', Vedainfo.in, 2020.

Pal Sanchari, '*J C Bose: The Little Known Story of How India's First Biophysicist Proved Plants Have Life*', The Better India, Banglore, 2016.

Pandit Sri Rama Rananuja Achary, 'Sukta Sangrah, Shrimatham, online, 2017.

Ramchander P.R, '*Śrī Mūkaṃikā Pañcaratna Strotam*', Strotra Ratna Blogspot, 2015.

Sengar Shweta, '*Man Arrested For Raping Seven Cows at a Shelter in Ayodhya*', India Times, 2019.

Shringeri Matha, *'History of Mathas'*, 2004.

Shringeri Matha, 'Matha-Ban on Fishing', 2019.

Shringeri Matha, '*Shri Bharti Teertha Mahasvami on Cow Protection*', Youtube, 2018.

Swami Nischalananda Saraswati, '*Dashnami Sampradaya Ka Mahatva'*, Youtube, 2017.

Swami Vivekananda, '*Complete works of Swami Vivekananda*', Partha Sinha Digital Publication, Online, 2019.

SUBRAMANIAN V, '*Shankara's Date: A Discussion on Sudhanva's Copper Plate*', 2015.

THE HINDU, 'Locust Swam Attack', 2020.

THE TELEGRAPH, '*Red Threat Spurs Seer Super Shield'*, Bhumbneshwara, 2008.

TOURMYINDIA, '*Rameshwaram*' 2020,

WALTERS HOLLY D, '*The Living Fossils*', The Fimmiliar Strange, 2018.